To Shahram and Cyrus,
great-grandsons of Andrei Prymak, Manitoba homesteader and
pioneer, who decided against taking monastic vows in the old country

MYKOLA KOSTOMAROV: A BIOGRAPHY

Печ со стали Ф. А. Брокгауза въ Лейпцигѣ

Н. Костомаровъ

THOMAS M. PRYMAK

Mykola Kostomarov:
A Biography

UNIVERSITY OF TORONTO PRESS
Toronto Buffalo London

© University of Toronto Press Incorporated 1996
Toronto Buffalo London
Printed in Canada

ISBN 0-8020-0758-9

∞

Printed on acid-free paper

Canadian Cataloguing in Publication Data

Prymak, Thomas M., 1948–
  Mykola Kostomarov : a biography

  Includes bibliographical references and index.
  ISBN 0-8020-0758-9

  1. Kostomarov, N.I. (Nikolai Ivanovich), 1817–1885.
  2. Nationalism – Ukraine – History – 19th century.
  3. Nationalists – Ukraine – Biography.   4. Historians –
  Ukraine – Biography. I. Title.

  DK508.47.K67P78 1996   947'.7107'092   C95-932111-X

Frontispiece: From *Literaturnoe nasledie N.I. Kostomarova* (St Petersburg: Stasiulevich, 1890)

University of Toronto Press acknowledges the financial assistance to its publishing program of the Canada Council and the Ontario Arts Council.

This book has been published with the help of a grant from the Canadian Federation for the Humanities, using funds provided by the Social Sciences and Humanities Research Council of Canada.

I wish good things to you, brothers,
and to the Land of Rus'.

Volodymyr Monomakh

I have a sort of partiality for the conquered.

Augustin Thierry

Contents

Preface

There is a story behind the writing of every book, and this one is no exception. My interest in Mykola Kostomarov is old, going back almost two decades to the time when I first began formal studies in Russian and East European history. In the 1975–6 academic year, I was a graduate student in the Soviet nationalities seminar led by Professor John Keep of the University of Toronto. At that time, I first became somewhat acquainted with the life and work of Mykola Kostomarov. Professor Keep was hoping to put together a volume of translated sources on the nationality question in imperial Russia and the Soviet Union and invited us, his students, to participate by selecting a document from our area of special interest to be included in the collection. My special interest was the triangle of Ukrainian-Russian-Polish relations that dominated the history of the western Ukrainian lands in the nineteenth century. Accordingly, I chose to translate Alexander Herzen's marvellous little essay entitled 'Russia and Poland,' in which the famous Russian journalist defied Russian public opinion and acknowledged not only Poland's right to an independent national existence, but also Ukraine's. Herzen dreamed too of some kind of loose, future Slavic federation. Kostomarov reacted enthusiastically to his proposals and penned Herzen a letter of support. That letter was my first exposure to Kostomarov's ideas, and they were not without effect on me. Professor Keep's volume on the nationalities question was never published, but my work on Herzen, which made direct mention of Kostomarov's reaction, eventually appeared in the Toronto-based *Journal of Ukrainian Studies*.

In the years that followed, I continued my work on the triangle of Ukrainian-Russian-Polish relations with a study of the pioneering

Ukrainian journal *Osnova* (*The Foundation*) and the attitudes towards the Poles found therein. My paper '*Osnova* and the Poles,' which further developed my ideas about Kostomarov, was presented to Professor Peter Brock's graduate seminar on modern Polish history, also at the University of Toronto. Thereafter, I put aside study of the Ukrainian-Russian-Polish triangle in the nineteenth century and spent several years working on the political career of the great Ukrainian historian Mykhailo Hrushevsky, who, it turned out, further developed or reformulated many of the ideas first proposed by Kostomarov. Other work occupied me for a few more years, but by 1989 I had begun research on a project concerning nineteenth-century Russian historiography and the national question. That project quickly evolved into a study of the life and work of Kostomarov. To do full justice to Kostomarov, I had of course to treat political, literary, and personal as well as historiographical themes. But the undertaking was much to my taste, and *Mykola Kostomarov: A Biography* is the result.

I will never forget the time I spent researching and writing the book, for those exciting years saw the final end of the long 'cold war,' the last great attempt to reform the U.S.S.R., the promulgation of 'glasnost' and 'perestroika,' the opening up of Soviet libraries and archives to Western scholars, the disintegration of the communist empire in Eastern Europe, the collapse of the Soviet Union, and the emergence of independent Ukraine and other states from its ruins.

Although I was unable to travel during much of the period and most of my research was carried out at the Robarts Library at the University of Toronto, I was able to make some use of the great libraries of Eastern Europe, Ukraine, and Russia through the interlibrary loan system. Through the system, I obtained important materials from such great repositories as the Vernadsky Library of the Academy of Sciences of Ukraine in Kiev, the Russian National Library in St Petersburg, and the Slavonic Library at the University of Helsinki. I thank all those institutions for the materials they sent me.

The research for *Mykola Kostomarov: A Biography* was undertaken with the help of funding from the Social Sciences and Humanities Research Council of Canada through a Canada Research Fellowship which I held from 1989 to 1992 at the Department of History, McMaster University, Hamilton, Ontario. I am grateful to both the Council and the history department for giving me the opportunity to carry out such a long and difficult but ultimately rewarding project. Special thanks to my colleagues Robert Johnston, John Weaver, and Dan Geagan for their help and encouragement. They made my stay at McMaster both fruitful and enjoyable. I also received much help and encouragement from George Luckyj, Professor Emeritus of Slavic Studies, University of Toronto, and Bohdan Budurowycz, Professor Emeritus of Slavic Studies, University of Toronto, who read the manuscript and suggested improvements. I am proud to have been associated with such distinguished and learned scholars, men whose wide European education and turbulent Continental experience brought a special authority and immediacy to bear on the questions of East European history we discussed together. Bohdan Klid of the Canadian Institute of Ukrainian Studies, University of Alberta, and Roman Serbyn of L'Université du Québec à Montréal also read the manuscript and suggested improvements. Svetlana Rubashkina of the Kuban State University, Krasnodar, took a special interest in my work and gave me some important leads. The Canadian Institute of Ukrainian Studies awarded me a grant to help with indexing and other matters. Violet Croydon of the Department of History, McMaster University, and Janet Kamienik and her colleagues of JMK Executive Services typed the manuscript. Theresa Griffin was my copy editor, Darlene Zeleney my editor *pro tem*, and Ron Schoeffel my general editor at the University of Toronto Press. Appropriate thanks are due to all those people and institutions. Of course, I take full responsibility for any mistakes that remain. I suspect, however, that Kostomarov would have been pleased to know that so many people took such care to tell the story of his life.

THOMAS M. PRYMAK
Toronto
June 1995

Introduction

Mykola Kostomarov (1817–85) was a leading light of the Ukrainian national awakening of the nineteenth century. He was a prolific historian who strove to write the history of the common Ukrainian people, and an original ethnographer forever seeking the mysterious 'soul' of that people. He was also a significant poet and writer who made a contribution to the development of the Ukrainian literary language, an educator who proclaimed his ideals from the lecterns of some of the most prestigious universities in Russia, and a publicist and ideologue who authored some of the most important political documents to be produced in Ukraine at a time when it was still generally known as 'Little Russia.' He was to guide the national awakening through many difficult years to a stage where it would one day be proclaimed a 'national movement.'

Kostomarov also played an important role in Russian life and letters independently of his involvement in Ukrainian affairs. He was the foremost representative of the so-called populist school of Russian historians, who put the nation or 'the people' (*narod*) at the centre of their story and relegated princes and tsars to a secondary place. He clearly shifted the focus of Russian history from external relations and diplomatic issues to 'internal' or social history, and in the process he elevated the principles of nationality, liberty, and equality and stressed the value of the native Slavic elements in Russian culture. Similarly, he made significant contributions to Russian life as an educator, an ethnographer, a journalist, and a literary and public figure.

It is the task of this book to tell the story of Kostomarov's life and his manifold contributions to Russian and Ukrainian history and culture. Kostomarov was primarily a historian, and an examination of his historical ideas plays an important role in the book. The study is not primarily a historiographical one, however, but a biography with an emphasis on Kostomarov's role in the cultural politics of his day and on his place in the Ukrainian national awakening. Kostomarov had an original and highly peculiar notion of Russian and Ukrainian national identity, and particular attention is paid to that aspect of his contribution to the Russian and Ukrainian cultural traditions.

My account of Kostomarov's life is based primarily on the writings of the historian himself. What I have done is to survey his narrative histories and methodically examine his more political writings and his historical polemics, which crystallize his views on most important matters. I have found his autobiographical writings, which exist in several forms and many editions, especially helpful, and in a way they have served as my starting-point and as a guide throughout. Kostomarov's *Collected Works*, which also exist in several different editions – one of them initiated while he was still a fairly young man – are also valuable to a prospective biographer and are used extensively in this book.

Kostomarov was such a prolific writer and so important an intellectual and public figure that detailed material about him began to appear immediately after his death. It included a new edition of his *Collected Works*, valuable firsthand testimonies from friends, acquaintances, and colleagues, encyclopaedia entries on him by men who had known him personally, and sections especially devoted to his life and work within larger and more general histories. As a rule, these essays tended to be sympathetic to Kostomarov, although they did not entirely lack a critical spirit. Moreover, some of the authors had had direct access to Kostomarov's as yet unpublished autobiographical writings, which turned out to be extensive. (A shorter autobiography appeared in 1885; a longer one in 1890.) Written with the tsarist censors in mind, these accounts, both Kostomarov's autobiographies and the works about him by others, breathed a fairly conservative spirit. In addition, there appeared a few rather negative biographical treatments, which called into question the historian's Russian patriotism and were obviously unsympathetic to Kostomarov and to the Ukrainian national awakening in general. Taken as a whole, these writings make up a kind of 'first wave' of materials for his biography.[1]

The great revolution of 1917–21 inaugurated a new phase in the study of Kostomarov's life and work. The old tsarist censors, to whom every prospective writer formerly had had to give some thought, were now gone, and the radical and oppositional nature of Kostomarov's legacy could be stressed clearly for the first time. New documents concerning Kostomarov's participation in the quasi-legal Cyril-Methodian Brotherhood now came to light, and a fuller profile of the historian's political and social ideals emerged.[2]

During the years that followed the revolution, Kostomarov scholarship made rapid advances. A new and fuller autobiography was published in Moscow in 1922, and this time discussion of the Cyril-Methodian Brotherhood and other political affairs was not omitted. This autobiography, the fullest ever to appear, also contained a lengthy memoir by Kostomarov's wife, Alina, and other personal materials. Moreover, during the same period, in Soviet Ukraine, the distinguished historian Mykhailo Hrushevsky (1866–1934) published a large collection of Kostomarov's rarer polemical writings (1928) and an extensive collection of his ethnographic works (1930), as well as numerous documents, letters, and other materials about Kostomarov. None of this material had appeared in the previous editions of his *Collected Works*. On a different level, however, and independently of this effort in Soviet Ukraine, in the 1920s the Ukrainian émigré historian Dmytro Doroshenko published a brief but well-balanced biography of the historian. These materials form a 'second wave' of sources for the Kostomarov biographer and are listed in full in the bibliography at the end of this volume.

During the late 1920s, the Communists consolidated their hold on the officially Soviet but still somewhat independent institutions of Russian and Ukrainian scholarship. In Moscow, the Institute of Red Professors under the guidance of the dean of Soviet historians, M.N. Pokrovsky (1868–1932), initiated a series of studies including a reanalysis of the work of the major pre-revolutionary historians. The work of Kostomarov and other historians of the so-called federalist school was analysed by M.A. Rubach (Rubanovych), who was able to see many 'progressive' and positive aspects in the historian's legacy. Rubach assigned Kostomarov to what he called the 'petty bourgeois federal-anarchist trend struggling against industrial and commercial capital,' gave him credit for his oppositional activities in the Cyril-Methodian Brotherhood, and acknowledged that he had sympathized with the enserfed peasantry and had championed republicanism against autocracy. However, Rubach also criticized Kostomarov for not giving proper attention to economic factors and for not properly defining and understanding the role of social classes in history. Rubach's extensive article was written in the mid-1920s and in spite of its clearly communist conceptualization was a fairly positive assessment of Kostomarov's life and ideas.[3]

The consolidation of power by Joseph Stalin in the early 1930s put an end to serious scholarship about Mykola Kostomarov. The Academy of Sciences of the U.S.S.R. and the Academy of Sciences of the Ukrainian Republic, within which men like Hrushevsky had worked, were thoroughly purged and 'sovietized,' and independent scholarship virtually ground to a halt. The school of Pokrovsky was suppressed, and the Russian imperial tradition partially rehabilitated. Centralization of power and Russification of the cultures of the non-Russian Soviet peoples became the dominant trends. The attitudes of the 1930s were inhospitable to the study of federalizing decentralizers of Kostomarov's type, and for a time all discussion of Kostomarov's legacy ceased. Then, in the early 1940s, the negative evaluation of Kostomarov which had emerged during the Stalin purges was systematized and codified in a major textbook of Soviet historiography by N.L. Rubinshtein. In this book, Kostomarov's 'idealism,' political moderation, and ethnographism were all thoroughly criticized, and he was labelled a 'liberal' and a 'bourgeois nationalist' who stood in opposition to all true 'revolutionary democrats.' Kostomarov's debunking of Russian national icons was declared 'national nihilism.' He was crudely lumped together with more conservative Russian historians and unabashedly proclaimed an adherent of the 'state school'; he was, in fact, declared more like the 'aristocratic' Nikolai Karamzin (1766–1826), against whose ideas he had struggled all his life, than like the relatively 'progressive' Vasili Kliuchevsky (1841–1911), who had actually borrowed some of his ideas from Kostomarov.[4]

This general state of affairs remained unchanged until the death of Stalin and the accession to power of Khrushchev somewhat changed the political climate in the Soviet Union. At that point, once again it became possible to say something positive about Kostomarov, and in a major re-evaluation of Russian historiography undertaken at that time, he was given some credit for his opposition to autocracy, although he continued to be criticized severely for his 'liberal' inclination towards compromising with the authorities, for his fabrication of a supposed theory of the 'classlessness' of the Ukrainian people, and for his idealization of the Cossacks and the 'democratic' nature of the Ukrainian nationality.[5]

The situation in Soviet Ukraine was even more complex. In particular, during the fragile but very real cultural renaissance which occurred in

Soviet Ukraine under the political protection of First Secretary Petro Shelest in the late 1960s, Soviet Ukrainian historians did their best to find a redeeming aspect to Kostomarov's activities, and a number of minor articles were published in an attempt to 'rehabilitate' him to a degree.[6] These efforts, however, never got very far since all attempts to create an independent Ukrainian intellectual tradition within the U.S.S.R. were crudely snuffed out during the ascendency of Brezhnev and Suslov. Shelest lost his position, and in the early 1970s a series of cultural purges took place. Thus, in 1971 the Russian historians V.E. Illeritsky and I.A. Kudriavtsev emphatically wrote:

Kostomarov was not a democrat by political conviction. He did not reflect the interests of the popular masses in their struggle for the destruction of their social yoke. The interests of the bourgeois-landlord liberal circles of Ukraine were expressed in his work. In the middle of the last century, those people demanded national autonomy for Ukraine within the bounds of the Tsarist Empire. In the historical views of Kostomarov, such desires found their expression in his idealization of Ukrainian history, of the national qualities of the South Russian nationality, of Cossackdom. However, at the same time Kostomarov half consciously tended to set the Ukrainian people against the Russians. That peculiarity of his view was later used by Ukrainian bourgeois nationalists, whose activities from the end of the nineteenth century against the proletarian movement in Ukraine and in Russia were thoroughly reactionary.[7]

Given this generally negative view of Kostomarov's life and work, it is understandable that throughout the 1970s and most of the 1980s very little of value was produced in the Soviet Union on the subject. When Kostomarov's achievements had to be treated – as, for example, in a general work by A.N. Tsamutali on ideological trends in Russian historiography – they were handled with great delicacy, and very little that was positive was said about the historian.[8]

It is thus somewhat surprising that in 1984 the Soviet Ukrainian historian Yu.A. Pinchuk managed to publish an entire book devoted to the historical views of Kostomarov. Although the book was largely devoted to some of the more specialized points of Kostomarov's historiographical heritage and obviously had been thoroughly emasculated by the various censors, it provided some basic information about Kostomarov's life and work, something that had long been absent from Soviet historical literature.[9] This was the state of Kostomarov studies in the Soviet Union on the eve of the Gorbachev reforms and the Soviet collapse.

The generally negative state of the Soviet scholarship was not without effect on scholars working in the West. In fact, not a single book was published on Kostomarov in the West after Doroshenko's pioneering Ukrainian-language study of the early 1920s. Even articles on Kostomarov were relatively few, most of them being published in the Ukrainian language by Ukrainian émigré scholars, such as those in the 1950s and 1960s by Volodymyr Miiakovsky.[10] For many years, the most extensive treatment of Kostomarov in English was the section on him in the indefatigable Doroshenko's 'A Survey of Ukrainian Historiography' (1957).[11] In 1966, however, Dennis Papazian, a graduate student at the University of Michigan, wrote a doctoral dissertation on Kostomarov in which was provided a new, non-Soviet view of the historian. Although Papazian, unaware of much of the work and published documentation on Kostomarov done by Hrushevsky and his colleagues in the 1920s, unnecessarily duplicated some of their work in the Soviet archives, he produced a new synthesis, and published a brief article in English on the Cyril-Methodian Brotherhood which was a first of its kind.[12] In general, however, Kostomarov and his work remained little known. The entry on Kostomarov in the multi-volume *Modern Encyclopedia of Russian and Soviet History* (1980) turned out to be a mere reprint and translation of a third-rate article by a little-known Soviet scholar.[13]

Considerable work on the Ukrainian national awakening was being done in the West, however, and this scholarship did not completely ignore the life and work of Kostomarov. George S.N. Luckyj in particular, beginning in the 1970s, published books in English on the national awakening between Gogol and Shevchenko, on the life of the historian's friend Panteleimon Kulish, and on the Cyril-Methodian Brotherhood, and an annotated translation of Pavlo Zaitsev's prestigious *Taras Shevchenko: A Life*.[14] All this material in some way touched upon the life of Kostomarov and was a help to the Kostomarov biographer.

Meanwhile, in the Soviet Union and in Eastern Europe the Gorbachev reforms gathered strength and the U.S.S.R. eventually came tumbling down. In 1991, Ukraine, along with many other former Soviet republics, declared state independence. Under the new conditions of intellectual freedom, Kostomarov scholarship once again began to flourish both in Russia and in newly independent Ukraine. New editions of classic works by Kostomarov appeared both in Moscow and in Kiev. The Russian editions, moreover, tended to stress the historian's contribution to Muscovite and Russian history, and the Ukrainian editions stressed his contributions to Ukrainian history and culture. Parts of Kostomarov's classic *Russian History in the Lives of Its Principal Figures,* for example, appeared in as many as five different editions.[15] Finally, in Moscow in 1991 and in Kiev in 1992, prominent articles appeared in the leading Russian and Ukrainian historical journals which fully 'rehabilitated' Kostomarov and acknowledged him as a major figure in Russian and Ukrainian culture.[16] They were closely followed by an important biography of the historian by Pinchuk, which gathered an impressive amount of interesting material on Kostomarov and generally painted him in a favourable light.[17] Pinchuk's biography was the first such work to be published since that of Doroshenko in the 1920s.

Pinchuk's book appeared as my own work, the first of its kind in a Western language, was nearing completion. It was not possible for me, therefore, to make full use of that work. I have tried to include some of the most interesting parts of Pinchuk's material which had not been readily available to me earlier. But in general my book was completed before I saw the Pinchuk biography, and my work is thus quite independent.

Mykola Kostomarov: A Biography is essentially, as the title indicates, an attempt at a biography, and its emphasis is on Kostomarov's manifold contributions to Russian and Ukrainian public life. As I mentioned earlier, it is not specifically a historiographical work, though some discussion of the scholar's historical ideas has been unavoidable. A certain amount of material about Kostomarov's personal life of course has been included; readers might find this material especially stimulating since there was much drama in Kostomarov's life. I have tried to keep the scholarly annotation to a minimum. Thus, numerous references to Kostomarov's *Autobiography,* which is a very rich source for his life story, have been omitted, and this work is cited only when absolutely necessary or when a direct quotation is given. Similarly, I have tried to keep the number of 'ibids' to a minimum when referring to other works. In the text, all titles of books, journals, and newspapers have been given in English translation with only a first reference to the Russian or Ukrainian original title where it seemed called for. Of course, the Slavic titles are given both in the notes and in the bibliography.

A word on the annotation. In the notes, I have tried to provide the reader with some general information on the publishing histories of Kostomarov's various works. That does not mean that I have actually seen all the works or editions listed. In general, I have consulted only the most recent or most available editions and have gleaned my bibliographical information from these later works or from Kostomarov's detailed personal bibliography, published in 1890. However, several important Kostomarov titles were not reprinted in any of the later collections, and I have had to consult them in the original. These titles are all listed separately in the bibliography at the end of the book. If a Kostomarov title from the notes is not listed there – as, for example, his articles in the rare literary almanac *The New Moon* (*Molodyk*) – then I have not seen it in the original. My principal sources, I must stress, were the great collections of the historian's works produced on the eve of the revolution and in the 1920s.

The transliteration of names and titles from languages which use a Cyrillic alphabet is always a problem for scholars working in the Slavic area. In general, I have used the American Library of Congress system for both Russian and Ukrainian, with certain simplifications. Soft-signs have been omitted. The only exceptions to this rule are in words with an overtly political meaning such as the proper name 'Rus'' or in somewhat peculiar names such as 'Soloviev.' In adjectival personal names, a final *y* has been considered sufficient: 'Mykhailo Hrushevsky' and not 'Mykhailo Hrushevs'kyi.' In the text, I use the more recognizable 'Yuzefovich,' while in the notes, for bibliographical reasons, I use 'Iuzefovich,' following the pure Library of Congress system.

Personal and place-names can also present a difficulty. In general, I use Ukrainian versions for those persons who identified most closely with Ukrainian culture, and Russian versions for those who identified solely with Russian. For Kostomarov himself, I tend to use the Ukrainian form, 'Mykola Ivanovych,' though at times, when he is acting in a purely Russian context, I leave the Russian form, 'Nikolai Ivanovich,' as is. Russian editions of his various published works, for example, bear this form.

For place-names, in general I use Russian forms for places in contemporary Russia, that is, the Russian Federation, and Ukrainian forms for lesser-known places in Ukraine. However, for cities and rivers with well-known forms in English, such as Kiev or the Dnieper, I retain these forms even though they are based on Russian equivalents. My goal in this case is simplicity, understandability, and clarity.

Finally, there is the matter of dating. The Julian calendar, used in the old Russian Empire, was twelve days behind our Western calendar in the nineteenth century. Since almost all the events discussed in the book took place in the Russian Empire, in Kharkiv, Kiev, Saratov, or St Petersburg, I have simply left all dates in the so-called old style. Only once, on the first page, where I mention the date of Kostomarov's birth, do I also give the Western or new-style date, in parentheses: 4 (16) May 1817.

MYKOLA KOSTOMAROV: A BIOGRAPHY

1

Youth and Education

Mykola Kostomarov, or Nikolai Kostomarov as he came to be known throughout Russia in the nineteenth century, was born on 4 (16) May 1817 in the manor-house of the village of Yurasovka, in the Ostrogozhk district of Voronezh province in the Russian Empire. This province was located in the upper reaches of the Don river valley. It was fertile and lightly forested steppe country populated for the most part by Ukrainian-speaking country folk and their partly Russified masters, whose ancestors had fled the historical Ukrainian lands to the west and settled as freemen and Cossacks in the 'Little Russian' region known as Sloboda Ukraine, which had been subject to the Muscovite tsar since the sixteenth century. Mykola's father, Ivan Petrovich, born in 1769, had served as a captain in the Russian army during the Russo-Turkish wars but retired at an early age to live on his estate at Yurasovka. Although he did not possess a large number of serfs – only three hundred according to his son's account – he was a substantial landowner, holding fourteen thousand desiatyns of fertile farm land sprinkled with meadows and forests. His historian son later traced the family history to an old boyar clan in Muscovy, one of whose members had fled to Lithuania during the time of Ivan the Terrible. This particular boyar's grandson, who was a native of Volhynia, in central Ukraine, joined the Cossack uprising of Bohdan Khmelnytsky against the Polish-Lithuanian Commonwealth and took part in the battle of Berestechko (1651), in which the Cossacks suffered a serious defeat. With many other Volhynian families, he fled eastward to the lands ruled by the Muscovite tsar and helped to populate the region called Sloboda Ukraine.[1]

Ivan Petrovich was a typical Russian country gentleman of the early nineteenth century. Though his education had not been thorough, he accepted the rationalist axioms of the eighteenth-century enlightenment and with a modest command of the French language took to reading the French *philosophes* in the original. His favourite writers were Voltaire, D'Alembert, Diderot, and the other encyclopaedists. Under the influence of these authors, he wavered between deism and atheism and with dubious success tried to apply his philosophy to his real life. 'In the political and social conceptions of my late father,' wrote Mykola Kostomarov many years later, 'there reigned a peculiar mixture of liberalism/democraticism with ancestral haughtiness.'

He used to love to lecture everywhere and to everybody that all men were equal, that hereditary distinctions were a superstition, and that everyone should live like brothers. However, that did not hinder him on occasion from displaying the whip to his social inferiors or from giving them a thrashing, especially in moments of anger when he could not control himself. But after each such transgression he would ask for forgiveness from the offended party and try in some way to make up for his mistake and distribute money and gifts. The servants enjoyed this to the degree that there were cases when they irritated him on purpose in order to make him angry and then make up with him later on.[2]

Whether Mykola exaggerated his father's egalitarian tendencies or not is unclear; in any event, Ivan Petrovich cared little enough about social distinctions to choose one of his own serfs, a Ukrainian girl by the name of Tatiana Petrivna Mylnikova, to be his wife. With marriage in mind, he sent Tatiana Petrivna to a boarding-school in Moscow to acquire an education befitting the wife of a country gentleman. But Napoleon's 1812 invasion of Russia and the burning of Moscow intervened, and Ivan Petrovich took Tatiana out of school and home to his estate in the south. They lived together in Yurasovka until the birth of their son, Mykola, after which they were formally married. The delay in the wedding ceremony was later to cost both mother and son dearly.

Mykola's early childhood was a fairly happy one. His father's estate was beautiful, with meadows, forests, a gently flowing river, and little islands covered with rich vegetation; all that inspired the boy, who would often read poetry under the trees with his father and sometimes imagine the islands in the river to be far-off places like Borneo, Sumatra, Celebes, or Java. But Ivan Petrovich was rather strict with Mykola. Under the influence of Rousseau's *Émile*, he taught his son to live close to nature, not even allowing him to bundle up properly when going outside in cold weather. Similarly, in accordance with Voltairean rationalism he would not allow the house servants to tell Mykola folk-tales about wood demons, house spirits, or witches.

When Mykola was ten years old, his father took him to Moscow to begin his formal education. He was enrolled at a boarding-school run by a Frenchman named Gay and soon impressed his instructors with his intelligence and astounding memory. Only his dancing teacher thought him a little backward.

In the summer of 1828, Mykola returned to Yurasovka fully expecting to go back to Moscow in the fall to continue his education. But a terrible incident occurred which was to change the course of his life. Ivan Petrovich had mortgaged his property and stored the money, which was to be used for his son's education and for improvements to the estate, in a trunk where he kept his valuables. Some unscrupulous house servants, encouraged by their master's teachings about equality and irreligion, decided to kill him and steal his fortune. One day, when Ivan Petrovich went out to the forest for his usual ride, these servants murdered him and bloodied his body so as to create the appearance of a riding accident. Meanwhile, Mykola and his mother waited for him to return. The hours passed and he did not arrive. It was time for supper but still there was no Ivan Petrovich. At length, a servant came and informed them that the horses had carried the master off. There was general commotion and a search was begun, during which the conspirators carried out their plan and took the money. Finally, a servant found Ivan Petrovich. Mykola and his mother were brought to the spot to find their loved one lying dead in a ravine, his head smashed and covered in blood. The scene made an indelible impression on the young Kostomarov, and years later his heart still quickened as he recalled it.[3]

Even the police did not suspect foul play. It was five years later that one of the peasants who had murdered the master became conscience-stricken and confessed to a priest and then to the authorities. The surviving conspirators were exposed and punished, but Mykola's life had been changed forever. Since his father had not married Tatiana Petrivna until after the birth of their child, young Kostomarov had been born into serfdom in the eyes of the law and had no rights to the family estate. Moreover, Ivan Petrovich's relatives soon arrived to claim their inheritance, and they were willing to use any means to get it. Mykola's mother's status as Ivan's legitimate wife could not be disputed, but the relatives insisted that since her son had been born before his mother was married, he was no more and should be treated as no more than a common serf. One of these relatives took Mykola as his personal lackey and treated him quite badly, seemingly in an attempt to frighten Tatiana Petrivna into giving up most of her share of her husband's estate. The stratagem, if that is what it was, worked. Tatiana Petrivna accepted a modest cash settlement of fifty thousand rubles and was assured of her son's freedom in return for all her rights to the inheritance. She then purchased a much smaller estate nearby and, although she now had only a few dozen serfs, was able to order things so that she could once again send her son away to complete his education.[4]

Mykola was placed in a small boarding-school in Voronezh, the capital of the province in which he lived. The school was directed by two teachers from the local gymnasium but could not compare with the expensive educational institutions of Moscow to which he would have been sent had his father not died. The local teachers were inadequate and the other students interested only in soldiering and hunting, and although Mykola impressed his mentors with his knowledge of geography and history, he was, as he later put it, 'relieved' to be expelled for breaking into a wine-cellar one night with his fellow pupils.[5]

In 1831, Tatiana Petrivna sent her son at his own request to the Voronezh gymnasium. He boarded with the school's Latin teacher, a certain Andrei Belinsky, a kindly old man from Austrian Galicia. Although he had been in Russia for over thirty years, Belinsky still spoke Russian with a strong Ukrainian accent, and according to his famous pupil he had little pedagogical talent. The other teachers seemed scarcely better and on the whole were more concerned with pleasing influential parents than with fostering the education of their pupils. In 1833, at the age of sixteen, Kostomarov was the only boy from his school to win admission to a Russian university.

Once again, Kostomarov did not set out for an expensive educational institution in the Russian north, but entered the University of Kharkiv, which had been founded in 1805 at the initiative of the nobility of Sloboda Ukraine and which displayed a marked local patriotism during the first decades of the century. Young Mykola passed his entrance examination without incident and along with a few other students took lodgings with a professor of Latin named Sokolsky. The Sokolsky family was very good to its young lodgers, and Kostomarov retained fond memories of the professor's wife, who fussed over her boarders and baked them fresh *pyrizhky* for breakfast every morning. 'Nadiia Omelianivna,' recalled Kostomarov many years later, 'remains in my memory as a typical kindly, old-fashioned Ukrainian lady. She spoke with every-one only in Ukrainian.'[6]

Kostomarov's first love during his early years in university was classical languages and literatures. That love inspired some of his antics at home. One time, his friends dragged him around the house by the heels in a re-enactment of a famous scene in Homer's *Iliad*. Sokolsky, sitting on the porch with some professor friends, was furious when the boys suddenly stormed by, but upon discovering the scholarly inspiration for the prank burst into laughter, and in the end all present had a good time.

Kostomarov's early love for antiquity was soon supplemented by an interest in modern literature. He continued to improve his French and was especially enraptured by the historical novels of Victor Hugo. At the same time, he tried his hand at writing poetry in Russian, using as models the works of ancient authors, especially Virgil.

In 1835, the atmosphere of the University of Kharkiv changed con-siderably with the arrival of certain professors who brought novel ideas to the institution and soon raised the level of academic discourse within it. Of them, the most important for the Historico-Philological Faculty, in which Kostomarov was registered, was M.M. Lunin, a 'universal' historian who had come from the University of Dorpat (Tartu) equipped with the latest notions of historical science. Mikhail Lunin, who had studied in Berlin under Savigny and von Ranke, was influenced by the philosophy of Hegel and greatly admired the work of Sir Walter Scott and the French romantic historians – such as François Guizot and Augustin Thierry – who were his younger contemporaries. Lunin taught ancient and modern history, and Kostomarov was clearly impressed by his treatment of older times, especially the struggle of Christianity against paganism. 'In general,' Kostomarov later recalled, 'this profes-sor's lectures made an enormous impression on me and caused a com-plete turn-around in my intellectual life; I loved history more than anything and from that time eagerly delved into the study of historical books ... I took up history with great enthusiasm and spent day and night reading the most varied historical books. I wanted to know the story of every nation, and I was no less interested in literature from a historical point of view.'[7]

During the same period, that is, beginning in the fall of 1835, Kosto-marov took lodgings with Petro Hulak-Artemovsky, a professor of Russian history at the university, who was already fairly widely known as a poet who wrote in the Ukrainian language. Hulak-Artemovsky's knowledge of Ukrainian was profound, and he dreamed of compiling a dictionary of the language, but Kostomarov thought his history lectures uninspiring and did not seem to get along with him very well. For a while, the young scholar tutored the professor's sons in history.

In 1837, Kostomarov graduated with the degree of 'candidate' and left the university to learn more about the non-academic world. On an adventurous whim, it seems, he decided to join the army. But he was not allowed to wear glasses in spite of his short-sightedness, and in general he displayed no aptitude for military life. He managed to put his time to good use, however, because Ostrogozhk, the town in which he was stationed, possessed rich military archives; over the course of a year, Kostomarov was able to compose a history of the local Ostrogozhk Cossack regiment. It was his first experience with real archival work.[8]

In the fall of 1837, the young scholar returned to the University of Kharkiv to continue his academic career. He attended lectures by Lunin and others. 'History was my most beloved subject,' he later wrote. 'I read a great many history books of every type, reflected upon them, and arrived at the following question ...':

Why is it that all the history books talk about the extraordinary historical characters, and occasionally about laws and institutions, but at the same time ignore the lives of the masses of ordinary people? The poor peasant, the working farmer, as it were, does not exist in history. Why does history not tell us about his way of life, his spiritual world, his feelings, and the means by which he expresses his happiness and his sadness? I soon became convinced that history must be studied not only from dead chronicles and writings, but also among living people. Could it not be that bygone ages are also reflected in the lives and memories of their heirs? It was merely necessary to seek, and certainly much would be found that scholarship had up to now overlooked. But where was one to begin? Naturally enough, with the study of my own Russian people. But in so far as I then lived in Little Russia I would begin with its Little Russian branch. This idea turned me towards the reading of the monuments of the national heritage. For the first time in my life, I got hold of the Little Russian songs published by [Mykhailo] Maksymovych in 1827 and the Great Russian songs of [I.P.] Sakharov, and I began to read them. I was struck and then carried away by the sincere beauty of Little Russian popular poetry. I had never suspected that such elegance, such depth and fresh feelings could be found in the creations of the [common] people who were so close to me and about whom I unfortunately knew nothing.[9]

Within a month, the young enthusiast had learned Maksymovch's collection by heart. He went on to study Maksymovych's second collection of Ukrainian songs, which was more sophisticated and included a number of somewhat longer historical dumas, or epic poems, dealing with the heroic days of the Cossacks. At this time, Kostomarov became acquainted with the work of I.I. Sreznevsky, a young professor of statistics at the university who had earlier become enthralled by Slavic, especially Ukrainian, historical poems and was just completing the publication of his wide-ranging collection on the history of the Zaporozhian Cossacks, entitled *Zaporozhian Antiquity* (1833–8). An acquaintance, A.L. Metlynsky, who was later to make his own contribution to Ukrainian literature, introduced Kostomarov to Sreznevsky, and the latter exercised a powerful influence on the young historian. From historical dumas and popular poetry, Kostomarov moved on to contemporary Ukrainian literature, and in a relatively short time he managed to read the modest corpus which then existed. It included the famous *Eneida* by Ivan Kotliarevsky, which Kostomarov had known in his youth but had been unable to understand before taking up the study of things Ukrainian. Not having at his disposal a dictionary of the 'Little Russian dialect,' as the Ukrainian language was then called in the Russian Empire – such a dictionary did not yet exist – Kostomarov eagerly peppered his manservant from Yurasovka and his friends and acquaintances with questions about the meaning of individual words and expressions. He made expeditions into the countryside around Kharkiv to collect songs, proverbs, and stories about the Ukrainian past, and he even frequented the local taverns, which turned out to be an ethnographer's paradise. After an expedition to Poltava, the site of the great battle (1709) between the armies of Tsar Peter I and King Charles XII of Sweden, he started to write a drama about their times, but he soon put it aside.[10]

During the course of 1837 and 1838, Kostomarov continued to improve his linguistic skills and in spite of his imperfect knowledge of the language took to writing poetry and other literary pieces in Ukrainian. Metlynsky and other friends scoffed at his attempts, but Kostomarov persevered and in three short weeks in February 1838 even composed a historical drama set in Cossack times. It was named *Sava Chaly* after its main character, and in private readings Sreznevsky praised the work. In the spring, Kostomarov went to Moscow with Metlynsky, who was travelling on an assignment in his capacity as a librarian at the University of Kharkiv. Kostomarov remained in Moscow for several months, during which time he sat in on some university lectures given by the historians Mikhail Kachenovsky and Mikhail Pogodin and the literary scholar S.P. Shevyrev. The historians did not impress Kostomarov but the literary scholar did, and he briefly played with the idea of taking a master's degree in Russian philology.[11] In the summer, he returned to his mother's home in the country, where he studied German and read Goethe and Schiller in the original. In the fall, he returned to Kharkiv, where, like his colleague Sreznevsky, he took up Polish and Czech. The young scholar was impressed by the Královédvorský manuscript, the ostensible collection of medieval Czech poetry forged by Václav Hanka on the basis of popular Czech verse. Unaware of the spurious origin of the verses, he translated some of them into Ukrainian.

In the spring of 1838, Kostomarov's first book, his historical drama *Sava Chaly*, appeared in print under the pseudonym Yeremiia Halka. Kostomarov's creation was based not on historical documents but on folk material collected by Maksymovych, Sreznevsky, and the Polish ethnographer Wacław z Oleska and was mistakenly set in the seventeenth century. (The historical Sava Chaly, as Kostomarov later learned, was a haidamak, or insurgent Cossack leader, of the eighteenth century.)[12]

Kostomarov's *Sava Chaly* went beyond much of the Ukrainian literature of its time in both form and content. Although it was based on folk material and its story had the characteristics typical of romantic tragedy, the play did not dwell on the customs and way of life of the Ukrainian country folk, as was usual in the Ukrainian literature of those days. Instead, it was a drama based on actual historical events which also explored questions of political loyalty and national contradictions. It was very favourably reviewed in the influential Russian journal *Notes of the Fatherland* (*Otechestvennye zapiski*), which did not yet see 'Little Russian' local patriotism as in anyway insidious, and it was reprinted in Odessa in 1875.[13]

Towards the end of 1839, Kostomarov's second volume appeared. *Ukrainian Ballads* (*Ukrainskii ballady*) was a small collection of poetry based on historical Ukrainian songs and some translations from the Královédvorský manuscript. It was followed a few months later by another booklet of poems, entitled *The Branch* (*Vitka*), containing similar material, with one of the poems dedicated to Sreznevsky, who was about to depart on a study tour of the Slavic countries outside the boundaries of the Russian Empire. The poems were typical products of the Ukrainian romantic literature of their day and, unlike the play *Sava Chaly*, did not go far beyond the imitation of folk poetry and other romantic models. They were, however, heartily welcomed by the small circle of Ukrainian enthusiasts in Kharkiv.[14]

Kostomarov continued to collect folk-songs and other material having to do with the Ukrainian past. 'More and more,' he later wrote, 'I was carried away by the Little Russian language. I was annoyed that such a beautiful tongue remained without any literary development and on top of that endured a prejudice which was completely undeserved.'

Everywhere I heard coarse comments and jibes at the Ukrainians [*Khokhly*] not only on the part of the Great Russians but also from higher-class Little Russians, who considered it permissible to scoff at the peasant and his means of expression. I considered that kind of attitude towards the people and its speech a deprecation of human dignity, and the more I heard such comments, the more strongly I identified with the Little Russian nationality.[15]

Throughout 1840, Kostomarov continued to interest himself in Ukrainian affairs while preparing to take the master's examinations in history at the University of Kharkiv. In November, he was examined by Lunin, who proved to be rather tough, Hulak-Artemovsky, who did not seem to take the process very seriously, and other professors. Having successfully completed his exams, Kostomarov began work on a dissertation and, manifesting a serious interest in religion, chose to study the history of the Union of Brest (1596), according to which the Orthodox church of the Ukrainian and Belorussian lands within the Polish-Lithuanian Commonwealth recognized the supremacy of Rome while retaining its separate rite and ecclesiastical organization. This was a subject of great contemporary significance, since Tsar Nicholas I, as part of his repressive measures against his Polish subjects for their rebellion of 1831, had in 1839 forcibly suppressed the 'Uniate' or 'Greek Catholic' church and compelled its adherents to return to Orthodoxy. The formal title of Kostomarov's dissertation was 'On the Reasons and Character of the Union in Western Russia.'[16]

While Kostomarov was thus working, he made the acquaintance of another enthusiast of the Ukrainian awakening, Oleksander Korsun, a landowner from Taganrog, who was himself a Ukrainian writer and who was preparing an almanac for publication under the title *The Sheaf* (*Snip*). Korsun had noted that *The Branch* had been published at the university printing house and went there to track down the unknown author. He found out where Yeremiia Halka, alias Mykola Kostomarov, lived, and visited him at his home. Kostomarov made a good impression on his visitor. Korsun later recalled that the history student was a man twenty-odd years old, with eyeglasses, fine features, and a somewhat girlish laugh. When enthusiastic about something, he quickly became agitated and developed a nervous manner. When Korsun suggested that Kostomarov contribute something to his projected almanac, the latter immediately agreed and handed over some of his verses – translations of Byron, from Czech, and some original poetry. The same evening, he also brought Korsun the unfinished manuscript of another play, entitled 'The Night at Pereiaslav,' a romantic tragedy in the Schillerian style set in Cossack times.[17]

A common love for the Ukrainian language and the fledgling Ukrainian literature soon bound the two men together, and together they discovered a fiery and melancholic new author who was to transform that literature into something more mature, more dynamic, and much more dangerous to the unity and peace of the Russian Empire. In the fall of 1840, Taras Shevchenko's first collection of poetry, published under the title *The Minstrel* (*Kobzar*), appeared and made an immediate and indelible impression on Ukrainian literary circles. 'One day I was walking with Mykola Ivanovych Kostomarov to the cathedral for the divine liturgy,' Korsun later recalled, 'when we dropped in at Aparin's bookstore. We asked if he had any new books, and Aparin showed us a thin book – *The Minstrel*. We sat down on a bench and continued to sit there right through the lunch hour. We read the entire book ... This was something quite special, new and original. *The Minstrel* stunned us!' Shortly afterwards, Kostomarov met Hulak-Artemovsky on the street and, dispensing with the usual pleasantries, in enthusiastic tones immediately began to tell him about *The Ministrel*. Such was the effect of Shevchenko's poetry on his contemporaries.[18]

During the winter of 1840–1, Kostomarov worked on his dissertation on the Union of Brest. In addition to the published history of Little Russia by Dmytro Bantysh-Kamensky, with which Kostomarov was already well acquainted, and the standard histories of Poland by authors such as Adam Naruszewicz, on which he relied quite heavily, the young historian made some use of various Polish chronicles, the description of Ukraine by Guillaume le Vasseur, Sieur de Beauplan, the collection of historical Ukrainian folk-songs by Wacław z Oleska, and the unpublished history of Ukraine which circulated under the name *History of the Ruthenians* (*Istoriia Rusov*) and was misleadingly ascribed to the late bishop Heorhii Konysky. This last history was a colourful work which reflected the local patriotism of the nobility of Left-Bank and Sloboda Ukraine – that is, the landed estate descended from the Cossack officer class of older times. The *History of the Ruthenians* served to balance the somewhat dry official history of Bantysh-Kamensky, which was heavily laden with loyalty to the Russian monarchy and reflected the unilinear and state-centred historical scheme of the St Petersburg court historiographer Nikolai Karamzin.[19]

Kostomarov's work on the church union was a thoroughly Ukrainian treatment which reflected the interests of the Kharkiv circles in which he moved, and bore little relation to Karamzin-style Muscocentric Russian history. Moreover, Kostomarov did not dwell on the politics of the church hierarchs, or even on the fiery polemics of ecclesiastical scholars, but instead, in accordance with his philosophy of history, put the entire people, the nation (*narod*), at the centre of his story. In Kostomarov's opinion, the story of the union was that of the popular struggle for the Orthodox faith against the Catholic Poles. He ascribed the inclination of the Orthodox clergy to accept the union to a deep moral decay, which he believed had set in in earlier centuries, and dared to criticize the ecumenical patriarch at Constantinople, and he wrote more or less in the spirit of the rationalist enlightenment in which he had been raised. According to Kostomarov, it was the church union and the struggle against it which displaced the traditional mistrust of Muscovite despotism among the Ukrainian population, which supplanted the overriding Kievan loyalties and love for independence of the churchmen, and which overcame the reluctance of the Ukrainian national leader, Bohdan Khmelnytsky, and inexorably led to the unification of Northern and Southern Rus' under the Orthodox tsar of Moscow. Kostomarov drew an especially dark picture of what he believed to be a short-sighted and ambitious Khmelnytsky, who dreamed of invading Poland but ended by submitting to Muscovy. 'The Little Russians wanted independence,' wrote the young historian. 'That was their popular demand; Khmelnytsky did not fulfil that demand at the moment when he could have.'[20]

In the spring of 1841, Kostomarov completed his dissertation and submitted it to the university faculty for examination. He then went on vacation to the Crimea, where, inspired by the architectural splendour of the former Khanate, the ruins of the ancient Greek colonies on the Black Sea coast, and the poetry of Alexander Pushkin, who had earlier visited those places, he wrote several verses in the Ukrainian language, extracts of which – including the poem 'To Maria Potocki' – he shortly afterwards published in the literary almanac *The New Moon* (*Molodyk*).

This almanac, published by Kostomarov's friend Ivan Betsky, appeared in four books between 1843 and 1844. It contained works by the veteran of writing in the Ukrainian vernacular Hryhori Kvitka-Osnovianenko, who had gained considerable fame for his sentimental short stories depicting country life in Little Russia; by Metlynsky, who had begun writing in Ukrainian under Kostomarov's influence; and by Shevchenko, Pushkin, and others. It also contained the innovative 'Survey of Works Written in the Little Russian Language.' by Kostomarov himself.[21]

Kostomarov's 'Survey' recounted the modest growth of literature in the Ukrainian vernacular from Kotliarevsky's time to his own; he considered Kvitka-Osnovianenko and Shevchenko 'without a doubt the best Little Russian writers' and devoted considerable attention to his romantic contemporaries. Kostomarov straightforwardly defended the Ukrainian language's antiquity, dignity, right to existence, and suitability for artistic creation. He thought that literature in the vernacular, both Russian and Ukrainian, rose naturally as a response to the spread of the national principle, and that if Ukrainians were to write in Russian rather than in their native language they would eventually have to give up their nationality – which would be a self-evident injustice. 'And so,' continued the young enthusiast, 'the idea of nationality, while thrusting Russian literature ahead, has created a separate section within it – Little Russian literature, which according to its character is purely Russian, but of its own nationality [*svoenarodnaia*].' He concluded: 'Many contemporary critics call this tendency to write in Little Russian an incomprehensible whim, but that way of thinking is groundless. [Writing in Little Russian] is an imperative of the time because it proceeds from that principle which gives life to contemporary society.'[22]

By the spring of 1842, Kostomarov's dissertation, 'On the Reasons and Character of the Union in Western Russia,' had been printed in a run of one hundred copies by the university printing house, and in preparation for the final defence, set for the sixth week of Lent, the author had distributed copies to faculty members and to his friends. Suddenly, however, the dean of the faculty quietly informed Kostomarov that the new Orthodox bishop of Kharkiv, Innokenty Borisov, had seen his work and had some serious reservations about it. The dean suggested that they visit Bishop Innokenty to discuss the work. During the discussions, Innokenty criticized what he believed to be the young historian's negative portrayal of the Orthodox clergy, in particular of the Patriarch of Constantinople. When Kostomarov began to back up his opinions with historical facts, the dean broke in and asked whether Innokenty had in

mind censorship or merely scholarship. The bishop replied, 'Only scholarship and in no way censorship.' The dean then suggested that the
matter was settled, since the approaching defence would cover scholarly
questions. The difficulty appeared to be resolved.[23]

But the day before his scheduled defence Kostomarov unexpectedly
saw a notice nailed to the university wall announcing its cancellation.
The dean informed the young scholar that Innokenty wanted a meeting
with the minister of public education, Count Sergei Uvarov, before the
defence was held. Kostomarov approached Innokenty in search of an
explanation, but the bishop seemed to be hiding something. Time
passed, and finally an order came from Uvarov's office in St Petersburg
that all copies of the dissertation be retrieved and destroyed and that
Kostomarov begin work on a new topic. The order was accompanied by
a report by Professor N.G. Ustrialov of the University of St Petersburg
which severely criticized Kostomarov's work, ostensibly for its poor
scholarship. So the young historian had to make the rounds asking for
the return of the copies he had earlier distributed. Many people made
excuses in order to keep their copies – Kostomarov retrieved fewer than
twenty of the original hundred; but all those recovered were solemnly
burned at a meeting of the university council.[24] 'The persecution of my
dissertation,' wrote Kostomarov with conviction many years later, 'was
understandably a result of the beliefs expressed in it that the spread of
the union was promoted by the ignorance, immorality, and laziness of
the Orthodox clergy, and, above all, in several places I aired ideas
which were more Protestant than Orthodox.'[25]

Undaunted by the unusual experience – even in the Russia of
Nicholas I – of having his scholarship committed to the flames, Kostomarov immediately set to work on an even more daring subject, but one
which, as he later recalled, 'had already been close to my heart for a
very long time.'[26] Kostomarov entitled his project 'On the Historical
Significance of Russian Popular Poetry' and worked on it with great
enthusiasm throughout the 1842–43 academic year. He had been collecting folk-songs and historical material for several years, of course, and
he welcomed the opportunity to delve more deeply into the subject. He
became especially interested in the symbolism of folk poetry, an area
that was still little explored. On 6 November 1842, he wrote to Sreznevsky: 'My dissertation is moving ahead, and most of all I want to work
on symbolism. The more I get into that subject, the more and more I
discover interesting things. Much that had been ambiguous to me has
now become clear ... Blessed be that moment when I was struck by the

happy thought of choosing this subject as the theme of my disserta-tion.'[27]

However, the work was not without difficulties. Some faculty mem-bers expressed dismay that peasant songs could be considered the subject of serious historical work. Even Hulak-Artemovsky, who had gained some renown for his contributions to Ukrainian literature, at first viewed the project with a critical eye, and he eventually approved of it only when he had seen the completed work. Furthermore, the young historian's personal affairs were not going well. He fell in love with a governess who, in turn, gave herself to another. When the man deserted her, Kostomarov challenged him to a duel. The university authorities found out, the duel was cancelled, and Kostomarov lost a part-time position he had held for a time as assistant inspector of students.[28]

None of the these personal or academic problems served to turn the young enthusiast from his goal. He buried himself in his work and as a result managed not only to complete his dissertation in short order but also to publish his first articles on historical themes in a later vol-ume of Betsky's almanac, *The New Moon*, and to begin collecting material for an in-depth study of Bohdan Khmelnytsky.[29] So enthusiastic was Kostomarov about his work that he sought out personal contact with everyone in the field who was available to him. For example, he wrote to Platon Lukashevych, marshal of the nobility of the Pereiaslav district and a distinguished ethnographer and folklorist who in 1836 had published a collection of 'Little Russian' and 'Red Russian' (that is, Galician Ukrainian) folk-songs. Kostomarov greeted him thus: 'God give you good health for your love for the fatherland. I too love that same Ukraine, and that same old Hetmanate, and those most noble hetmans, and the brave young Cossacks, and your songs, and your language, and everything that there is good and your own about you, and not foreign or stolen.'[30]

By the end of 1843, 'On the Historical Significance of Russian Popular Poetry' had been examined and approved by the faculty committee and printed by the university press. The formal defence was set for 13 January 1844. In the days before the defence, Sreznevsky, who had returned from his study tour abroad to accept a position as professor of Slavic languages at Kharkiv, and Lunin, who liked Kostomarov's disser-tation very much and shared his ideas about introducing the popular element into historical science, both proved great supporters. Kostoma-rov even read parts of the work to Sreznevsky in order to get his critical comments.[31]

Kostomarov's finished work began with a statement of his thesis that folk poetry was an important historical source, though one that should be used with great care since folk-songs often contain fantasies of various sorts. As a source for the study of the people's view of itself, however, folk-song was unsurpassed; it was only necessary to establish that such a source was truly of folk origin. Kostomarov went on to discuss the poetic symbolism of folk poetry, especially symbolic references to plants and animals. He examined purely historical songs and recorded one that he himself had discovered – a duma about galley-slaves on the Black Sea – though he did not describe where, how, or from whom he had gotten the epic song. With regard to Ukrainian history, Kostomarov stated his belief that folk-songs established four basic Ukrainian types: the Cossack warrior; the carter, or *chumak*; the vagrant, or *burlak*; and the villager or agriculturalist. He went on to assert that these types reflected the course of Ukrainian history from the high summer of Cossackdom, so to speak, through the autumn of the *chumak* and *burlak*, to the cold winter of agricultural serfdom. Finally, Kostomarov stated that he, like the Moscow Slavist Osyp Bodiansky before him, thought Ukrainian folk poetry richer and more dramatic than Russian folk poetry, which, he claimed, was limited to the family sphere and displayed a natural monarchism and high regard for ritual.[32]

Kostomarov's oral defence of this dissertation did not proceed without incident. One of his official opponents, a certain Professor Yakimov (Sreznevsky was the other), took out of context a few lines from a verse quoted by Kostomarov, and demanded to know their poetic value. But Lunin rushed to the aid of the young scholar and asserted that poetry should always be viewed as a whole. Towards the end of the defence, Bishop Innokenty arrived and attempted to compare folk poetry to that of the Holy Scriptures, but he was soon silenced by Hulak-Artemovsky. The thesis was accepted, and in due course Kostomarov received his master's degree from the university.[33]

The reviews of Kostomarov's dissertation began to appear during the following months. Some were quite negative. The progressive 'Westernizing' critic of *Notes of the Fatherland*, Vissarion Belinsky, seemed to see no value at all in Kostomarov's work and disparaged the very subject matter. 'In our time,' he began, 'if an author does not wish or is unable to speak about anything in particular, Russian folk poetry is always an excellent way of getting out of the difficulty. What can be said about this subject has already been said. But Mr Kostomarov has not given up on it, and he has published a whole book full of words about Russian popular poetry in which it would be difficult to find any content.'[34] Belinsky's idiosyncratic conservative counterpart, Osip Senkovsky, who was of Polish gentry origin, was even more critical, mocking what he believed were the fashionable references to Herder, Niebuhr, and Thierry and accusing Kostomarov of trying to find 'the historical significance of white wine and pretty girls in the philosophy of coachmen.'[35] Sreznevsky, however, published a positive as well as quite lengthy review of Kostomarov's work. He thought the work had great significance not only in Slavic but in general European scholarship and believed that men like the Grimm brothers, Sakharov, and the Slovak scholar Jan Kollár should take note of it. Sreznevsky congratulated Kostomarov for studying popular poetry found among the people themselves rather than only in books, but he also had a few criticisms. He took Kostomarov to task for ignoring fables and prose tradition, which, he believed, often differed from folk poetry only in external form; he did not like Kostomarov's emphasis on Ukrainian at the expense of Russian folk poetry; he partly disagreed with Kostomarov's treatment of symbolism, especially his neglect of mythology; and he wished that Kostomarov had turned his attention also to pre-Christian relics in the folk tradition and arranged the products of that tradition in the order of their creation.[36] Sreznevsky's observations may have been a reworking of points made by him at the defence. Certainly, Kostomarov took them seriously: with the exception of the prose fables, on which the historian was never actually to write, his next ethnographic projects addressed those very subjects.[37]

The successful defence of his second dissertation and the acquisition of the master's degree brought Mykola Kostomarov's formal education to an end; the first chapter of his personal life ended with it. This chapter had begun with a fairly happy childhood in the Province of Voronezh, where amid the quiet beauty of the Sloboda Ukrainian countryside he was taught to respect the principles of the eighteenth-century enlightenment. He was brought up speaking Russian but was surrounded by the rich folk culture of a people who not so long before had migrated to the area from the heartland of old Ukraine. An education in Moscow or St Petersburg might have turned him into a typical Little Russian country gentleman of his time, but the sudden death of his father deprived him of the financial means to obtain such an education. He was left with small-town schools and a provincial university. But he did well at both and soon displayed a serious interest in classical antiquity. Then Lunin turned his thoughts towards history, while Gogol, Maksymovych, and Sreznevsky awakened in him an interest in his native land. Since written material about Ukrainian history was scarce, Kostomarov, like a handful of others around him, turned for inspiration to the living traditions of the Ukrainian people. He began to collect folk material and to experiment with writing in the Ukrainian vernacular.

Kostomarov's background was not the best for a budding Ukrainian writer. His vocabulary was limited and his themes were the stock ones of the era. Yet he believed the new principle of nationality would inspire all contemporary culture, and he wanted to see Ukrainian literature develop to its fullest possible extent; his very first published works were something new for Ukrainian literature. 'There was in these verse creations,' observed the western Ukrainian writer Ivan Franko some three-quarters of a century later 'something that distinguished them from all other contemporary Ukrainian works, something energetic although restrained, in any case something of character, although not shiningly so.'[38] Kostomarov was not an instant success as a Ukrainian writer, but neither was he a complete failure.

Scholarship offered more solid prospects. Kostomarov's academic work, of course, reflected his interest in nationality and the common people. His first dissertation was a study not so much of church history as of the common man in action, a study of the days of Khmelnytsky, when Cossacks ruled; and for Kostomarov the concepts of *kozachestvo* (Cossackdom) and *narod* (the people) were closely intertwined, as were the concepts of *narod* (the people) and *bednyi muzhik* (the poor peasant). His focus was therefore strikingly different from that of Karamzin and official Russian historiography, which concentrated on rulers and relations between states. Karamzin, so to speak, dealt with 'external' history, while Kostomarov dealt with the 'internal.' Bantysh-Kamensky, who authored the first modern published history of Little Russia, and Hulak-Artemovsky, who taught Russian history at Kharkiv, were both devoted followers of Karamzin. By contrast, in his first serious historical work – his thesis on the church union – Kostomarov proved that he was not. For whatever reason, this first work, which was based largely on secondary sources and which the historian later admitted was somewhat flawed, was nipped in the bud.[39]

Kostomarov, not intimidated by this set-back, immediately turned to an even more adventurous theme: the historical significance of Russian – in actual fact, Ukrainian – popular poetry. It was the first time anyone had written a thesis on an ethnographic subject in a Ukrainian university. Yet as Bodiansky, Maksymovych, and Sreznevsky had shown, ideas about nationality and popular poetry were in the air. The well-spring of this movement was the German philosopher of history Johann Gottfried Herder (1744–1803), who thought that historical progress occurred in stages, that culture was manifested in the national spirit, in which language played an especially important role, and that true poetry originated not in the cultivated elite but in the common folk. Herder saw a bright future for the Slavic peoples, whom he believed closer to nature than their Western neighbours, and he predicted that Ukraine in particular would become 'a new Greece.' It comes as no surprise, therefore, that Herder's ideas were in vogue in Kharkiv during the first decades of the nineteenth century, and that Kostomarov absorbed them so thoroughly. In his work on the historical significance of Russian popular poetry, Kostomarov explicitly referred to various Western European authors, including Sir Walter Scott and 'the undying Herder.'[40] Many years later, Kostomarov observed that in his early work on Russian folk poetry he had tried to show 'the historical importance of folk-songs not in the sense that they could provide important and reliable material for the exposition of factual history, but rather in that they reveal the national psychology to us and inform us about those impressions which nature, historical circumstances, and social stratification have made on the spirit of the people.'[41] It was a principle that he would continue to develop throughout his academic and public life.

2

Schoolteacher and University Professor

Kostomarov remained in Kharkiv for several months after the successful defence of his master's dissertation. Lunin, who clearly saw much promise in his young protégé, tried to have Kostomarov sent on a study tour of Western Europe in preparation for a professorship at Kharkiv. Lunin wanted to see him appointed to the new chair of modern history then under discussion, but the objections of a majority of the professors forced him to abandon that plan. Lunin's conservative colleagues seemingly could not stomach Kostomarov's predilection for the common people, his excursions to taverns and the villages in the pursuit of his academic interest, and his writing in a language they thought little more than 'gibberish.' Moreover, it was rumoured that he was 'given to free thinking.'[1]

Unable to teach at the University of Kharkiv, Kostomarov briefly considered going to St Petersburg to continue his work on Bohdan Khmelnytsky in the public library there. But he decided to stay in Ukraine and, since his financial resources were not great, approached Prince Tsertelev, the assistant curator of the Kharkiv school district, about finding a position in the neighbouring Kiev school district, where he thought he might continue to gather firsthand material about Cossack times. Tsertelev was aware of the reasons for Kostomarov's desire to teach in Ukraine and immediately wrote to Kiev. An answer came swiftly. The aspiring historian was offered a position as a history teacher in the gymnasium in Rivne, in Volhynia, on the Right Bank of the Dnieper River. The town was near the field of Berestechko, the site of one of the great battles between Khmelnytsky and the Poles, and Kostomarov eagerly accepted. On 7 October 1844, three days after formally receiving his master's degree, the young scholar said goodbye to his mother and friends and set off for Kiev and Rivne.[2]

He arrived in Kiev a few days later, and immediately went to see the assistant curator of the school district about his appointment. Mikhail Yuzefovich received Kostomarov warmly and told him that he had read his dissertation on Russian popular poetry and liked it very much. He was aware, it seems, of the young scholar's reasons for wanting a position in the Kiev area and approved of them. While visiting Yuzefovich, Kostomarov made the acquaintance of another young Ukrainian writer, Panteleimon Kulish, then a school inspector in Kiev. 'At that time,' wrote the latter in his memoirs, 'at Yuzefovich's I met the master of arts of Kharkiv University, M.I. Kostomarov, who was engaged with him in a wide-ranging conversation about the Cossacks, in whom we were all very much interested ... I joined the conversation and delivered a long passage from some chronicle. Kostomarov was stunned by this knowledge of Little Russian literature, and so from our first exchange we became close friends.'[3] From Yuzefovich's, the two Cossack enthusiasts took a walk around Kiev. They visited the ancient church of Saint Sophia, at that time still in bad repair, and then went to Kulish's home. When the conversation turned to historical songs, Kulish brought out the enormous pile of papers which made up his collection. Thereafter, the two men saw each other almost every day and enthusiastically exchanged notes on the glories of Cossack history. Kulish also introduced Kostomarov to Maksymovych, who lived in the old city in a modest wooden house with a garden. At the initiative of Kulish, the three men developed a plan for the publication of a scholarly periodical specializing in Ukrainian history and culture, and on 23 October, Kostomarov wrote to Sreznevsky in Kharkiv to enlist him in the enterprise. Though nothing was to come of the idea for several years, Kostomarov was obviously stimulated by Kulish, whom, as he wrote to Sreznevsky, he thought 'educated, gifted, with a deep knowledge of Ukraine.' 'We used to talk throughout entire summer nights,' Kulish later recalled of his new friend. 'In our walks at night ... we might have seemed drunk to a passing observer. And we were drunk, but not with wine.'[4]

Only one shadow fell upon Kostomarov during this first visit to Kiev. His former mentor, Mikhail Lunin, at that time was in Kiev, on his way home from a voyage abroad in search of a cure for a serious sickness. On 14 October 1844, Lunin died, and on 17 October he was buried in the old cemetery in Kiev.[5]

A few days after Lunin's funeral, Kostomarov set off for Rivne. The weather was bad, and he made the whole journey in rain. However, that did not stop the young Cossack enthusiast from collecting ethnographic material and visiting various historical sites along the way. He stopped at the burial mound of the legendary Cossack Nechai, who was purported to have carried off a great treasure stolen from various Polish lords; he saw the castle of the princes Koretsky, which had been ruined during the Khmelnytsky rebellion; and he visited the town of Ostrih, its ruined Orthodox church and tower, and the ruins of nearby Jesuit, Carmelite, and Capuchin religious houses. The Capuchin house had been destroyed only in 1841, after the suppression of the Greek Catholic church. The continuously bad weather, the muddy roads, and the greasy taverns put Kostomarov in a bad mood. He was especially repelled by the Jews who ran the taverns. 'For five days,' he wrote to a Kharkiv friend upon arrival at his destination, 'I floated from Kiev to Rivne through a vast ocean of the thickest mud ... Only the high burial mounds ... the remains of old fortresses, and the crucifixes placed along the roadside by the pious Catholic gentry somewhat raised my soul from loathing.'[6]

Kostomarov's first impressions of Rivne were also gloomy. Rivne was a typical medium-sized Right-Bank-Ukrainian town. It had come under Russian rule only in 1793, as a result of the second partition of Poland, and the urban population was still predominantly Polish and Jewish. The gymnasium where Kostomarov was to teach had been founded a few years earlier with the help of a bequest from the wealthy Lubomirski family. It was an impressive building with a large columned portico, but it was the only cultural institution in the town. There were about three hundred students, almost all Polish Catholics with a sprinkling of students of Jewish origin. By contrast, the faculty was almost exclusively made up of 'Little Russians,' or Orthodox Ukrainians, mostly from the Left Bank.[7] During his stay in Kiev, Yuzefovich had promised Kostomarov that he would eventually transfer him to Kiev; as early as 10 November 1844, the council of the University of Saint Vladimir in Kiev was considering an application from the young schoolteacher for a position as teaching assistant in history.[8]

In spite of difficulties, Kostomarov made good use of his time in Rivne. Every week he delivered fifteen lectures in history and assigned and corrected his students' work; occasionally he prepared longer historical discourses as well. Both the principal and the local school inspector were impressed with his pedagogical abilities. 'Master Kostomarov,' reported the latter, 'devotes himself to scholarship with a special love and has already displayed his exceptional gifts with several historical compositions. Without a doubt, he has all the qualities necessary to make a very good teacher.'[9]

Kostomarov enjoyed teaching and liked most of his students, whom he thought industrious and intelligent. He also got along with most of his fellow teachers, including a relative of Kulish who was given to singing Ukrainian folk-songs, but he did not find his colleagues up to his own academic level. When he asked his pupils to collect folk-songs and other ethnographic materials during their vacations, he felt once again that that kind of pursuit did not enjoy the respect of most of his colleagues. They could say nothing, however, because it was generally known that the new teacher was proceeding, as he wrote to a Kharkiv friend, 'with the support of Yuzefovich.'[10] Given that many of the central events of Ukrainian Cossack history had taken place in the Province of Volhynia, it was not long before Kostomarov had collected a great mass of new historical material of folk origin.

During the Christmas vacation, Kostomarov visited the sites in neighbouring towns. They included the Dermansky Monastery and the town of Hoshcha, which in the sixteenth century had been the site of an Arian school. (The Arians were a radical Protestant sect who flourished in the Polish-Lithuanian Commonwealth before the Counter-Reformation.) During the Easter holidays in 1845, Kostomarov visited the town of Kremenets, which had been the home of a well-known Polish lyceum before the insurrection of 1831, and travelled to the famous Pochaiv Monastery (Pochaivska Lavra) in western Volhynia, which attracted pilgrims from across the border in Austrian Galicia. Kostomarov spent the entire Easter weekend at Pochaiv, where he was deeply inspired by the divine service. He made the acquaintance of the archimandrite, Hryhori Nemolodovsky, a Ukrainian who had earlier served at Kaniv and who knew many stories about the monastery. Kostomarov scanned the ancient library, visited the shrines, and saw the holy relics, including the icon of the Mother of God, who was purported to have made a miraculous appearance and saved the monastery from the Turks during the siege of 1675. The young scholar noted the great respect which drew Orthodox Christians, Greek Catholics, and Roman Catholics to this place of pilgrimage, and later he recalled that the pilgrims from Austrian Galicia were of exactly the same language and nationality as those from Volhynia.[11]

From Pochaiv, Kostomarov went on to the town of Vyshnevets, the ancestral home of the great Wiśniowiecki family, who at one time had held enormous estates on both the Left and the Right banks of the Dnieper River. Originally Orthodox, the family was converted to Catholicism in the early seventeenth century and became Polonized; one of its most famous scions, Jeremi Wiśniowiecki, became a deadly foe of Khmelnytsky and the Cossacks. The town and ancestral palace were now held by Count Mniszek, who allowed Kostomarov to see his palace and portrait gallery. The latter contained a number of interesting items including contemporary portraits of various members of the Wiśnio-wiecki family, of Khmelnytsky, and of the so-called false Dmitri, who with Polish and Cossack support had briefly ruled in Moscow during the Time of Troubles (1605–6).[12]

From Vyshnevets, Kostomarov returned to Kremenets in search of a manuscript history of Ukraine about which Count Mniszek had told him. The young scholar could not track it down, so he went on to the field of Berestechko, where he mapped the terrain and traced the location of the Polish and Cossack camps and the movements of the Polish, Cossack, and Tatar armies during the great battle of 1651.[13]

Throughout these tours of Ukrainian points of interest, Kostomarov took copious notes and, as was his custom, made talking to the common people an object. He was profoundly saddened by their lot and wrote to a friend that he thought 'punitive exile would have been easier for them.'[14] It was his first real experience of the kind of Polish landlord and Jewish leaseholder who had held sway under the old Commonwealth, and many years later he recalled the powerful effect it had had upon him. 'In Rivne,' he wrote, 'I began to look unfavourably on the Polish landlords and the Jews. In talking constantly with the people, I had many opportunities to be convinced how impoverished and downtrodden the people of Volhynia were. After I left that area, Russian landowners, in comparison with Polish ones, seemed almost human beings, and the people themselves seemed livelier and more vital to me as I approached Great Russia.'[15] Kostomarov was obviously relieved when, at the end of the school year, he received word that he was to be transferred to the prestigious First Kiev Gymnasium.

At the beginning of the summer vacation, he returned to his home in Voronezh province by way of Kiev, Hlukhiv, and Kursk. He lingered for a while at the Divnogor Monastery on the Don, the setting of which he considered one of the most beautiful in all Russia, and in August he returned to Kiev. At first, he took up quarters in the old city; later he transferred to a place near Khreshchatyk Street, where he lived with the student Panas Markovych, a passionate advocate of Ukrainian ethnography who was later to marry the writer Marko Vovchok (Mariia Vilinska). Kostomarov also accepted part-time teaching positions at two boarding-schools for women. One of them was run by a Frenchman named Demelien, a relative of the revolutionary Robespierre, and the other by the widow of Bohdan Zaleski, a prominent writer of the Ukrainian school of Polish literature.[16]

Once again, Kostomarov proved a great success as a teacher. His lectures made an indelible impression on the young Nikolai Ge, for example, who would one day become a close friend and one of Russia's better-known painters. 'Mykola Kostomarov was the most loved teacher for everyone,' Ge later recalled. 'There was not a single pupil who did not become engrossed in his stories of Russian history.'

He made the whole city love Russian history. When he entered the class, everyone froze as if in church, and there flowed a rich, living picture of life in old Kiev. Everyone was all ears. But suddenly – the bell would ring and everyone, both teacher and pupils, was sad that the time had passed so quickly. Mykola Ivanovych never asked too much of us, and he never gave away high grades for free. Our teacher used to throw a piece of paper at us and mutter: 'Here, we have to set the grades. Do it yourselves.' And no one would grade himself too high. ... Kostomarov's lessons were like church holidays; everyone awaited them. He made such an impression that the teacher who replaced him later on did not give history lessons for a whole year, but simply read from various Russian authors, saying that after Kostomarov he could not teach us history. He made the same impression at the boarding-school for women and later on at the university.[17]

At Demelien's boarding-school, however, Kostomarov's young female pupils were conscious of other things besides his teaching abilities. The girls noticed both their teacher's good looks and his absent-mindedness with respect to his dress. They were taken aback by his nervous mannerisms and by what they considered his strange habits. To the girls, Kostomarov's writing was illegible and he himself 'funny looking,' always dressed in what appeared to be a 'sack.' The near-sighted teacher was called a 'scarecrow' by his young protégées. Nevertheless, they instinctively liked him. [18] One of them, Alina Leontievna Kragielska, one of the best students in the class, attracted Kostomarov's special attention. 'This was a young girl of melancholic disposition,' he later recalled, 'very capable, one of the kind of people whose feelings were always of the highest order.'[19] He was to meet her again.

In November 1845, Kostomarov received a letter from his mother complaining that she was having difficulty running the estate in Voronezh province on her own. Since it was not easy for the schoolteacher to travel such a distance to help his mother, he decided to sell the land and buy something a little closer to Kiev. In December 1845, he travelled to Voronezh, sold the property, and returned to Kiev via Kharkiv. On the return journey, however, he caught a severe cold, and he arrived in Kiev in bad condition. He could not live in his own frozen quarters, so he stayed a few days in a third-rate hotel on Khreshchatyk Street. After that, an acquaintance, M.I. Hulak, a recent graduate of the University of Dorpat who was then living in Kiev, invited Kostomarov to stay with him until his mother should arrive. The young school-teacher was so sick that he had to undergo a throat operation and spent several weeks in Mykola Hulak's apartment recovering. He was unable to work during that time, so together with Hulak, who was also a Slavic enthusiast, he spent his time learning Serbian. A common friend, Vasyl Bilozersky, who had just finished studies at the university and was looking for a teaching position in Kiev, often visited them. Markovych too eventually returned to Kiev and joined the circle.[20]

The idea of the renaissance of the various Slavic peoples and the notion of Slavic unity, at that time enjoying fresh new vigour, animated their conversations. 'Our friendly discussions,' Kostomarov later wrote, 'most often took us to the idea of Slavic unity':

In our imaginations the idea of Slavic unity was not bounded by the spheres of science and poetry, but began to be manifested in the forms in which, so it seemed to us, it had to be embodied for future history. Without our con-sciously willing it, the federal structure began to appear to us as the most fortunate trend in the social life of the Slavic nations. We saw all the Slavic peoples united with each other in a federation – similar to that of the ancient Greek republics or the United States of America – in which all of them would be strongly tied to each other, but in which each would preserve its autonomy.

However, a federation of various peoples in national units of unequal size did not seem desirable to the young Slavic enthusiasts. 'How could one truly have a union based on mutual equality,' asked Kostomarov, 'when on the one hand there was the minute size of the Lusatian [Sorbs] and on the other hand the great mass of the Russian people with the wide expanse of its fatherland?'

We came to the conclusion that together with the preservation of the rights of nationalities, another division of the parts of the future Slavic state would be necessary for its federal structure. In such a way, the idea arose for the administrative division of lands settled by Slavic peoples without regard for which nationality occupied this or that portion of a wide expanse of territory. We could not work out the details of our imagined federal structure; we left its actual creation to future history. [But] in all parts of the federation we foresaw the same basic laws and rights, the same weights, measures, and currency, the absence of customs barriers, freedom of trade, the general abolition of serfdom and all forms of slavery, a single central power which would handle external relations and the army and navy. [We foresaw] the full autonomy of each member concerning internal institutions, internal administration, the judiciary, and national education. The most immediate and correct means of attaining this goal in the distant future was seen in the education of society in the spirit of such ideas, and therefore it was considered necessary that there should be people in the universities and other institutions of learning who would be dedicated to these ideas and able to pass them on to the younger generation. The idea appeared of creating a society whose task would be to spread the notion of Slavic unity both by means of education and by means of literature.

Kostomarov proposed to his friends that the society should have a constitution which stressed full freedom of religion and nationality and should never accept the idea that the end justifies the means. The emphasis would be on education and literature. 'My comrades sincerely accepted these ideas,' Kostomarov continued, 'and a name was proposed for our society – that of Saints Cyril and Methodius, the Slavic apostles.' When the ailing scholar recovered from his illness and returned to his teaching duties, the intensity of the discussion diminished somewhat, 'but,' he concluded, 'the dream of Slavic unity and a Slavic federation remained for us a testament for life.'[21]

   At the beginning of February 1846, Kostomarov's mother arrived. The two began to live together, in an apartment rented from the Sukhostavsky family on Khreshchatyk Street, and the young scholar's life quickly took on a more orderly form; gone were the uncertainties and frequent changes of residence typical of bachelor life. It was not long, moreover, before Kostomarov discovered that the Ukrainian poet Taras Shevchenko, whom he had praised in his outline of Ukrainian literature published in Kharkiv a few years before, was living a short way down the street from him. Shevchenko had spent the winter as the honoured guest of various wealthy landowners in the provinces of Chernihiv and Poltava and had come to Kiev in search of a position in which his talents as a painter would be put to good use. He had quickly found work, as an artist sketching architectural monuments with the Archeographic Commission and as a teacher of painting at the university. In April, Shevchenko visited Kostomarov in the company of a common friend, and the two men immediately took a liking to each other. Kostomarov was particularly struck by what he later called Shevchenko's simple intelligence, his sadness, his humour, his idealism, and his lack of hypocrisy. A few days later, Shevchenko visited Kostomarov a second time and amid the spring blossoms of the Sukhostavsky garden read him some of his unpublished poetry. This was the time of Shevchenko's greatest creativity, the time when he composed his fiery and melancholic political poems – *The Dream* (*Son*), *The Caucasus* (*Kavkaz*), and *The Heretic* (*Ieretyk*) – and Kostomarov was utterly enraptured. 'Terror seized me,' the young historian later wrote. 'I saw that Shevchenko's muse had torn asunder the curtain draped over the life of the people. It was terrifying and sweet, painful and tempting, to look inside.'[22] Thereafter, the two men met frequently for tea in the garden, and eventually their conversation turned to the idea of Slavic unity, about which Shevchenko seemed enthusiastic. That brought them even closer together. Kostomarov also told Shevchenko about the Cyril-Methodian Brotherhood, and Shevchenko soon met the other members and joined the circle, though he seems to have been impatient with some of its tactics. Certainly there were some disagreements between the two men.[23]

At the beginning of May 1846, Kostomarov was informed that Saint Vladimir's University in Kiev was interested in taking him on to fill the chair of Russian history recently left vacant as a result of the death of Professor V.F. Dombrovsky, a man who had earlier supported Kostomarov's bid to join the university as a teaching assistant. On 4 June, Kostomarov delivered a trial lecture on the origins of Russian history. The young scholar argued that Russian history began with the first Slavic settlements on 'Russian' soil, and claimed that the Huns were partly descended from Slavic refugees who had fled the onslaught of the Goths. His presentation was heavily sprinkled with quotations from ancient Greek and Latin authors and impressed the faculty favourably. Kostomarov was unanimously elected. It was one of the happiest days of his life; after leaving the university, he strolled about the city with Shevchenko, who, delighted with Kostomarov's appointment, sang Cossack love songs without regard for passersby.[24]

Shevchenko, it seems, made a profound impression on all the Cyril-

Methodians. Kulish, then living in St Petersburg, was in touch with his Kievan friends and was aware of Shevchenko's influence. He later wrote, 'All of us knew Shevchenko's works by heart and were enchanted with them.'

All of us, especially Kostomarov, were influenced by his works. Shevchenko, who had been brought up reading the *History of the Ruthenians* by Konysky, turned us into people who hated the Muscovites and all those who were responsible for the sufferings of our native Ukraine. We considered the Muscovites a rough people, incapable of anything cultured. We used to call them nanny-goats [*Katsapy*]. Shevchenko was full of sarcasm, tales, and anecdotes about these poor Great Russians ... In many things, Shevchenko naturally fell under the influence of Kostomarov, but all the same Kostomarov was not free of the influence of Shevchenko.[25]

In contrast to this evaluation of relations between Kostomarov and Shevchenko by Kulish is Kostomarov's late assertion that Shevchenko was free of all national enmities and had breathed only love for his fellow man in their conversations. 'In spite of his heated advocacy of the [common] people,' wrote Kostomarov in the introduction to a later edition of Shevchenko's collected poetry, 'in his conversations with me Shevchenko did not reveal that rage against the oppressors which was expressed in his [poetic] works on more than one occasion. On the contrary, he breathed a spirit of love and a desire to resolve all national and social misunderstandings. He dreamed of universal liberty and the brotherhood of all peoples.'[26]

Kostomarov and Shevchenko saw each other less frequently in the summer of 1846. Shevchenko, on the historian's advice, went off to paint the historical monuments of the Ukrainian countryside, while Kostomarov went to Odessa to bathe in the Black Sea. In Odessa, at the theatre, the scholar met his former pupil Alina Leontievna Kragielska, who was visiting the town with her mother and sister. The young couple got along well, and when they returned to Kiev in the fall, Kostomarov began to visit the Kragielski family. Alina would play the piano for her former teacher, and he would often recite poetry, especially Adam Mickiewicz's *The Ancestors* (*Dziady*) and *Konrad Wallenrod*, which he knew by heart, his performances greatly pleasing Alina's mother, who was of proud Polish background. Alina later recalled that the couple especially enjoyed listening to music together and that Kostomarov was particularly fond of Beethoven, Liszt, Rossini, and

Schubert. When Franz Liszt gave a concert in the Great Hall of the University of Kiev, Kostomarov and Alina made certain they were present. In February 1847, Kostomarov proposed to Alina, and though Alina's mother was hesitant on account of the historian's personal idiosyncrasies and democratic views, she eventually consented, and 30 March was set as the wedding date.[27]

At about the same time, Kostomarov published another research article on Ukrainian history in the Cossack period. The tone of the article was somewhat different from that of his historical works of the Kharkiv period. 'Thoughts on the History of Little Russia' delved into the pre-history of the Khmelnytsky era, stressed the Slavic and Ukrainian roots of the Cossack phenomenon, and argued that the native population of Kievan Rus' had not been completely destroyed during the Mongol ascendency but had survived to form the kernel of a resurgent Ukraine during the Cossack era. This position was plainly at odds with the Polish theory that early modern Ukraine had been repopulated under Polish auspices and that the Poles had a special civilizing mission in the East. (It similarly contradicted the view of certain Russian observers, who stressed what they regarded as the Asian character of Cossack society.) Kostomarov's article had a polemical tone which had not been present in his Kharkiv historical writings and was probably prompted by patronizing remarks about Ukrainian history made by Poles with whom he had come into contact since his moves to Rivne and Kiev.[28]

In the fall of 1846, Kostomarov began to teach at Saint Vladimir's University. He was well received by his colleagues and seemed to enjoy his work. He frequently visited Maksymovych and discussed with him the various problems of Russian and Ukrainian history. 'To speak the truth,' Kostomarov later wrote of the elder Ukrainian historian, 'he was not a great scholar, but was very wise and dispassionate concerning those questions which were well known to him.'[29]

During this period, Kostomarov was so busy preparing his lectures that he had little time for mixing with colleagues or students, with many of whom he shared no strong interests. Nevertheless, he did have an opportunity to observe the general characteristics of the Kiev student body. Many of the students were of Polish background from the Right Bank, and the whole student body was sharply divided into 'Catholics' and 'Russians,' as they were called. Governor-General Bibikov kept a close watch on the university, and when rumours reached him that the Polish students were gathering in secret societies to discuss political questions, he threatened to close down the institution. In spite of the Russifying efforts of the authorities, however, Polish remained the preferred language of the local cultured classes and was even spoken by many of the Ukrainian villagers who were serfs of the Polish gentry. These political tensions, Kostomarov later remarked, had a strong dampening effect on intellectual life at the university.[30]

In general, however, the young professor was able to follow his interests with regard to his teaching duties. He lectured on 'Russian' history – what today would be called 'Ukrainian' history – and Slavic mythology. His historical ideas were still in the process of development, but his militant democratism was already evident, and at times it roused the ire of some of his contemporaries, even Ukrainians like Kulish, who thought that his historian friend mistakenly identified the Ukrainian nation solely with the peasant classes. Kulish concluded a letter to Kostomarov, 'I do not accept your division into chosen and unchosen [peoples], and I fear that with such a view of history you will end up in the deepest darkness.'[31]

Like his views of history, Kostomarov's ideas about ethnography continued to evolve. They were clearly reflected in his lectures on Slavic mythology delivered at the university during the second half of 1846. At the beginning of 1847, he had the lectures printed in book form in the Old Slavonic Cyrillic script, the use of which probably reflected his interest in religion and pious attitude towards Slavic antiquity, an attitude which can properly be referred to as his 'Byzantinism.'[32]

In his work on Slavic mythology, Kostomarov discussed general questions – the feast days in the calendar of the pagan Slavs, pagan rites in general, and those of ancient Rus' in particular. Although he admitted that the ancient Slavs had many Gods, relying on Procopius and Helmold he stressed the importance of the cult of the sun and of celestial bodies and from there claimed that the ancient Slavs anticipated the purer monotheism of later times. He also underlined the yearly cycle of the death and resurrection, the winter and summer of the physical world, which, in his own words, 'is the incarnation of the divine being on earth, of beneficience, suffering, and victory.' Ancient Slavic mythology, in Kostomarov's view, was thus a 'natural' religion which anticipated the Christian theology of the incarnation.[33]

Kostomarov's study of Slavic mythology was only one aspect of his interest in Slavic culture and in religion in the wide sense of the term. Private discussions about Slavic unity and the initiation of the Cyril-Methodian Brotherhood were others. In the absence of a department of

Slavic studies in the university – there was some talk of founding such a department, but the idea had not yet been realized – the private discussions took on considerable importance. By the time of the approach of the Christmas season in 1846, Kostomarov's secret society for the promotion of Slavic federalism had already been in existence for some while. It was during this Christmas season that Mykola Savych, a friend of Kostomarov's from Kharkiv, arrived in Kiev on his way to Paris and the two men went to visit Hulak. Shevchenko was also present, and the friends engaged in a wide-ranging discussion which included the Slavic idea; in particular, they discussed the notion of a future federation of the Slavic peoples and the means whereby they might broaden the ranks of their secret society. Shevchenko, especially, spoke in terms that would have been quite unacceptable to the authorities. The 'brethren,' as they called themselves, spoke freely, not suspecting that through the walls of Hulak's apartment their conversation was being overheard by a young student named Petrov. The next day Petrov approached Hulak and expressed a keen interest in the ideas of Slavic solidarity and a Slavic federation. Hulak told the student about the Cyril-Methodian Brotherhood and eventually showed him a copy of Kostomarov's tract on Slavic federalism, which he had copied out for himself. Bilozersky also had a copy, but he was in Poltava at the time, serving as a teacher at a cadet school. Savych was so taken with the idea of a secret Slavic society that he changed his plan to go to Paris and decided instead to make a tour of the various Slavic lands in order to recruit members.[34]

The enthusiastic discussion during the Christmas season seemed to dissipate somewhat during the following months. At the end of January, Hulak and Shevchenko both left Kiev. Hulak travelled to St Petersburg, where he intended to continue his studies, and Shevchenko went to visit his friend Viktor Zabila in Borzna. At about this time, Kulish, who had just married Bilozersky's sister, Oleksandra, arrived in Kiev with his bride. Bilozersky himself also arrived, intending to go abroad with Kulish and Oleksandra. The Imperial Academy of Sciences was sending Kulish to foreign lands to study Slavic languages, and after a few days the small party of Ukrainians departed for the West. Meanwhile, Kostomarov was busy with his own betrothed, Alina. He visited Alina and her family every evening. One day, he gave her a copy of his book on the church union and a copy of *The Branch*; Alina's mother, not impressed, complained that one was not 'Polish' and the other just 'the songs of country bumpkins' (*khokhlatski pesni*). Young Alina was surprised when Kostomarov presented her with a copy of *On the Imitation of Christ* by Thomas à Kempis, complete with an inscription on the importance of the example of the Saviour in married life. Alina despaired of reading the book before the wedding, but Kostomarov insisted and all went according to plan. The young scholar was in good spirits as his wedding day approached.[35]

Kostomarov's wedding day heralded the end of the second period of the young historian's life, extending from his departure from Kharkiv, through his experience in Rivne, to his years as a teacher and university professor in Kiev. He had set out from Kharkiv with a good education and a burning interest in the Slavic awakening and the literary rebirth of the Ukrainian people. In Kiev, he met others who shared his interest in popular historical songs and Ukrainian literature. Though this first visit to Kiev was brief, it was memorable and pregnant with implications for the future.

From Kiev, Kostomarov went on to Rivne, in Volhynia, where he took up a position teaching school. He excelled in his chosen vocation and made a favourable impression on his superiors. Moreover, he was able to make good use of his time in Volhynia in visiting the sites of some of the great events of Cossack history in the days of Bohdan Khmelnytsky. The new teacher continued to collect folk-songs and enlisted his students in the enterprise. At the end of 1845, when he was transferred to Kiev, he arrived in the city with a certain amount of practical experience of the descendants of the Ukrainians, Poles, and Jews who had once populated the Polish-Lithuanian Commonwealth. He had also been exposed to the ruins of castles and churches and to the functioning monasteries, all of them physical reminders of that vanished polity. They were not without effect on the formation of his sense of national identity and the development of his historical ideas.

Kostomarov had left Kharkiv a romantic democrat interested in the history of the common folk, who had preserved the language and traditions of a people regarded as a branch of the Russian people that had lost its independent place in history. In Kiev and in Volhynia, Kostomarov's ivory-tower love of the common people and their Cossack ancestors and his bookish distaste for Polish landlords were sharpened by immediate contact with poor country folk still suffering terribly under the yoke of contemporary serfdom. Unpleasant experiences with Jewish tavern-keepers and Polish landlords caused him to adjust his intellectual positions, and a newly defensive polemical tone marked the texts of some of his historical publications. Nevertheless, he continued to meet new people and to acquire new manuscripts, and they expanded the base for his historical writings. Personal contact with Polish intellectuals, while often abrasive for this Russified native of Sloboda Ukraine, was not without its benefits.

In Rivne and in Kiev, Kostomarov quickly proved himself a success as a teacher and lecturer. Moreover, he immediately became the central figure in a group of young colleagues and students who were keenly interested in the ideas of Slavic unity and the Ukrainian awakening. Largely under the influence of Kostomarov, this group of friends formed a secret society or 'brotherhood' for the promotion of their ideals. At the same time, Kostomarov met Shevchenko, who immediately became a new inspiration for the circle and who would have a lasting influence on the historian, even in his professional activity. Many years later, Kostomarov reflected on the reciprocity of poetry and history and the special significance of Shevchenko for him. 'Poetry,' he wrote, 'always marches ahead, always dares some bold act; history, science, and practical work follow in its footsteps ...'

Taras's muse has broken some underground dam, closed by many locks for centuries, buried in the soil, deliberately ploughed and cultivated, so that the very memory of the place where this underground stream flows is hidden from younger generations. Taras's muse daringly entered this cleft with an inextinguishable torch and opened up the way for sunlight, fresh air, and human curiosity. It was easy to step into this subterranean place when air reached it. But what human power can withstand the ancient vapours, which in a trice kill all the forces of life, extinguishing all earthly fires! ... But poetry is not afraid of the deadly vapour, if it is true poetry. And no historical or moral carbonic acid will extinguish this torch, since this torch is aflame with an immortal fire – the fire of Prometheus.[36]

Such was the nature of Shevchenko's influence on the small circle of Slavic enthusiasts and Ukrainian activists gathered in Kiev; such was the power of Shevchenko's influence on Kostomarov.

That did not mean that Kostomarov was without his doubts. He was, after all, the son of a Russian landlord who had been raised to speak and write Russian and not Ukrainian. But unlike Sreznevsky, who was of similar background and steadily drifted away from the Ukrainian movement after his initial period in Kharkiv, Kostomarov came into close contact with Shevchenko and Kulish, who changed the nature of his national consciousness and left an indelible mark on his personal identity. 'Why do you say that you are not a Ukrainian?' Kulish admonished him in the spring of 1846. 'We are giving you citizenship rights. Besides, your mother is Ukrainian. I could not love you as much as I do if I did not regard you as Ukrainian. Can you possibly reject a name so precious to us?'[37] Kostomarov's reply to Kulish's admonition has not been preserved, but from the young historian's central role in the Cyril-Methodian Brotherhood it is clear that he would not go the way of Sreznevsky and, despite his imperfect knowledge of the Ukrainian language, was determined to make a positive contribution to the awakening of the Ukrainian people within the context of the general Slavic revival. The means by which he intended to do so is made apparent in the program and the strategy of the Cyril-Methodian Brotherhood.

3

The Cyril-Methodian Brotherhood

Kostomarov was carried away by his enthusiasm for history and the Slavic world during the 1846–7 academic year. He attacked his work of preparing lectures in Russian history and Slavic mythology with a vengeance. He later recalled: 'In accord with my passionate nature, I did not follow the golden mean but gave my whole soul to [the cause]. My idea of founding a society drove me to fanaticism. I spread it wherever I could: among the students in my department, in private conversations with university professors, and even at the theological academy.'[1] Young colleagues like the schoolteacher Dmytro Pylchykiv were also successful at influencing the youth, and several younger members were recruited into the Cyril-Methodian Brotherhood.

Certain elements in Kostomarov's background prepared the way for this semi-conspiratorial work. One of the most important was the example of the secret Decembrist Society, which had risen against Tsar Nicholas I in 1825 but had quickly been put down. Several of its leaders had been hanged. The cult of the Decembrists, and their reputation of having been 'martyred' for the sake of Russian freedom, continued long after the suppression of the uprising, which had taken place in both St Petersburg and Ukraine. One of the Decembrist leaders, Kondrat Ryleev, had been stationed in the Ostrogozhk district, where Kostomarov had been raised. Ryleev married a local girl, often summered at his family's Sloboda Ukrainian estate, and acquired a lasting interest in Ukrainian history which was clearly reflected in his literary work. His tragic death by hanging was long remembered by his contemporaries, and his influence must still have been felt in the Ostrogozhk area while Kostomarov was living there.[2] Indeed, Kostomarov seems to have had a lively interest in the Decembrist movement at the time and had in his possession in Kiev an old issue of a newspaper in which the punishment of the Decembrist leaders was announced.[3] Moreover, Kostomarov's colleague Shevchenko had been familiar with the Decembrist legend since his residence in St Peterburg, and other Cyril-Methodians such as Bilozersky, Hulak, and Hulak's cousin the student Oleksander Navrotsky were associated with the literary salon of the Poltava cultural figure Sophie Kapnist, who was the daughter of a well-known Ukrainian autonomist and had been a personal friend of several Decembrists.[4]

The Decembrists and the Cyril-Methodians had certain characteristics in common. Not only were both conspiratorial underground brotherhoods aiming at eventual political change, but the southern branch of the Decembrist Society contained a wing, made up principally of Polish landowners from the Right Bank, which espoused a philosophy of Slavic unity. The Society of United Slavs, as it was called, also advocated the abolition of peasant bondage. 'The aim of the society,' according to *The Russian Invalid (Russkii invalid)*, which was probably the newspaper of which Kostomarov had an issue in his possession, was to unite the eight Slavic tribes in a common alliance and in a republican system of government, while preserving the independence of each. These were enumerated on an octagonal seal as Russia, Poland, Bohemia, Moravia, Dalmatia, Croatia, Hungary and Transylvania, and Serbia with Moldavia and Wallachia.'[5] There is little doubt that the ideas of the Society of United Slavs did not die with the suppression of the Decembrist revolt.

It was only a few years after the suppression of the Decembrists that the Poles of the western provinces of the empire rose to re-establish the Polish-Lithuanian Commonwealth. But the unsuccessful conclusion of that venture did not put an end to the political activities of various Polish factions scattered throughout the Lithuanian, Belorussian, and Ukrainian borderlands. From the political centres of the Polish emigration in Western Europe, emissaries were sent to create underground organizations in various Polish provinces under Russian rule. The illegal works of the Polish national poet Mickiewicz were widely read. Kostomarov, of course, was well acquainted with the poet's *The Ancestors*, which dealt with the sufferings of Lithuania under Russian rule and may well have evoked parallels in his eyes with his native Ukraine. In 1838, the Polish revolutionary emissary Szymon Konarski was arrested in Vilnius (Vilna), and a vast conspiracy reaching across the borderlands was uncovered. In Kiev, where Konarski also had an organization, hundreds of Polish students were arrested, and the university was temporarily closed down. At one point during his travels in Volhynia, Kostomarov himself was briefly mistaken for a Polish emissary.[6]

Several such Polish patriotic organizations had considerable influence in Ukraine. The Society of United Brethren spread the idea that through Christian love and education Poland could be resurrected, and the Brotherhood of Saint Stanisław advocated a similar program for all the Slavic lands with suffering Poland as the centrepiece.[7] Though there seems to have been no direct connection between these Polish conspiratorial societies and the Cyril-Methodians, there was a certain concurrence of ideas, and Kostomarov and his friends had personal contact with many Poles. Kostomarov and Shevchenko, for example, befriended an elderly Pole who had once served Catherine II as an envoy to the Slavs of the Ottoman Empire. His task had been to raise an insurrection against the Turks, and in his old age he remained a Panslav who dreamed of a union of Slavic republics.[8]

In general, however, Kostomarov remained fairly suspicious of cooperation with Polish conspiratorial societies. On one occasion, Shevchenko introduced him to a young Polish friend, Julian Bielina-Kędrzycki, a typical representative of patriotic Kievan Polish youth who later joined in the insurrection of 1863 against the Russian Empire. The conversation, which was carried on in Russian although all three men could speak Ukrainian well, began cautiously, on the subject of the university, the professors, and so on. It then passed to painting and related subjects. At length, Shevchenko turned to Kostomarov: 'Mykola, say what you have to say!' Kostomarov looked troubled but finally began. He talked about how the Germans, the Latins, and the Anglo-Saxons were united while the Slavs all went their own ways. Shevchenko urged him on again, asking him to reiterate the ideas he had discussed earlier with Kulish. Kostomarov cautiously continued, saying that a scholarly brotherhood should be formed which could lead the way in propagating Slavic unity. But then he unexpectedly added that all the Slavs, in his exact words, 'must unite under one Orthodox tsar and in one Orthodox faith.' Shevchenko, to whom Kostomarov's caution and insincerity before the Pole was entirely unexpected, exclaimed, 'You, Mykola, want to lead all the Slavs into one priest-ridden house!' Bielina-Kędrzycki could also feel that Kostomarov was dissimulating, and the conversation was brought to a conclusion.[9]

While Kostomarov's relapse was surely a self-protecting form of dissimulation, his broader religious sentiment and Byzantine sympathies were very real. He infused these religious feelings into his organizational and ideological work on behalf of the Cyril-Methodian Brotherhood, and since he was the brotherhood's major theoretician, to some extent they came to be shared by all the members. Many years later, Kulish described the youthful idealists in the following terms:

[At that time,] Ukrainian songs and the literature of the Ukrainian people inspired youthful minds in Kiev with a salutary thought: to raise their nation out of the darkness which was destroying its well-being and making it impossible for spiritual forces to overcome the decay ... The Kievan youth we are talking about was deeply enlightened by Holy Scripture; it was a youth of great spiritual purity and was enthusiastic about spreading the gospel of neighbourly love ... The teacher of the Kievan group ... was He Himself [that is, the Christ]. They were all equal, and he was the first among them, who was their servant.[10]

Such was the tenor of the men who founded the Brotherhood of Saints Cyril and Methodius. But Kulish left for St Petersburg before the constitution and ideological documents of the society were formulated. These documents, composed by Kostomarov himself, give a fuller and more exact picture of the ideals and direction of the brotherhood.

The 'statute' or constitution was basic. It contained six important points:

1 We hold that the spiritual and political union of the Slavs is the true destiny to which they should aspire.
2 We hold that at the time of their union each Slavic tribe [or nation] should be independent, and we acknowledge these tribes to be the South Russians [that is, the Ukrainians], the North Russians together with the Belorussians, the Poles, the Czechs with the Slovaks, the Lusatians, the Illyro-Serbs with the Croats, and the Bulgarians.
3 We hold that each tribe should be ruled by the people and should observe the complete equality of citizens according to their birth, Christian faith, and status.
4 We hold that the government, legislation, and right to private property and to education of all the Slavs should be based on the holy religion of our Lord, Jesus Christ.
5 We hold that, in this condition of equality, education and pure morals should be a stipulation for participation in a government.
6 We believe that a general Slavic council made up of the representatives of all tribes should come into being.[11]

The six points contained in the constitution of the brotherhood were very general. Their fundamental intent was to state the desire for Slavic unity, for general equality among persons and nations, and for moral purity in government. The constitution differed from the statement of goals of the earlier Society of United Slavs in that the 'South Russians' or Ukrainians were specifically enumerated as one of the independent and equal Slavic nations. The constitution of the Cyril-Methodian Brotherhood was further refined in a second document, also composed by Kostomarov, entitled 'Principal Rules.' The rules were set forth as follows:

1 We found a society (brotherhood) with the goal of spreading the ideas set forth in the Constitution (Statute). The principal means of doing so is through the education of youth, the publication of literature, and the expansion of the membership. The Society is named after its patrons Cyril and Methodius, accepting as its sign/symbol a ring or icon with the names and pictures of those saints.
2 Each member of the Brotherhood takes an oath upon his entry that he will live by his abilities, work, property, and social contacts for the goals of the Brotherhood. If any member of the Brotherhood should be perse-cuted and even undergo torture for the sake of the ideas of the society, then in accordance with the oath he has taken he will not give away any member, any of his brothers.
3 In the event that any member falls into the hands of enemies and his family is left in need, the Brotherhood is obligated to help it.
4 Each member accepted into the Brotherhood can himself accept a new member and is not required to give his name to other members of the Brotherhood.
5 We accept as members Slavs of all nations [narodiv] and all callings (all service and social estates).
6 Full equality of rights must reign among all members.
7 Because the Slavic peoples confess different religions and have prejudices against one another, the Brotherhood will strive to get rid of all feelings of national and religious animosity among them and will propagate the idea of reconciliation of the differences between the Christian churches.
8 The Brotherhood will strive to root out serfdom and all discrimination against the lower classes and spread education everywhere among the masses.
9 Both the Brotherhood as a whole and each individual member must order his activity in accordance with the Gospel laws of love, humility, and

forbearance. The Brotherhood considers the principle 'The end justifies the means!' atheistic.

10 Several members of the Brotherhood who happen to find themselves together in one place can hold their meetings and approve separate measures for their work, although their decisions should not contradict the main ideas and rules of the Brotherhood.

11 None of the members should say anything about the existence and composition of the Brotherhood to anyone who has not become a member of the Brotherhood and shows no promise of joining it.[12]

The principal rules of the Cyril-Methodian Brotherhood were thus a reiteration and refinement of the constitution of the society and at the same time set forth in greater detail an outline for its practical organization. Most significant were the clear statements in favour of religious tolerance and the abolition of serfdom.

Kostomarov developed the ideas of the brotherhood somewhat further in two emotional 'appeals' which he wrote as literature to be distributed among trusted friends and potential members. These two appeals or proclamations were the 'Proclamation to Brother Ukrainians' and the 'Proclamation to Brother Russians and Poles.' In the first, Kostomarov reiterated the call for Panslavic unity and once again listed the Slavic nations. The exact names of the nations listed in the proclamation, however, differ somewhat from those listed in the constitution of the society: they are the Muscovites (not the 'North Russians,' and there is no mention of the Belorussians), the Ukrainians (that is, *Ukraintsi*, not 'South Russians'), the Poles, the Czechs, the Slovaks (now separate from the Czechs), the Croats, the Illyro-Serbs (now separate from the Croats), and the Bulgarians. In the 'Proclamation to Brother Ukrainians,' Kostomarov altogether neglected to mention the tiny Lusatian Sorb population of central Prussia.[13]

After listing the various Slavic nations with whom the Ukrainians were to unite, Kostomarov in rather vague terms proposed a model government for the Panslavic union. There was to be a central parliament, or *sejm*, with an administrator elected each year, and every member republic also would have an administrator elected each year. Neither birth nor wealth would elect deputies to parliament, but popular choice made according to the intelligence and culture of the electors; the Christian faith was to be the basis of all law. 'This, brother Ukrainians on both sides of the Dnieper,' concluded the proclamation, 'is what we offer for your consideration. Read it through carefully and let each person think how to attain it and how it would be better. They say, ''The more heads, the more reason.'' If you think about it, when the moment comes to talk about it, the Lord will give you the wisdom and the understanding.'[14]

The 'Proclamation to Brother Russians and Poles' paralleled the proclamation to the Ukrainians in that it too outlined most of the central ideas of the brotherhood. But this proclamation expressed an especially strong spirit of reconciliation according to which oppressed Ukraine forgave her more powerful neighbours for all past grievances. 'Brother Great Russians and Poles!' it began,

Ukraine, your beggarly sister, speaks thus to you who have crucified her and cut her to pieces, but she does not remember the harm which has been done to her and sympathizes with your misfortunes and is ready to sacrifice the blood of her children for your liberty. Read through this fraternal message. Examine the great work of your common salvation. Awaken from your sleep and your lethargy. Drive from your hearts the absurd hatred for one another planted by the tsars and the lords for the destruction of your common liberty. Be ashamed of the yoke which weighs upon your shoulders, and of your own corruption. Curse the sacrilegious name of the worldly tsar and the worldly lord. Drive from your hearts the spirit of unfaith inculcated in you by the Germans and the Romans, and the harshness inspired by the Tatars. Dress yourselves in your own Slavic love for humanity. And remember your brothers who suffered both in the silken chains of the Germans and in the clutches of the Turks, and let the goal of the life and activity of each of you be the common Slavic union, general equality of rights, brotherhood, and the peace and love of our Lord Jesus Christ. Amen.[15]

In addition to the two proclamations, Kostomarov penned a number of smaller items which also revealed a great deal about his notion of Panslavism. In a private but incomplete note on Panslavism, for example, he set forth the idea that the Slavs were just entering the historical stage, whereas the Greeks, Romans, and Germanic peoples had already made an honourable contribution to civilization but, knowing that, had become proud and fallen into inequity (*nespravedlivost*) in their dealings with other nations. That was, in the historian's thinking, against the law of God. In Kostomarov's view, the Slavs were victims of such pride and should plainly reject it. Similarly, in an unfinished story bearing the title *Panich Natalich*, Kostomarov urged the Slavs to put aside their animosity towards one another and join together in true

Christian love. Then, he predicted, the teaching of the Saviour would become the law of the land; the curing rays of science and art would reach the lowly peasant cottage. And the Slavs, free, noble, and burning with love of the Lord, 'the one Tsar and teacher,' would gather from the banks of the Volga, the Danube, the Vistula, the Ilmen, from the Adriatic to Kamchatka, and would come to Kiev, 'the great city, the capital of the Slavic race.' And there, a hymn of praise in all the Slavic languages would rise to the Lord while the ancient bells of Saint Sophia sounded out. 'Believe me,' Kostomarov concluded, 'it will come to be, to be, to be!'[16]

In the constitution, rules, and proclamations of the Cyril-Methodian Brotherhood and in his various other writings, Kostomarov outlined his vision of Slavic rebirth and unity, freedom and independence, social equality and religious tolerance and adopted a theory of progress in which the Slavs in general and the Ukrainians in particular, though oppressed in the past, had a bright future. That future, which Kostomarov and his friends believed was linked to the spread of literacy, education, and literature in the native language, still required its narrator. Kostomarov's colleague Mykola Hulak alluded to that requirement in a letter to Markovych in which he described a conversation with their common friend the landowner Tarnovsky. Kostomarov himself is mentioned in the letter. 'In our conversations,' wrote Hulak, 'Tarnovsky could not but touch upon our literature.'

Among other things, he asserted that our literature has already passed through the period of its epic development. Although we do not have a Homer, we do have our dumas and historical songs, which are true Homeric rhapsodies. The natural and progressive development of the language now requires that poetry pass into prose, the duma into historical relations. We have our homerics; let us now have a Herodotus. Mykola Ivanovych [Kostomarov] is entirely in accord with these thoughts. He has even promised to finish writing something in Ukrainian, not in the vulgar tongue but in a fine yet simple and popular way. In a word, it has to be a work written not only for the sake of our literature but also so that it will occupy an honourable place among the best creations of the human intellect. Then a wide arena will be opened for our philosophy. The language will be worked out to the degree that not only our native as well as universal history but even high-quality scholarship will be taught in this language. Obviously, that will be the very last period of development. When it will come we do not know, but when we apply the efforts of our friends to that goal, the impossible becomes possible. According to this theory, drama will make its appearance among us later on.

Hulak's correspondent, Markovych, who was also a great enthusiast of the Ukrainian language, replied to Hulak that he agreed with Tarnovsky's theory of the development of Greek literature. 'But allow me to suggest,' he continued, 'that Herodotus knew the Greek language much better than Kostomarov knows the Ukrainian language. I do not know the Greek language, but I do feel something for the Ukrainian, and I can make some judgment about writers who write in it. Kostomarov hunts simplicity, but snares coarseness and distaste [hrubist i nesmak].' Markovych then contrasted what he thought were Kostomarov's awkward Ukrainian verses with the natural simplicity of Shevchenko's poetry, his rough use of participle and tone with the smooth flow of the writings of Shevchenko and Kulish. Markovych then suggested that it was not Kostomarov but rather Kulish or even Bilozersky who should be put to the task of writing a work of history in Ukrainian.[17]

As it turned out, Markovych's suggestions went unheeded. Neither by character nor by profession was Kulish or Bilozersky a historian. But Kostomarov was. Moreover, he also had the enthusiasm and the ability to carry out Tarnovsky's plan. The result was the most impressive and most detailed document to come from the pen of a Cyril-Methodian. Contemporary observers were sometimes to refer to this document as the 'Law of God' [Zakon Bozhii]; on the strength of both its content and its significance with regard to the development of Ukrainian national consciousness, Kulish and later generations have called it Books of the Genesis of the Ukrainian People (Knyhy buttia ukrainskoho narodu).[18]

The work took the form of a quasi-religious history of mankind. It was written in archaic, religious-style language and told the story of mankind from its creation, through the Hebrews, Greeks, and Romans, to the Germans, French, and Slavs. The central idea of the work was that the heavenly King is the one Lord of mankind and that all forms of idolatry and worship of earthly kings lead to the decline, enslavement, and destruction of peoples. Thus, the Hebrews were the chosen people because they alone worshipped the one true God; but when the Hebrews set up kings before them and fell into idolatry, they declined as a people, and the Greeks took the lead. The Greeks achieved their leading role through their sense of freedom and equality, and they gave mankind the arts and the sciences. But the Greeks too were idolaters and enslaved a part of their own people, and thus they fell before the

Macedonians and the Romans. Rome had been a republic but with the passage of time was transformed into an empire, and eventually the Roman emperor made so bold as to call himself a god. So the true Lord, the Heavenly Father, sent his Son, Jesus Christ, to be an example for mankind. The early Christians followed his example, lived as brethren, held everything in common, and practised humility, and they were persecuted for it. Eventually, however, the Roman tribe – the Italians, French, and Spanish – accepted Christianity and made a useful contribution to history. But those people in their turn 'invented a head of Christianity, the Pope, and that Pope imagined that he had power over the entire Christian world.' Their doing so led to the appearance among the Germans, who accepted the holy faith better than the Greeks or Romans had, of Luther, who taught that Christians must live as they once had. But philosophers appeared who rejected the faith and preached self-interest. The French slew their king and fell into the worse bondage of worshipping national honour, and the English worshipped gold. Among the Slavs, however, who are the younger brothers of the Latins and the Germans, a different situation obtained.

The Slavs, according to *Books of the Genesis of the Ukrainian People*, at first had neither kings nor masters and worshipped one God. When the apostles Constantine (Cyril) and Methodius appeared among them and translated the Holy Scriptures into the Slavic language, the Slavs accepted the Christian faith 'as no other people had.' But even they eventually accepted kings and masters, and their misfortunes began. In Poland, the masters hanged and killed without regard for law, while in Muscovy the tsar kissed the hand of the Tatar khan so that he might keep the Christian people in captivity. Ukraine, however, loved neither tsar nor Polish lord and established a free Cossack Host and brotherhoods of true Christians; and the Cossacks rose to drive out the Polish lords and joined with Muscovy as one Slavic people with another. Soon, however, Ukraine perceived that once again she had fallen into captivity, for the Muscovite tsar was 'an idol and a torturer.' Ukraine therefore tried to free herself from Muscovy, but after many travails only found herself divided among the Poles and the Muscovites. She was tortured by a tsar (Peter I) who built his new capital on Cossack bones and a tsarina (Catherine II) who destroyed the Cossack Host and once again set up lords over the common people. And these lords soon turned into Frenchmen and Germans because the true Slav loves no lord but 'is mindful of the one God, Jesus Christ, King of heaven and earth.' Ukraine was put into her grave but did not die. She anticipated

Polish strivings for freedom and equality (in the Polish national insur-
rections) and Russian efforts to establish a republic (in the Decembrist
uprisings). Using Germans, the despotic tsar now ruled the three Slavic
peoples. But he will not prevail:

Ukraine will rise from her grave and again will call to her brother Slavs, and
they will hear her call, and the Slavic peoples will rise, and there will remain
neither tsar nor tsarevich, nor tsarina, nor prince, nor count, nor duke, nor
Excellency, nor Highness, nor lord, nor boyar, nor peasant, nor serf, neither
in Great Russia, nor in Poland, nor in Ukraine, nor in the Czech lands, nor
among the Croats, nor among the Serbs, nor among the Bulgars. And
Ukraine will be an independent republic in the Slavic union. Then all the
peoples, pointing to the place on the map where Ukraine will be delineated,
will say: Behold, the stone which the builders rejected has become the cornerstone.[19]

On this optimistic note, *Books of the Genesis of the Ukrainian People* ended.

Kostomarov's *Books* was obviously meant to fill that need for a historical vision of the Ukrainian people discussed in the letters of Hulak
and Markovych. Using simple language but an exalted biblical tone, the
historian sought to break through the barrier separating Ukrainian
vernacular poetry from common academic prose and dignify the Ukrainian language through the creation of an inspired work of historical
discourse. The language and message were simple enough to be understood by the common Ukrainian layman yet elevated and distinguished enough to serve as a model for future prose compositions of a
more practical character. Though marked by occasional infelicities and
lapses into Russian, the document seemed capable of achieving those
goals.

Moreover, the *Books* was the culmination and final synthesis of the
ideas of the Cyril-Methodians. Though Kostomarov was certainly the
ultimate author, the final work was produced only after many hours of
intense discussion among the various members of the brotherhood.
Shevchenko's influence perhaps sharpened Kostomarov's criticism of the
tsar and his stress on the hardships of the common folk.[20] Although the
work was composed in Ukrainian for distribution among the Ukrainian
people, the Cyril-Methodians also produced copies in Russian for distribution among the Russians; Hulak carried such a copy with him to
St Petersburg. Translation into the other Slavic languages was probably
also envisioned. Certainly Kulish and Bilozersky took a copy with them

on their way to the West. It is therefore not making too great a claim to say that *Books of the Genesis of the Ukrainian People* was the most important document produced by the Cyril-Methodian Brotherhood.

That did not mean that it was an entirely original work, however. One can see traces of Czech Slavophilism, of the democratic Christianity of Félicité de Lamennais, and of the utopianism of the Polish emigration in the ideology of the Cyril-Methodians. Mickiewicz's famous *Books of the Polish People and of the Polish Pilgrimage* (*Księgi narodu polskiego i pielgrzymstwa polskiego*) above all was an inspiration to and a model for Kostomarov. Mickiewicz's work was published in France in 1832 and was meant to infuse a sense of patriotism and morality in the Polish émigrés, who were at that time badly divided along political lines. Before Kostomarov, Mickiewicz contrasted monotheism and the rule of the tsars; he saw partitioned Poland as the suffering Christ among the nations, criticized the Western nations, and urged his fellow émigrés or 'pilgrims' to forget their squabbles and adhere to the highest moral standards in order to resurrect the Polish state. Only then would Christendom know true peace. Deeply influenced by his ideas, Kostomarov adapted them to a Ukrainian context in his *Books of the Genesis of the Ukrainian People*. Of course, the Orthodox Kostomarov gave a slightly different interpretation of the history of Christianity from that of the Catholic Mickiewicz, was much more critical of the old Polish-Lithuanian Commonwealth, and in the end envisioned a new era for Slavdom rather than for all mankind, but he retained much from Mickiewicz's *Books*, especially in the first half of his narrative. At times, Kostomarov almost repeated Mickiewicz word for word. Thus, concerning the Western nations, the two texts read as follows:

Mickiewicz	Kostomarov
I tak zrobili królowie dla Francuzów bałwana, i nazwali go Honor ...	... frantsuzy ... menshe shanuvaly Khrysta, nizh chest natsionalnu ...
A zas Anglikom zrobił król bałwana ... która sie nazywał dawniej Mamonem.	... a anhlychane klianialys zolotu i mamoni ...
(And so the Kings made an idol for the French, and they called it Honour ...)	(... the French ... revered Christ less than they did their national honour.)

(And the King made an idol for the   (The English bowed down to gold
English ... which was formerly   and Mammon ...)[21]
called Mammon.)

Moreover, both texts speak of the nation as lying in the grave but not dead. Poland will be resurrected to free all the peoples of Europe; Ukraine will arise to call forth all the Slavs. Both books saw the world's rulers in a negative light, but Kostomarov's condemnation of kingship is more militant than Mickiewicz's, and his stress on the innate goodness of the the Slavs is missing from the Polish work. In Kostomarov's *Books*, of course, Ukraine replaces Poland at the centre of future European history.

The noble vision of *Books of the Genesis of the Ukrainian People* and the other programmatic documents of the Cyril-Methodian Brotherhood highlighted another stage in the life of Mykola Kostomarov. He had come to Kiev with all the innocence and enthusiasm of youth and deeply inspired by a sense of the awakening of the Slavic peoples throughout Eastern Europe. He had discovered the Ukrainian people in Kharkiv, but in Kiev that discovery was moulded into a definite plan for the cultural and political rebirth of the people. The rebirth was to proceed from certain qualities intrinsic to the Ukrainian people itself, especially its spirit of democracy and freedom from idolatry, but the Ukrainian people would lead the other Slavs in a coeval rising and become the cornerstone of a free and equal federation of Slavic nations.

Most notable in Kostomarov's programmatic documents, especially *Books of the Genesis of the Ukrainian People*, was his definite use of the words 'Ukraine' (*Ukraina*) and 'Ukrainians' (*Ukraintsi*). In the 1840s, those terms had a primarily geographical and regional ring to them and were without the full national or ethnolinguistic meaning they were to acquire over the course of the next century. But Kostomarov anticipated their use by making the Ukrainian people not only a full and equal member of the Slavic family of peoples but also the centerpiece of the projected Slavic federation. In other words, in Kostomarov's uncensored vision of the 1840s the Ukrainian people formed a nationality in its own right, and one, moreover, that was on a par with the other recognized nationalities of the world.

In the *Books*, Kostomarov named certain characteristics of the Ukrainian people that he regarded as significant with respect to Ukrainian history and to the role the country would play in world politics in the future. He believed that the Ukrainian people had a quality of religious-ness that gave better expression to Christian ideals than could be found among the apostate Latin or Germanic peoples or among the aristocratic Poles or monarchical Great Russians. This quality consisted of an abhor-rence of idolatry and master-worship and was most clearly manifest in the religious and social ideals of the freedom-loving and egalitarian Cossack brotherhood. In Kostomarov's view in the 1840s, the Cossack brotherhood was a central event in the history of the Ukrainian people.

That brotherhood, according to Kostomarov, was thoroughly egalitar-ian, and a similar spirit of egalitarianism ran clearly through all the documents of the Cyril-Methodians. In *Books of the Genesis of the Ukraini-an People*, it was given a formulation which can be described as un-equivocally anti-monarchical and even republican; it culminated in the prophecy that Ukraine would one day form 'an independent republic in the Slavic union.' During the months and years following, Kosto-marov's uncensored vision of freedom, independence, fraternity, equal-ity, and republicanism was to be put to a severe test, as he strove to live, work, and write in the tsar's conservative empire. How much of his vision would survive the tsar's censors and police was an open question.

4

Arrest, Imprisonment, and Exile

During the winter of 1846–7, Kostomarov continued to work hard at his university duties and simultaneously prepared for his wedding. He moved into a new apartment with a beautiful view overlooking the Dnieper, ordered a piano from Western Europe for his fiancée, and went with Shevchenko to inspect a small estate outside Kiev which he was interested in buying. The owners of the estate, two elderly spinsters, were captivated by Shevchenko's personality but could not reach an agreement with Kostomarov, and no deal was concluded. On the way back to Kiev, Kostomarov's, carriage fell through the ice while crossing the Dnieper, and both Kostomarov and Shevchenko got drenched. Hot tea mixed with rum warmed their return home, however, and no harm was done. Shortly afterwards, Shevchenko travelled to Chernihiv province to visit some friends.[1]

Kostomarov was left in Kiev to make the final arrangements for his wedding. Spring came early that year, and as his wedding day approached the young scholar was filled with excitement and hope for the future. One day, while visiting Yuzefovich's office, he received a note from the civil governor, Funduklei, saying that he wished to see him. Kostomarov was then reading Funduklei's *Description of the City of Kiev* but because of the wedding preparations had not been able to finish the work. He decided to visit the governor later on, when he had time to do so. The next day, Kostomarov received a courier from the widow Zaleska, at whose school he had been a teacher; she wished to see him immediately. He replied that he would come to see her the next day. After delivering Kostomarov's reply, the courier quickly returned to him to insist, not tomorrow, but today! Kostomarov therefore went off to Zaleska's house but did not find her at home, and so returned to his wedding arrangements. Little did he suspect that both those people were trying to warn him of impending disaster.[2]

The Friday before the Sunday of his wedding, which was to take place on 30 March, the young scholar went to church to settle some final matters with the sexton. He returned home late in the evening and was getting ready for bed when he heard a knock on the door. It was his old patron, Yuzefovich, the deputy superintendent of the Kiev school district, who had come to warn him that he was under suspicion and was about to be searched by the police. Yuzefovich said that if Kostomarov had anything incriminating, he should destroy it immediately. The scholar had nothing in his apartment but recalled that in the pocket of his topcoat was the rough draft of his manuscript on Slavic federalism. He drew it out and went to get some fire in which to burn it. But Yuzefovich took the document from him and assured him that everything was all right and that he would look after it. He then departed as suddenly as he had come.

Doubtless, Kostomarov was left aghast. He had no time to recover, however, for shortly afterwards the expected police officials arrived at his door. In walked Governor Funduklei, School Superintendent Traskin, Major-General Belousov, and Police Chief Galiadkin and demanded the keys to his apartment. They began to go through his belongings. Seeing the enormous bulk of the scholar's papers, Traskin exclaimed in French, 'Damn it, it will take ten years to go through these papers!' On the desk, however, lay an old newspaper containing the article announcing the punishment of the Decembrists. Glancing at it, Belousov remarked insinuatingly, 'Now it is clear what you have been up to!' The officials collected Kostomarov's papers and carried them off. Kostomarov too was led off, with barely time to kiss his mother's hand goodbye. It was cold and trembling with fear.[3]

Kostomarov's study was sealed, and he was taken to Funduklei's offices, where the governor seated him in a room, offered him a cigar, and left, closing the door behind him. Kostomarov waited and smoked. After some time, Pisarev, who was a member of Governor-General Bibikov's staff, Belousov, and Traskin entered the room, and the interrogation began.

The inquisitors asked Kostomarov if he knew Hulak. 'I know him, ' answered Kostomarov. 'What is your relationship with him?' asked Pisarev. 'Very good. Friendly,' he answered. 'But,' replied Pisarev, 'he has submitted a denunciation of you to the Third Department [of Police] and in this denunciation has included a manuscript which you had given to him. So you also have a copy of it. Can you give your word of honour that you do not know anything about this manuscript?'

Kostomarov was certain that Hulak would never denounce him to the police and also knew that only an hour before he had given the original of his Slavic manuscript to Yusefovich for safe keeping. Therefore, he firmly replied, 'I can and I do.' 'Look over here. What is this?' Pisarev then asked, showing him the same document he had just given Yuzefovich. Kostomarov turned white, trembled, and fell against the table.[4]

He was then taken to a jail in the Podil district of the city and placed in a dirty little cell, where he spent the night and the next day. He could neither eat nor sleep, and nothing they offered him seemed clean. In the morning, the police chief, Galiadkin, came in, looked around, and said: 'How was your night, Professor? Today was supposed to be your wedding day! It was probably not as nice as it would have been in the company of a young girl!' He turned and walked out.

At six in the evening, at Kostomarov's request, he was allowed to say goodbye to his mother and his financée at his apartment. They were, of course, in tears. Kostomarov too wept and, embracing his betrothed, said: 'I am not a criminal, believe me, I am not a criminal! I love you, my Alina, and I will go to my grave with this love.' He asked nothing of either his mother or Alina. The police officials rushed the farewells, and in the company of two soldiers Kostomarov was carted away to St Petersburg. The next day, the police returned to his apartment and confiscated the remainder of his papers and his library.

When Kostomarov and his keepers were only a few miles out of Kiev, they met the young Cyril-Methodians Andruzhchenko and Andruzsky, who were returning to Kiev after the holidays, and Kostomarov succeeded in warning them that the brotherhood had been discovered. But as soon as they arrived in Kiev, they too were arrested. Shevchenko was also arrested on the way to Kiev, where he was to have attended Kostomarov's wedding. Kulish and Bilozersky were arrested in Poland just as they we about to leave the Russian Empire. Markovych, Hulak, Navrotsky, and other members of the brotherhood were also taken. They were all sent to St Petersburg, where they were confined in the Peter and Paul fortress.[5]

Though they did not know it at first, all of them had been arrested as a result of a denunciation of the brotherhood by the University of Kiev student Aleksei Petrov, who had overheard the private conversations of the brethren during the previous Christmas season through the wall of Hulak's apartment. He had thereafter befriended Hulak and pretended to be sympathetic to the cause. On 28 February 1847, Petrov had reported the existence of the Cyril-Methodian Brotherhood to Kostomarov's former patron, the deputy superintendent of the Kiev school district, Yuzefovich. Yuzefovich, it seems, was upset by the discovery of such an apparently conspiratorial organization among his trusted employees and immediately released Shevchenko from his position on the Archeographic Commission. On 3 March, Yuzefovich and Petrov had reported the matter to Superintendent Traskin, and at that time Petrov had put his denunciation in writing. Traskin immediately had sent Petrov's report to the military governor-general of Kiev, Bibikov, who was then on a visit to St Petersburg. On 17 March, Bibikov had informed Count Orlov, the chief of police, who then had considered the matter with the head of the Third Department, General Dubelt. The two men had decided that they had a serious matter on their hands, involving possible harm to the state. The heir to the throne, Alexander, had been informed of the situation, and immediately an order had gone out to conduct an investigation and arrest all those persons implicated in the brotherhood.[6]

The police had conscientiously followed their orders and arrested all those they believed were members of what they called the 'Ukraino-Slavic Society.' Hulak had been the first to be arrested, then Kostomarov, then the others. The police did their best to get voluntary 'confessions' from the arrested men and played on their consciences and their emotions. They also brought in loyal priests to play on the religious sentiments of the subjects.

The reactions of the arrested men varied. Most of them behaved in a noble manner and refused to implicate or blame their fellows in any way. Hulak was especially firm, refusing to say anything whatsoever. Shevchenko too was solid, Kulish somewhat less so. Kostomarov, however, nervous and unstable at the best of times, had been psychologically devastated by his arrest on the eve of his wedding day and by his betrayal by Yuzefovich. When the time for interrogation came, he was in no condition to resist his tormentors.

He talked. But he did so as cautiously as he could in the difficult circumstances. During the first interrogation, that of 15 April 1847, he held up surprisingly well. He claimed that he knew nothing about a secret Cyril-Methodian society and explained that his very real interest in Panslavism had never gone beyond intellectual and cultural curiosity; that is, it had not yet become political. He explained his Panslavism in the most innocuous terms possible, as a belief that all the Slavs should be united under the sceptre of the Russian tsar. Moreover, he stressed his Great Russian background and tried to distance himself from everything Ukrainian. When asked about *Books of the Genesis of the Ukrainian People*, which the investigators referred to as the 'Law of God' (*Zakon Bozhii*), he replied that he had translated part from Polish but had found it originally partly in Ukrainian and that he did not share the ideas expressed in it. He maintained that the author was a certain de Balmain and that his own copy had originally been entitled *Podnestrianka*. In other words, Kostomarov also tried to distance himself from the highly incriminating *Books* by stressing its similarity to Mickiewicz's work and by inventing an author or translator for it. In fact, Kostomarov knew that de Balmain, a former friend of Shevchenko's, was not the author and was, moreover, safely dead.

With respect to his friends and colleagues, Kostomarov stressed the academic side of their discussions about Panslavism and Ukrainian affairs and said that he had discussed such matters with Maksymovych and Yuzefovich among others. He said that Hulak was a rather strange fellow whom he had not taken seriously, especially when talking about founding a society; that Kulish was given to praising Ukraine but that he had frequently quarrelled with him; and that he did not see Shevchenko very often and that Shevchenko was not much interested in the Slavic question. 'He did not really care that much about Slavdom,' Kostomarov concluded. 'Neither in a good nor in a bad sense. But he was a fiery and extreme Little Russian, although he never spoke of Little Russia in the form of a state.'[7]

Two days later, Kostomarov was interrogated a second time. On that occasion, however, his nerves did not hold up well: his behaviour was obsequious towards the regime and a betrayal of the confidence of his comrades. When asked about the signet ring inscribed with the names of Cyril and Methodius and about his leadership of a 'moderate wing' of a Slavic society which displayed liberal tendencies and was opposed to the monarchy, Kostomarov replied that he had dreamed up the ring only out of respect for the Slavic saints and that he was nothing more than a simple scholar. 'I can only reply,' he said, 'that I loved to be engaged in Slavic literature, philosophy, and history. I thought about the unification of the Slavs, but never separated this thought from a second, holy, and sincere one; namely, the desire for the glory and supremacy of the legal tsar and father and for my Russian homeland. Never in my life have I rejected the monarchical form of government.' Kostomarov then asserted that he was simply repeating ideas about

Panslavism that had appeared in official journals published by the government such as *Journal of the Ministry of Public Instruction.*

In replying to further questions about his comrades, Kostomarov strove to distance himself as far as possible from what the interrogators would most certainly think were their undesirable views. He said that Kulish was consumed by a fanatic and exclusive love for Little Russia; that the student Posiada was a liar if he had said that he, Kostomarov, had spoken about forming a Slavic society; that Hulak was given to childish dreams and had displayed an inclination towards liberalism which he brought to Kiev from Dorpat, where he had been a student; that Savych was little known to him but had been messing with French communist ideas and considered it possible to share everything, even women; and that he, Kostomarov, had kept Shevchenko's verses only for their linguistic interest and did not share their 'vile ideas' (*gnusnykh myslei*). He claimed further that he did not remember where he had gotten *Books of the Genesis of the Ukrainian People* from and that, like many other Ukrainian historical manuscripts in his collection, he did not know who its author was.[8]

It was clear that Kostomarov, who was normally a highly strung individual, was not in good psychological condition when he was returned to his cell. He thought that reading would relieve the strain, and one time when General Dubelt was inspecting the prisoners, he asked him for some books. 'It is not permitted,' the general responded. 'You, my good friend, already know a lot more than you should. And you want to know more and more!' 'It is the sin of Adam, Your Excellency,' answered Kostomarov despondently.

During the following weeks, Kostomarov's psychological state grew worse and he fell into a deep depression. His condition so deteriorated, in fact, that a doctor was called in to have a look at him. The doctor confirmed the symptoms of depression (*priznaki omracheniia uma*) and suggested that he be taken to a hospital. He was not, but by 7 May he had collected himself sufficiently to request that he be allowed to make a new confession. His earlier testimony, he claimed, was filled with errors due to his confused state of mind.[9]

On 7, 9, and 24 May, Kostomarov once again answered a series of questions about the Cyril-Methodian Brotherhood put to him by the Third Department of the tsar's police. Once again, he tried to make the society sound as harmless as possible. He stressed its academic basis and claimed that a true society, in the fullest sense of the word, had never formally existed. This time, however, he said nothing against his former comrades, and in general he stressed the legal nature of their common interests. Accordingly, he claimed that Hulak and Bilozersky had never spoken to him against the existing order; that Shevchenko had never said anything suggesting ill will and had merely joked with him about Little Russians; and that Savych was little known to him and should not have been accused by him of holding communist ideas.

Kostomarov also changed his story when asked about the origin of *Books of the Genesis of the Ukrainian People*. He now claimed that, if he remembered correctly, he had obtained the manuscript originally from a certain Khmelnytsky, who had lived with him briefly in Kharkiv, and that he had kept it because of its historical and linguistic interest. However, he also added that he believed it to be of Polish origin since it reflected the radical ideas of Polish revolutionaries such as Adam Mickiewicz and Joachim Lelewel. He added that many Poles from Ukraine – men like Czajkowski and Zaleski – dreamed of Ukraine's former glory and sought to resurrect the country. When Kostomarov was told that Hulak had already confessed to being the author of the document, the historian replied that it was not true and that Hulak had probably said this to help him out.[10]

The tsar's police also personally confronted Kostomarov with the student Petrov, who had first denounced the brotherhood to the authorities; with the student Andruzsky, who had accused Kostomarov of wanting to resurrect the old Ukrainian Cossack order; and with his former comrades Bilozersky and Hulak, whose stories differed somewhat from the historian's. Petrov had claimed that in his lectures Kostomarov had colourfully depicted the murders of the grand princes of old Rus', but the historian responded, quite logically, that that was impossible since none of those grand princes had ever been murdered in a popular uprising. Moreover, he was able completely to refute Andruzsky's testimony, and the young student, according to Kostomarov's later recollection, broke down entirely under his assertions. Similarly, Kostomarov held to his story before his friends Bilozersky and Hulak. He was, moreover, profoundly impressed by Hulak's behaviour and concluded, 'Hulak was a true and practising Christian.'[11]

While Kostomarov and his friends were being held at the Third Department in St Petersburg, his mother, Tatiana Petrivna, and his fiancée, Alina, together with Alina's mother, arrived in the capital. In only a few days, with the help of Kostomarov's faithful manservant, Foma, they had succeeded in travelling by carriage some 1,230 versts (about 1,000 kilometres), from Kiev to St Petersburg. (There was as yet

no railway to speed from them on their way.) At one of the way sta-
tions a short distance out of Kiev, they had spotted a cart accompanied
by two soldiers. It was Shevchenko, also being taken to the capital.
Tatiana Petrivna had been the first to recognize him. Shevchenko had
approached them and mournfully said: 'Here we have Mykola's mother
and his dear young betrothed. Oh, how sad, how very sad! What grief
for his mother and girl!' Shevchenko had kissed the women, and the
two parties once again had begun to go their separate ways. However,
before they had separated completely, Shevchenko had succeeded in
telling the women that he did not grieve for himself because he was
single. 'I grieve for Mykola because he has a mother and a beloved one
and he is guilty of nothing except having befriended me. Forgive me,
dear mother, and do not bow before me!'[12]

Upon his arrival in St Petersburg, Shevchenko too was incarcerated
by the Third Department and interrogated. But he was allowed to have
a Bible and some paper on which to write. From his cell window he
could see people come and go, and on 19 May, after having written six
short poems, he chanced to see Tatiana Petrivna coming to visit her son.
He was immediately seized by the touching theme of mother and son
joined in tragedy and composed the following poem:

To N.I. Kostomarov

The joyful sun passed in and out
Of vernal clouds that danced about;
The prisoners were served, like me,
With thin, distasteful mugs of tea;
While all around the trampling ranged
Of blue-clad warders being changed.
To the great door, the key's shrill jars,
And to the heavy window-bars
I had grown used, and felt no more
Deep anguish for the days of yore,
The buried and forgotten years
And all the torment of my tears.
Them in abundance have I shed
Upon this desert, waste and dead,
Where not a plant salutes the view,
Not even one dry stalk of rue.
My native thorp I called to mind:

But who were those I'd left behind?
My parents, both lay buried deep ...
And rankling griefs my senses sweep
That no one there remembers me.
Your mother then, dear friend, I see
Who, black as earth, walks weak with loss
As if she just had left her cross ...
My thanks to God were boundless then
As the most fortunate of men
In having no one thus to share
My shackles and my goal's despair.

St Petersburg (citadel), May 19, 1847

Shevchenko hid this poem with several other compositions and managed to preserve them for some years.[13]

At about the same time, the police investigation into the affair of what they called the Ukraino-Slavic Society was completed, and the police chief, Count Orlov, composed his final report, which he submitted to the tsar. Orlov concluded that Hulak, Bilozersky, and Kostomarov were the ones who had laid the basis for the society, which, he thought, had in fact existed for a time as an actual organization. According to Orlov, the conspirators were basically scholars, with no connection with the military and therefore no opportunity to organize anything in the way of an insurrection. (Such a possibility had been charged by the student informer, Petrov.) Nevertheless, Orlov considered the offenders dangerous men since they could influence young minds in an unhealthy direction. Orlov then suggested what he regarded as the proper punishment for each of the offenders. 'Kostomarov,' wrote Orlov to Tsar Nicholas I, 'took part in the Ukraino-Slavic society, thought up the idea of the ring and the name of the Society of Saints Cyril and Methodius, circulated the criminal manuscript of the *Law of God*, and although he later openly admitted that, still, he is more culpable in so far as he was older in years than any of the others and was obliged by his professorial rank to turn young people from an unwanted direction; for Kostomarov, one year of incarceration in a prison to be followed by penal exile in government service in one of the Great Russian provinces. He should not be allowed to engage in scholarship and should be put under close police supervision.' The tsar pencilled in on the margin of this sentence, 'To the Province of Viatka.'[14]

On 30 May, the tsar's sentences of the various men implicated in the Cyril-Methodian Brotherhood were pronounced on all the offenders, who were assembled for the occasion before Count Orlov and General Dubelt. The heaviest punishment was meted out to Shevchenko, who had deeply offended the government by his derogatory verses about the tsar and his family. He was condemned to life service as a common soldier in Central Asia and was to be kept under the strictest surveillance and prohibited from writing or painting. Hulak was given three years' solitary confinement in the Schlisselburg fortress, to be followed by punitive exile; Kulish was given four months' imprisonment, followed by exile to Vologda; Bilozersky, four months' exile to Petrozavodsk; and all the accused were barred from returning to Ukraine. The works of Kostomarov, Shevchenko, and Kulish were to be no longer permitted to circulate.[15]

Later the same day, Kostomarov was transferred from the Third Department to begin serving his term in the Peter and Paul fortress. He was introduced to the commandment, a General Skobelev, who happened to be an old friend of Alina's late father, and then taken away to his cell. It was a fairly large room with a bed, a simple oak table, a chair, and a single window. The guards took away their prisoner's clothes and eyeglasses and dressed him in an ill-fitting prison uniform. His mother was allowed to see him once a week in the presence of the commandant or another officer.

On 14 June, he was permitted to see his mother and to bid farewell to Alina and her mother. It was a sad occasion. Kostomarov's eyeglasses still had not been returned to him, and he could recognize his visitors only when they spoke to him. Alina's mother promised that after Kostomarov had served his year in prison, he would be allowed to marry her daughter. Before Alina left St Petersburg for Kiev, she gave a message to Kostomarov through Tatiana Petrivna to keep healthy and never give up hope. In fact, it would be many years before they met again.

The outside world was not wholly ignorant of the arrest of Kostomarov and his circle. In Russia, rumours spread about the uncovering of a separatist Ukrainian plot by the tsar's police, and in Germany the press reported the arrests and stressed the Panslavic sympathies of the arrested men.[16] While these various rumours spread among the general public, Kostomarov settled down to his new life as a prison inmate.

Kostomarov's regime remained severe at first, his only relief being the weekly visits of his mother, who visited him every Friday. Days passed into weeks, and weeks into months. Eventually Skobelev, who seemed to take pity on his scholarly prisoner, allowed him tea to drink, cigars to smoke, and books to read. These last were brought to him by Tatiana Petrivna, who continued to see him only in the presence of a supervising officer. Eventually, he was allowed paper and a pencil with which to write. He was given borshch and cornmeal to eat and on special days was allowed dumplings.

The unfortunate scholar resolved to put his time in prison to good use and began the study of ancient Greek, with which he was already somewhat acquainted. After intensive study for several months, he had mastered that difficult language to the extent that he was able to read Homer in the original, only occasionally glancing at a Latin translation. Simultaneously, for intellectual relief as he later recalled, he studied the much easier Spanish language. He made rapid progress in Spanish and before long had read almost all of *Don Quixote* in the original. In February 1848, however, he began to have health problems again. He was brothered by headaches, nervous attacks, and even hallucinations. The doctor in charge ordered him to stop his study of Greek and to bathe his head in cold water. Every day, he was allowed into the garden for a bath. The warder, a great believer in hydrotherapy, encouraged these experimental treatments, and indeed in a short time the overwrought scholar began to recover. Thereafter, he took to reading French novels and systematically went through the works of George Sand. As spring approached, the days grew longer and the atmosphere more cheerful. Kostomarov anxiously awaited 30 May 1848, the day on which he was to be released.[17]

At six o'clock on the morning of 30 May, Kostomarov's jailers brought him his suitcase, computed the bill for the tea and cigars he had consumed in prison, and led him away to the Third Department offices. He was placed in a well-furnished room with an open window and an unarmed soldier at the door and was asked to wait. After about an hour's time, General Dubelt arrived and briefly interviewed him. Kostomarov remained in this room for fourteen days.

During his time at the Third Department, the historian's mother came to see him every day. He was given food from the best restaurants and enjoyed wine with his supper. He was also given a box of Havana cigars. The window of the room was always open, and there is no doubt that this transition period improved his spirits considerably.

It seems that word of Kostomarov's apparently delicate state of health had reached the highest quarters. One day, he was taken to the administrative offices and told that the tsar himself had ordered Count Orlov to ask him if he would like to be sent somewhere that would be warmer than Viatka and if he was in need of money. Kostomarov thanked his custodians and said that he would like to be sent to the Crimea, where he could follow his physician's suggestions about therapeutic bathing. His request was forwarded to Count Orlov and to the tsar, one of whom is reported to have responded: 'There is too much poetry there. It would be better if he chooses among one of these four cities of southeast Russia: Astrakhan, Saratov, Orenburg, or Penza.'[18] Considering the matter carefully, Kostomarov chose Saratov, which was located in the middle Volga region and provided an opportunity for him to continue his water therapy. The authorities agreed, and he was given three hundred rubles to help him along. His mother had already been paid his professor's salary for the previous year.

Before being sent to his chosen place of exile, Kostomarov had one last meeting with General Dubelt, who seems to have treated him with a certain amount of consideration. 'We have done everything we could for you,' the general said to Kostomarov. 'But, of course, you cannot expect to get too much more. You should know, my good friend, that ordinary people care for their own interest, and this gets them suitable position, place, wealth, and comfort. But those who are dedicated to high ideals and try to change humanity – as you yourself know, it is written of them in the Holy Scriptures, "They walk about in the skins of goats and live in puppet shows and on the edge of worldly disasters."' Dubelt then showed Kostomarov a letter which Count Orlov had written to his future employer and custodian, the governor of Saratov. The postscript read: 'I ask you to be gentle with him for he is a good person. He made a mistake and has now sincerely repented it.'[19] Dubelt also told Kostomarov that he could choose his route from St Petersburg to Saratov and stop somewhere along the way if he wished.

On 15 June, Kostomarov, in the company of a military officer and soldier, said goodbye to his mother and set off for Saratov. He had chosen a route through Novgorod, which interested him because of its great historical significance, and he dallied in that city for a few days visiting various churches and monasteries. Novgorod so delighted Kostomarov that he composed a poem in honour of the city and read it aloud to his bemused warders. Kostomarov's party then passed on to Tver, which had been severely hit by a cholera epidemic. The prisoner's coachman died of the disease before his very eyes. In Moscow, the party passed piles of dead loaded onto a cart. The entire country between Moscow and Saratov also had been severely struck by the disease, but the young scholar managed to arrive safely in Saratov on 24 June. He immediately reported to the governor of Saratov, M.L. Kozhevnikov, and presented his papers to him. There is no doubt that the letter from Count Orlov asking Kozhevnikov to be gentle with the former prisoner worked its magic. He was treated quite civilly. 'I had been under constant police supervision for over a year,' Kostomarov later recalled, 'and after leaving the governor's residence, I was finally alone, without an escort.'

The officer who had brought me invited me to go to the hotel with him, but I was so delighted by my liberty that at first I wanted to run off to some unknown place, only later going to the hotel. And that I did, and not knowing where I was going to, ran off in the opposite direction from the hotel. Later on, I had to ask passers by where the hotel was, and I was barely able to find it. The officer who had brought me to Saratov left the next morning. I found myself in an entirely unknown city, in a strange district where I had neither friends nor acquaintances.[20]

Kostomarov eventually found an apartment and began to settle down to his new life in exile. After his initial burst of enthusiasm – helped along, no doubt, by the governor's polite reception of him – the dreariness of life in a small provincial town began to set in.

Kostomarov was certainly not impressed by Saratov. It was a small city of twenty-five thousand people, with muddy streets, no sidewalks, no impressive buildings, and no bridge over the Volga. Moreover, when Kostomarov arrived, a cholera epidemic was raging, and about a hundred people were dying every day. When an army officer who had just arrived from St Petersburg collapsed next door to Kostomarov's hotel room, the young exile, who was already more than slightly hypochondriac, was thoroughly frightened by the consequences of his unknowingly having chosen such an unhealthy place in which to live. He considered himself brave in eating local berries with cream, a dish which, he was informed, might taste good but was quite dangerous. However, within a month or two, his devoted mother arrived in Saratov, and the young exile's life took on more orderliness.

In accordance with the regular conditions of penal exile, Kostomarov was required to serve somewhere in the imperial bureaucracy in Saratov. The governor gave him various light duties to perform as a secretary – first in the criminal, then in the secret, department – but Kostomarov quickly showed himself unsuited to bureaucratic work. He could not sit calmly in the office but would pace about the room, or suddenly throw up his hands and rush out to the street. 'What a strange man!' one of his fellow office workers later recalled. 'It was said that he behaved like this because he was profoundly upset on account of his betrothed, whom he deeply loved but who had betrayed him when he had been condemned to the Peter and Paul prison. It was said that she had married another.'[21]

In fact, for a long time Alina was not told that Kostomarov's place of exile had been changed to Saratov, and she continued to write to him in Viatka. Her mother had turned decisively against the historian and did everything possible to keep the two from communicating with each other. Eventually, Alina managed to correspond with Kostomarov surreptitiously for about two years. The historian treasured her letters and read and reread them until they fell to pieces from handling. Alina similarly treasured Kostomarov's. Both of the separated lovers were eventually found out, and their unsympathetic mothers put an end to the romance. Alina was forced to marry a man named Kysil but never forgot her first love. The heartbroken historian similarly kept alive the memory of his beloved. They were to meet again many years later.[22]

During his brief and unsuccessful career as an administrator, Kostomarov was given some work regarding an Old Believer sect, members of which were among the inhabitants of the Saratov district, and the work aroused his interest in the history of the sect. It was his first real contact with Great Russian as opposed to Ukrainian country folk, and apparently the over-enthusiastic Kostomarov once again ruffled the feathers of his rather staid fellow bureaucrats.[23] He was eventually relieved of the work and left with the job of serving as 'official translator.' But since there was no translating to do in the middle of the Russian steppes, Governor Kozhevnikov appointed Kostomarov editor of the local government newspaper, the *Saratov Provincial News* (*Saratovskie gubernskie vedomosti*). Once again, however, Kostomarov proved himself a poor administrator, often not reporting for work on account of his 'delicate' health. He was soon relieved of his editorial duties.[24] In general, Kostomarov's first years in Saratov were difficult ones in spite of the goodwill of the governor. The distraught historian quickly proved himself an unreliable and incompetent administrator who could not get along with his colleagues, and a nervous city intellectual who, in the words of an acquaintance named Bezruchkov, 'was considered a madman by everybody.'[25]

Bezruchkov, however, was nowhere near the truth. Kostomarov

shunned the company of most provincials because they offered him no intellectual stimulation and he did not share their interest in drinking or rural sports. He spent most of his free time studying and writing. And during his quiet isolation in Saratov he produced marvellous things.

In 1849, for example, he wrote a long dramatic piece on the life of the ancient Roman historian Cremutius Aulus Cordus (d. 25 A.D.). In the play, which takes place in Rome during the reign of Emperor Tiberius, there are three acts – 'The Informers,' 'The Tyrant,' and 'The Historian.' The truthful historian Cremutius Cordus is set against the all-powerful tyrant Tiberius. Cordus is persecuted and condemned without hope only for telling the truth.

There is no doubt that Kostomarov's play was written as an exercise in autobiography during a very difficult time in his life. The tale showed, moreover, that his subservience to the autocratic power of Nicholas I and his officials was limited and that he was beginning to recover his courage. Kostomarov had been badly bent by his terrifying arrest and his year in prison, but he remained unbroken. He dedicated his play 'To the memory of 14 June 1847,' the occasion of his last meeting with his beloved Alina, added a quotation from Mickiewicz on beauty remembered, and quietly waited for a time when circumstances would allow publication.[26] At about the same time, moreover, he wrote to his friend Vasyl Bilozersky asking him to subscribe to the German newspaper *Allgemeine Zeitung* because he wanted, as he put it, 'to study systematically the revolutions of 1848.'[27]

Nor did Kostomarov abandon his old historical interests. In spite of his isolation in a small provincial town in Great Russia where there were no significant libraries, Kostomarov immediately returned to his study of the era of Bohdan Khmelnytsky and the great Ukrainian revolt against the Poles. Many of his books and papers, including his vast collection of Ukrainian folk-songs, had been returned to him after his release from prison, and he wrote to old friends and acquaintances asking them to send him additional material. In particular, he wrote to the Polish aristocrat Count Konstanty Swidzinski, to whom he had been introduced by Kulish in Kiev and who possessed an enormous private library and had a special interest in history and archaeology. 'The Count,' Kostomarov later recalled, 'responded to my request more kindly than I had hoped': 'One after another he sent me Latin and Polish books illuminating the era of Bohdan Khmelnytsky. With the help of those works, I was able not only to continue my historical composition but even to bring it to such a state that only a little polishing was needed to complete it. And that I put off until such time as I was free and had the opportunity to go to those cities where the appropriate libraries and archives were located.'[28] Kostomarov thus had available to him not only the traditional sources and the histories composed by Russian and Ukrainian chroniclers and scholars, but also the many Polish and Latin sources sent to him by Swidzinski and the collections of folk material compiled by Sreznevsky and others. In widening the field of his sources, he was amassing material for a treatment of the Ukrainian struggle for social, religious, and national independence from the Polish-Lithuanian Commonwealth that was potentially more vivid and more panoramic than any that had come before it. The basic work was completed within a few years.

But Kostomarov did not confine himself to purely scholarly pursuits during this period. He also made the acquaintance of whatever educated society was to be found in the locality and soon discovered a number of kindred spirits. A circle of Polish political exiles predominated among his early Saratov friends. They were highly cultivated people with whom Kostomarov could discuss history, politics, and literature, and although their Polish patriotism often ruffled Kostomarov's Russian/Ukrainian feathers, his disputes with them always ended on a friendly note. One of the Poles, a certain Meletowicz, who shared some of Kostomarov's Panslavic sympathies, became the historian's closest friend and reminded him of what he believed was the pure Slavic goodness that reigned in Poland prior to the restricting influence of the Catholic baroque and its 'Jesuitical' casuistry. But Meletowicz's untimely death from cholera put an end to their promising relationship.[29]

Kostomarov also befriended a number of educated Russians. Among them were Arkhimandrite Nikanor (later, archbishop of Kherson), who was deeply impressed with Kostomarov's piety and knowledge of Holy Scripture; there was also I.U. Palimpsestov, who had long theological discussions with the historian and was similarly impressed with his religious commitment. Palimpsestov later recalled that Kostomarov could recite the Gospels and the letters of Saint Paul by heart and had an abiding love for Church Slavonic, which he thought should be taught in elementary schools for the common people. Palimpsestov also recalled that although Kostomarov was knowledgeable in Catholic and Lutheran theology, he always retained a special, if unusual, affection for Orthodoxy. 'This church,' he said of the Orthodox to Palimpsestov on

one occasion, 'can be called a true church of the people; it is understandable both to a poorly developed man and to a man with higher
education, to both children and old people. This is the kind of church
that Christ wanted to found.'[30]

Kostomarov's religious sentiments, however, remained unconven-
tional for quiet Saratov. He loved to spice his informal conversations
with maxims in Church Slavonic, but he retained serious reservations
about the centralized, hierarchical organization of the official Russian
Orthodox church. 'He went to church almost every day,' Arkhimandrite
Nikanor later recalled, 'but he was far from believing everything he
heard.'[31] Friendships with other persons in Saratov, such as the Russian
cultural historian A.N. Pypin, indicate that Kostomarov never limited
himself to circles in which religious commitment was paramount.

Saratov, moreover, was not devoid of women, and Kostomarov's love
for Alina was soon sorely tested. In 1850, for example, the historian
frequented the home of one Russian family with a number of eligible
daughters. One of them, Natalia Stupina, an intelligent, ruddy, round-
faced girl whom Kostomarov thought 'a purely Great Russian type,'
attracted the special attention of the scholar, and the talk of marriage
which followed greatly pleased the historian's hopeful mother. But for
one reason or another the relationship did not work out, and, like the
unfortunate Alina, the young Natalia eventually married another.[32]

Misfortune in love did not improve Kostomarov's spirits. He believed
that his health was deteriorating and utilized the services of certain
quack doctors, who only made the situation worse.

At about the same time, the spring of 1851, the young N.G. Chernyshevsky arrived in Saratov to teach at the local gymnasium. He made
a point of introducing himself to the historian, of whom he had been
told by Sreznevsky. To Kostomarov, Nikolai Chernyshevsky seemed an
intelligent and handsome youth with whom he could discuss politics
and literature; to Chernyshevsky, Kostomarov appeared a learned and
attractive intellectual who was wasting away in the provinces. 'You,
Izmail Ivanovich,' Chernyshevsky wrote to their common friend Sreznevsky, 'had so spoken to me about Nikolai Ivanovich's intelligence and
character that as soon as I arrived in Saratov, I rushed off to visit him.'

I found him a man to whom I could not but be attracted. Naturally, he is
very homesick in Saratov, and for this reason I serve as a diversion for him.
So I spend a lot of time visiting him. He is expecting permission to leave
here and live in one of the capitals; perhaps he is even expecting permission

to continue his service in his former vocation, if not as a professor then at least as a librarian or the editor of a journal or something like that. Nikolai Ivanovich has decided against serious work as a civil servant and against remaining in Saratov for any length of time. It is to be hoped that he will quickly get the necessary permission because he has succeeded in impressing the governor and other people who are necessary to him. But for the time being he is living in Saratov without any definite occupation – he serves as a translator in the provincial administration simply in order to be counted as a civil servant.

Chernyshevsky continued on a more intimate note:

Naturally, seeing his career shattered, his beloved occupation torn from him, and, at least for a time, his goals in life displaced, Nikolai Ivanovich is homesick and depressed. He tries to keep himself busy but the impossibility of seeing his work in print deprives him of all enthusiasm. Thus, he wrote a history of Bohdan Khmelnytsky, and the censor tore it to pieces so that it made no sense. Since he did not wish to ruin his work, he put it away in a drawer. But the history throws new light on the situation in seventeenth-century Little Russia and on its annexation to Russia. For a long time, that put him off further work.

Chernyshevsky concluded by telling Sreznevsky that recently Kostomarov had somewhat recovered from his depression and had begun to work on the era of Ivan the Terrible. 'I am happy about that,' he wrote, 'because only work can somewhat dissipate his homesickness and get rid of the spiritual depression, which has a bad effect upon his health.'[33] In the meantime, Chernyshevsky discussed politics and played chess with Kostomarov, and Kostomarov placed his hope in the distant future.

Kostomarov also continued to make new acquaintances. In 1852, he met another interesting woman, Hanna Paskhalova, with whom he developed some common intellectual interests. The two studied natural history and astronomy together, and at one point Kostomarov even built a hot air balloon. He also involved himself in spiritualist seances and theories of animal magnetism, which raised the eyebrows even of some of his closest friends. Moreover, although the historian read Humbolt with enthusiasm, he did not give up his interest in folklore, and together with Paskhalova he visited the countryside to gather folksongs. But Paskhalova's mother did not relish her daughter's star-gazing in the attic and singing peasant songs with the strange historian, and Chernyshevsky took it upon himself to warn the couple of her disapprobation, even suggesting that they get married. 'In general, Chernyshevsky and Paskhalova did not much like each other,' Kostomarov later concluded.[34]

In the summer of 1852, the historian was given permission to visit the Crimea for a holiday. He travelled for a while with an Italian named Amoretti, who taught French in Kharkiv. Amoretti shared Kostomarov's love for the Ukrainian people, and the two men proved to be good companions. At Kerch, they observed some archaeological excavations, and in the Crimea they visited various cities including Bakhchisarai and spent some time on the beaches. Upon his return to Saratov, Kostomarov once again took up his study of ethnography.

In the spring of 1853, Hanna Paskhalova departed for St Petersburg, and Kostomarov turned to more purely historical work. From the study of printed documents and manuscript materials which he found in local churches, Kostomarov began to reconstruct the social history of Muscovy before the eighteenth century. He discovered much new documentation on the Old Believer schism and a valuable manuscript on Ivan IV's *Stoglav*, or special church council, and he quickly acquired an interest in the Cossack and peasant revolts of Stenka Razin (1630–71) and Emelian Pugachev (1742–75), which had taken place largely in the Saratov region. Those subjects drew Kostomarov's attention for several years.[35]

At about the same time, Kostomarov changed his living quarters. He had found a well-equipped, spacious apartment in a medium-sized, two-storey building located in a quiet suburb at the edge of the city. He chose the quarters because their quiet helped him concentrate on his learned pursuits. But they had the added advantage of belonging to N.D. Prudentov, a local notable in charge of the archives at the nearby church administrative office. The two men became good friends, and Prudentov eventually helped Kostomarov gather archival material for his historical work touching upon the Saratov area, in particular for the history of the Cossack revolt of Stenka Razin.[36]

Also in 1852, the scholar became involved in a local murder case, in which three Jews were accused of killing two young Christian children and dumping their bodies into the Volga. Blood was found on one of the Jews, a book refuting the ancient blood libel – the idea that Jews sometimes used Christian blood in their religious rites – was found in the possession of the other, and the investigator sent by the central authorities asked Kostomarov to write a historical report on the subject.

The governor of Saratov, Kozhevnikov, had broken the rules by allow-ing some Jews to settle in his province, which lay outside the official 'Pale of Settlement,' and he desired the historian to refute the blood libel. But after several months of studying Jewish history, Kostomarov produced an equivocal report which noted the existence of human sacrifice in the ancient Near East and the recurrence of the blood libel in Western Europe during the Middle Ages, and concluded that the existence of a sect with such practices was not impossible. Kozhevnikov tried to persuade Kostomarov to alter his report, but the historian angrily refused. As a result of the affair, Kozhevnikov lost his job, the investigator from St Petersburg was briefly appointed deputy-governor, and a new governor named Ignatiev was sent to Saratov. As for the unfortunate accused, their case dragged on for several years. It even reached the Senate, which declared that there was insufficient evidence against them, and then the State Council and the tsar, who finally condemned them to penal servitude. Though Kostomarov found the affair unpleasant, he never changed his position on the question of blood libel, a fact that considerably irritated his progressive friend Chernyshevsky.[37]

In 1854, the historian had another disturbing experience. Without signing his name to the submission, he published in the *Saratov Provincial News* some of the folk-songs that he and Paskhalova had collected. But someone, it seems, was upset by the impious and somewhat risqué tone of the verses and reported the matter to the St Petersburg author-ities, who thereafter made a complaint to the paper and fired the local censor. Kostomarov himself, however, managed to escape unscathed.[38]

In spite of his difficulties with the central authorities, Kostomarov was able to get along with the new governor, who, of course, owed his position partly to the historian's report in connection with the blood libel case. Ignatiev gave Kostomarov full freedom and appointed him head of the local Statistical Committee. It was not long, moreover, before Hanna Paskhalova returned from St Petersburg with her new husband, Danylo Mordovets, who was promptly appointed Kostomarov's aide on the committee. Kostomarov and Mordovets had a common background – both were of partly Russified Ukrainian ancestry – and common interests in literature, history, and folklore. Like Kostomarov, Mordovets was acquainted with Aleksandr Pypin and Izmail Sreznevsky, and like Kostomarov, at one point he had translated the Královédvorský manuscript into Ukrainian. The two men became close friends.[39]

In the summer of 1855, Saratov was plagued by a number of fires which destroyed large parts of the town. One great blaze reached the windows of Kostomarov's apartment and sent his mother and neighbours fleeing. Kostomarov, however, stood by impassively, oblivious to the danger to his furniture and possessions; he held his manuscript of Bohdan Khmelnytsky under his arm and, as he later wrote, recalled the saying of the classical sage *Omnia mea mecum porto*, 'Everything I have I carry with me'!

It was suspected that arsonists had started the fires, and rumours among the common people held that Russia's enemies in the Crimea, the 'Anglo-French,' were responsible. One day, Kostomarov accidentally came across a wild crowd of Russians beating up a man whom the people accused of being an 'Anglo-Frenchman' and an arsonist. The man turned out to be a poor Georgian seminarian, whom the crowd quickly freed upon the historian's intervention. In the general atmosphere of hysteria then prevailing in Saratov, even the educated classes had their prejudices and suspected that the Polish exiles had started the fires. Once, Kostomarov himself was taken for such a Pole.

After some time, the fires in Saratov ceased and the population calmed down. In March 1855, following the death of Nicholas I and the accession of the new tsar, Alexander II, Kostomarov requested permission to visit St Petersburg on family business. The atmosphere was conducive to change, and in the fall he was given permission to visit the capital for a duration of four months.

Kostomarov's journey to St Petersburg as winter approached was an exciting one. In the towns and cities along the way, people were engaged in animated conversation about the accession of the new tsar and the renewal of Russia. 'People,' he later wrote, 'were discussing the swift conclusion of peace [with the English and the French] and the transfer of the government's and society's attention to the internal well-being of Russia.'

It was a truly poetical time. It seemed as if all egoistic impulses had dissipated; people stopped thinking only of their own benefit. On everyone's mind and on everyone's tongue was the renaissance of Russian society to a different life which people desired but had never yet experienced. All spoke of their faith in the good intentions and intelligence of the new emperor, and they were already speaking occasionally of the liberation of the people from serfdom at the first opportunity.[40]

Life in St Petersburg itself was equally animated. Kostomarov quickly ran into old friends from Kharkiv, Kiev, and even Saratov. He met Sreznevsky, who had been in the capital for some time, Bilozersky, who had returned from exile, and Chernyshevsky, who had recently moved to St Petersburg; Chernyshevsky introduced him to the radical young literary critic Nikolai Dobroliubov. Kostomarov similarly met Kulish, also returned from exile, who introduced him to Sergei and Konstantin Aksakov; they were conservative Moscow Slavophiles with whom he was able to discuss 'Slavic' ideas.

Scholarship, however, consumed most of the historian's four months in St Petersburg. Day after day, he spent long hours in the great Public Library, where he examined rare books, manuscripts, and brochures for information with which to complete his study of Bohdan Khmelnytsky. The work went smoothly, and in short order Kostomarov was able to present his manuscript to the authorities and ask for permission to have it published.

The censor whom Kostomarov approached, a man named Freigang, stunned the historian by telling him that publication of his work – Kostomarov had given it the innocuous title 'The Age of [Tsar] Alexei Mikhailovich' – was impossible since the late emperor, Nicholas I, had issued a secret order that none of Kostomarov's works should be published. The historian immediately approached his former warder, General Dubelt, and asked him to do what he could to have the order rescinded. Dubelt complied, but he made it clear to the censors that they were to be very strict with Kostomarov's work, which touched upon the delicate question of Ukrainian nationality and Ukrainian independence and contained lively descriptions of civil conflict. As a result, the authorities specified that it could appear only in measured doses, in article form, scattered through one of the journals. But they further specified that it must appear in parts of no less than three chapters, since if the chapters appeared separately, the country folk could misinterpret them. Kostomarov also had to revise several dozen pages describing attacks by peasants on their noble masters. Nevertheless, the historian must have been elated when his masterpiece finally appeared in the prestigious journal *Notes of the Fatherland* under the relatively unambiguous title 'Bohdan Khmelnytsky and the Restoration of Southern Rus' to Russia.'[41]

But even that title did not do justice to Kostomarov's theme. For it was not the restoration of Southern Rus' to Russia that was the historian's major point, but the Cossacks' struggle against Poland for their religious, social, and political liberty and for independence. Kostomarov's description of the sorry plight of Southern Rus' under the Poles is very vivid: the church was degraded, the Cossacks humiliated, and the population enslaved. Bohdan Khmelnytsky's personal injuries at the hands of the Poles reflected the injuries of the entire Ukrainian people, and at his call they rose up to a man. Kostomarov puts into the hetman's mouth a moving speech at the outset of the rebellion. In that speech, Khmelnytsky states that the struggle is not simply a war for glory and booty, to which the Cossacks are well accustomed, but a struggle for honour, liberty, and faith, a struggle for 'our livelihood, our wives, and our children'; it is a struggle, in other words, to defend 'our mother Ukraine.'[42]

It is not Bohdan Khmelnytsky himself, however, who emerges as the principal hero over the course of the narrative, but the Ukrainian people. Indeed, the hetman is not portrayed in the brightest of colours: he is old and experienced rather than young and dashing, cold and calculating rather than warm and exuberant, cunning and reserved rather than honest and open. From the Jesuits, says Kostomarov, Khmelnytsky had learned to hide his true feelings and keep his own counsel amid potential adversaries. He could deal with two or three parties at the same time and allow none of them to discover his real intentions. It was this realistic politician who led Ukraine out of the Polish-Lithuanian Commonwealth, through the complex world of international combinations, and finally into Muscovy's all too welcoming embrace.

In his work, the 1859 book edition of which was entitled simply *Bohdan Khmelnytsky*, Kostomarov captures the reader's attention immediately and holds it completely to the end of the narrative. He does so through the frequent use of commonplace detail, anecdote, direct quotation, and dialogue taken straight from the Ukrainian and Polish chronicles or, more frequently, reconstructed on the basis of material found in them. Some of the dialogues, especially the speeches of Khmelnytsky, are even in vernacular Ukrainian rather than literary Russian. Kostomarov's sentences are short and direct, his narrative filled with movement. *Bohdan Khmelnytsky* is a book replete with suspense, drama, and pure action. The clash of great armies is its stuff; religious, social, and political freedom its ideals. During the long, tension-filled moments before the battle of Berestechko, Kostomarov, echoing the Polish chronicler, sums up the essence of the conflict. 'It was a majestic sight,' he writes. 'On the field as far as the eye could see stood countless ranks of the three hostile peoples. Each stood ready to do battle for what was most dear to it: the Poles for the fatherland, the Tatars for glory and profit, and the Cossacks for independence.'[43]

Kostomarov's use of the sources is particularly notable. Having spent long years in exile and never having had the opportunity of using the archives of Moscow and St Petersburg, he relied heavily on the Polish and Cossack chronicles. But of these he made good and original use. He was especially entralled, of course, by the Cossack chronicles, particularly the chronicle of Hrabianka, the triumphal tone of which he imitated, and the chronicle of Velychko, which he had helped prepare for publication in Kiev in the 1840s, shortly before his arrest and exile. His debt is clear not only in his general narrative but also in his interpretation of important events. For example, in his treatment of the Council of Pereiaslav (1654), as a result of which Ukraine acceded to Russia, Kostomarov stresses the Cossacks' demand that the tsar's representatives swear to preserve traditional Cossack rights and privileges just as the Cossacks would swear loyalty to the tsar. Then he states that although his Karamzinite predecessor Bantysh-Kamensky had written that only the Ukrainians swore the oath, the Cossack chronicler Velychko, who was well informed, relates clearly that the tsar's men in turn swore an oath to uphold the ancient rights of 'all Little Russia and all of the Zaporozhian army.'[44] In such a way, Kostomarov, managed to inform his readers, in spite of the vigorous red pencils of the tsar's censors, that he valued Ukrainian liberty highly against the imperial Russian as well as against the vanished Polish state.

Bohdan Khmelnytsky was an immediate success. The historian's friend Chernyshevsky, who reviewed the work for the progressive journal *The Contemporary (Sovremennik)*, was captivated by the learning and lucidity displayed therein and firmly declared that it 'necessarily assured its learned author a first place among our historians.'[45] Another acquaintance, the Slavist and ethnographer A.A. Kotliarevsky, who was of Ukrainian background from the Poltava area, noted, 'This excellent historical work unites the attraction of a novel with the strict precision of history.' He continued by saying that Kostomarov was primarily 'a historian artist,' who dissolved himself and his modern prejudices in his material and let the historical events speak for themselves. He thereby reduced national passions and lead mankind along a more tolerant road. Kostomarov's book, concluded an exuberant Kotliarevsky, was so well written that it was the first work of Russian history which could be read 'by all lovers of *serious* reading.'[46] Meanwhile, another critic, the progressive journalist G.Z. Eliseev, writing under the pseudonym

Grytsko, declared that 'the entire history of Little Russia should be given such a careful and dispassionate treatment as we have before us in *Bohdan Khmelnytsky*.'[47]

It was some time before Kostomarov could sit back and enjoy the reviews. While *Bohdan Khmelnytsky* was still being printed, the historian returned to Saratov, where he put in order the remaining material he had gathered at the St Petersburg Public Library. Much of it concerned trade and commerce in old Muscovy, and Kostomarov was quickly approaching the point where he could complete another stout volume, on that subject. Moreover, a short time later he published a penetrating article on a Great Russian poem of the seventeenth century, *The Tale of Woe-Misfortune* (*Povest o Gore-Zlochastii*), which his friend Pypin had discovered in his presence some months before, in an old manuscript collection. Kostomarov was greatly impressed by this unique monument of Old Russian literature, by its popular verse form, its popular language, and its unusual theme. Though there is no doubt that it was the poem's combination of folk and high literary qualities that so excited his admiration, he concluded, quite correctly, that it was more a literary work than a piece of folklore.[48]

But Ukrainian topics still attracted Kostomarov's special attention. For example, in 1856, when Panteleimon Kulish published his encyclopaedic two-volume miscellany on Ukrainian ethnography entitled *Notes on Southern Rus'* (*Zapiski o iuzhnoi Rusi*), the historian quickly penned a book-length review of the work which criticized its shortcomings but praised its detail, especially its original orthography, which for the first time accurately reflected the sounds of spoken Ukrainian and answered the fundamental question as to the delineation of the 'Great' and 'Little Russian' languages. 'With his basic knowledge of the history, ethnography, and language of the South Russian region,' wrote Kostomarov of his old colleague, 'citizen Kulish is at the present time the single writer in whom we place our hope for the development of the Little Russian word and the expression of the Little Russian element in Russian literature.'[49] It was the beginning of the reign of the new tsar that allowed Kostomarov to hope that such a literature could eventually flourish.

The beginning of the new reign also affected Kostomarov's legal status. After his coronation as Alexander II, the new tsar issued a manifesto which decreed liberty for a large number of political prisoners, and Kostomarov was one of them. He was called into the governor's office and told of his liberation from police supervision and compulsory residence in Saratov. The only limitation was that he would still be prohibited from teaching or lecturing. Nevertheless, after eight full years of restriction he was finally free and could travel. He immediately made plans for a visit to Western Europe, and in the meantime he completed his 'Outline of the Trade of the Muscovite State in the Sixteenth and Seventeenth Centuries.'[50]

From the time of his arrest in Kiev in the spring of 1847 until his release from penal exile nearly ten years later, Mykola Kostomarov had undergone many shattering experiences. The sudden shock of his arrest and betrayal on the eve of his wedding day, the trials and tribulations of his interrogation by the tsar's political police, the painful isolation of prison, and the difficulties of penal exile had all placed their imprint on his life and personality. Given his nervous disposition and delicate psychology, each and every event was bound to take its toll.

The first blows fell heaviest and hardest. Kostomarov was almost completely shattered by Yuzefovich's betrayal of him and by his sudden arrest. He was confused, inconsistent, and obsequious during his interrogation. He refused to recognize the seriousness of his transgression and, in the most difficult moments, betrayed the confidence of his friends and tried to transfer responsibility for his actions onto them. After a while, shame at his behaviour overtook him, and Kostomarov ceased to point his finger at his former colleagues. But during his time in the hands of the Third Department he abased himself repeatedly before his tormentors and expressed nothing but love and admiration for the Russian autocracy. His psychological instability grew worse under pressure.

Nevertheless, Kostomarov survived. He spent his year in prison fruitfully and busied himself with the study of language and literature. He remained obsequious to the authorities and suffered further attacks of hypochondria brought on by self-imposed mental stress, but he continued to recover. By the time of his release from prison, he had won a measure of respect and sympathy from his unsuspecting warders, and succeeded in getting himself exiled to one of the most pleasant retreats in European Russia.

Kostomarov took full advantage of the unexpected opportunities of exile in Saratov. He cultivated the friendship of the local intelligentsia, continued his scholarly work with the help of learned correspondents, and made his way onto the right side of the local authorities under whose supervision he had been placed.

The fruits of his efforts were not long in coming. Within a short period of time, Kostomarov had completed his masterpiece on the life and times of Bohdan Khmelnytsky, made contacts which were later to stand him in good stead, and received permission to visit the Crimea and St Petersburg.

Underneath this veneer of accommodation, however, Kostomarov had not forgotten the dreams of his youth. The value he placed on freedom continued undiminished. Many years later, Mordovets recalled how he and the historian 'had played the roles of Cossacks in captivity' during their years in Saratov.[51] Kostomarov's drama on Cremutius Aulus Cordus showed that he still abhorred the unlimited authority of the tsar, and his work on Bohdan Khmelnytsky revealed that he had not abandoned his interest in and devotion to Ukraine. Those were themes that he would enlarge upon in an even more vibrant fashion once he was granted full freedom to do so.

5

Liberty

In the spring of 1857, Kostomarov was finally able to realize a dream of long standing and set off on a tour of Western Europe. First, however, he visited Moscow and St Petersburg, where he had his eyes examined for a visual problem that had been troubling him. He was told that he had a bad case of cataracts and faced blindness if he did not take certain measures. The two physicians he saw further advised him to bathe in the sea and visit the baths while in Western Europe. Before leaving, he found time to visit various friends in the capital, including his old colleague Bilozersky and the legal historian K.D. Kavelin, whom he had first met in Saratov a year or two previously. Kavelin, a professor of law at the University of St Petersburg, had drawn up a memorandum on the emancipation of the Russian peasantry from serfdom, a subject about which everyone was talking, and was at the height of his fame. There is no doubt that the two men discussed the issue before Kostomarov set off for Western Europe.[1]

The historian began his tour with a short visit to Finland and then Sweden. In Stockholm, the Russian consul, Prince Dashkov, helped him gain entry to the state archives, where he searched for material on Russian and Ukrainian history. But the brevity of his visit and his inability to read Swedish severely limited him, and he was able to discover only a few interesting Latin, French, and German documents about the Time of Troubles in old Moscovy and the era of the great Northern War (1700–21), during which the Ukrainian hetman Mazepa, in alliance with the Swedes, revolted against the exacting rule of Peter the Great. Kostomarov was impressed by the free access he was given to Swedish state documents, but he later recalled that the Lutheran Swedes were not entirely open in religious matters and actively dis-

criminated against Catholics, whom they did not allow to build churches or testify in court.

From Sweden, Kostomarov sailed to Germany, where he visited
Lübeck, Hamburg, and Kiel and took a boat up the Rhine. He was
impressed by the old castles and other antiquities along the banks of
that great European river but did not think the general view superior
to the one along the Volga or the Dnieper. From Germany, he went to
France, where he spent some time bathing in the sea at Dieppe. Then
he travelled to Switzerland and northern Italy; in Venice, the mosaics
in the Basilica of Saint Mark reminded him of the mosaics in Kiev's
Saint Sophia. From Italy, he went to Ljubljana in Slovenia (then under
Habsburg rule). There, when he inquired about Slavic books from a
German bookseller, he was informed scornfully that the Slavic languages were in decline and that such Slavic 'stupidities' were a thing
of the past. Nevertheless, Kostomarov was able to see the German's
stock of Slavic books and even purchased a few of them. He noticed
that the common people of that eastern Alpine region still spoke a
Slavic tongue, which he found strange yet not entirely foreign to him.

From Slovenia, Kostomarov went on to the capital of the Habsburg
monarchy, Vienna, which impressed him deeply. He visited some spas
in the area and was delighted by the city's cleanliness and fresh air.
Then on to Prague, which at that time still had a predominantly German flavour. In Prague, he sought out the venerable patriarch of the
Czech national awakening, Václav Hanka, who, upon discovering that
the man standing before him was the Ukrainian translator and publisher
of his Královédvorský manuscript, gave him a guided tour of the
ancient Slavic capital. Hanka also provided Kostomarov with copies of
all his major publications. Only the same German disdain for the Slavic
tongues that Kostomarov had found in Ljubljana clouded his pleasant
stay in Prague.

From the capital of Bohemia, Kostomarov travelled to Dresden, Berlin,
and the port of Stettin (Szczecin), where he boarded ship for the return
to St Petersburg. After a week in St Petersburg, he returned to Saratov
via Moscow. He had spent several months touring Western Europe,
where he had seen much that made an indelible impression on him. Not
least was the low esteem in which the Slavic peoples were held by the
ruling Germans of Central Europe.[2]

Kostomarov was in good spirits upon his return to Saratov, where he
greeted his beloved mother warmly. From her, he learned that the
newly liberated Shevchenko had stopped to visit her on his way back

from exile in Central Asia. She had greeted the poet with tears, and when they had recalled their last meeting, in May 1847, they both had 'wept like children.' Shevchenko had left her the poem he had dedicated to Kostomarov in St Petersburg some ten years earlier, and then departed for Nizhny Novgorod, where he awaited permission to return to the capital.[3]

His spirits refreshed by the good news about Shevchenko and by his own leisurely voyage through Western Europe, Kostomarov returned to his work on Russian history with a passion. He buried himself in the study of the social history of old Russia, began to write a history of the home life and morals of the Great Russian people, and, despite the official ruling prohibiting him from teaching, established contact with the nearby University of Kazan with a view to eventual appointment to the faculty. His detailed proposal for the establishment of a new position in the field of old Russian social history was favourably received, as was his impressive literary and scholarly publishing record. The university council voted fifteen to two in favour of Kostomarov's election to the Kazan faculty, and the minister of education, E.P. Kovalevsky, was sympathetic and willing to do his part towards a revision of Kostomarov's legal encumberments. Kovalevsky requested that Kostomarov's former custodian, Ignatiev, provide him with a favourable report on the historian's conduct in Saratov, which would enable the minister to approach the tsar confidently for a revocation of the teaching ban. Ignatiev did so, but the matter eventually went to the tsar's police agency, the Third Department, which secretly vetoed any change in Kostomarov's status, and his application was left hanging for some time.[4]

In April 1858, Kostomarov began writing a study of the revolt of Stenka Razin. He had been gathering material for the project for many years and even at this late date continued to collect relevant folklore in the Saratov area, where much of the action had taken place. In May, he made an ethnographic expedition to the southern region of the province and visited the many Russian and German sectarian settlements concentrated in that part of the Russian steppe. He thought the German colonies most peculiar, little models of Germany set down in the heart of Russia. Among the Russian sectarians, he spent most time with the Molokans, a branch of the Old Believers; among the Germans, he was most struck by the communistic Herrnhutters, a radical Protestant group. In the middle Volga town of Tsaritsyn, he found an old Russian man who had lived through the rebellion of Emelian Pugachev and was able to give an eyewitness account of the revolt in the town. The old man also provided the historian with vivid legends about the time of Stenka Razin. However, when his rustic source also claimed to have participated personally in Razin's revolt, which had occurred some two hundred years before, Kostomarov had second thoughts about his veracity. Nevertheless, he included some of the Razin legends in his book, the first draft of which he quickly finished upon his return to Saratov.

Kostomarov's *The Revolt of Stenka Razin* was much shorter and simpler than his book on Bohdan Khmelnytsky. It was just as lively, however, with plenty of dialogue and vivid descriptions of both the bloody course of the revolt and the cruel repressions which followed it. Its use of folk-song, in fact, is even more marked and extensive than that of his work on Ukrainian history. Kostomarov was explicit about the causes of the revolt and discussed in detail the expansion of central rule and the imposition of serfdom from the time of Tsar Boris Godunov. He saw Razin's revolt as a throwback to the earlier *veche* period of Russian history, when personal liberty was still ascendent, but also as a mere flash in the night, a passing meteor which promised much but yielded nothing. Razin himself was strong and brave, but inconstant, terrible, and bloodthirsty, a man without a heart. 'He hated everything that stood above him,' wrote the historian, 'the law, society, the church; that is, everything connected with the awakening of humanity. His fearless will trampled on everything. Compassion did not exist for him. Honour and magnanimity were unknown to him.' Kostomarov ended by quoting one of his rural informants to the effect that Razin was the scourge of God and will come again. He will come before the Judgment Day, and 'may the good Christian man not live to see that day when Stenka will come again.'[5]

In the summer of 1858, having finished his work on Stenka Razin, Kostomarov temporarily moved to St Petersburg, where for a while he shared quarters with N.V. Kalachev, a fellow historian with whom he discussed various questions of ancient Russian history. He began work on a novel entitled *The Son (Syn)*, about a landowner's son who goes over to the rebels during the revolt of Stenka Razin. (The historian had conceived the idea for the novel in listening to the stories of the people during his tour of the Province of Saratov.) Shortly afterwards, Kostomarov published this novel in a journal edited by Nikolai Kalachev.[6]

At about the same time, Kostomarov heard that Shevchenko had moved to St Petersburg and was living at the Academy of Arts, where, as an artist of the Academy, he was given the use of a studio. Early one morning after his usual dip in the Neva River, the historian went to see him. 'Good health to you, Taras!' Kostomarov exclaimed as he entered the studio. Shevchenko took two steps back and looked over his unexpected visitor in wonder as he said, 'May I ask whom I have the honour of meeting?' 'Do you not recognize me?' Kostomarov asked incredulously. 'No,' was the response. 'It cannot be,' Kostomarov stubbornly continued, 'look closely, listen to my voice. Remember the past ... Kiev, Petersburg, the place of chains!' Shevchenko began to examine the historian from all sides, and finally, shrugging his shoulders, said: 'No. Excuse me. I cannot recognize you.'

For some time longer, the historian tried to get Shevchenko to recognize him, and the poet slowly became less formal and more familiar and begged him to torture him no longer but to tell him who he was. Finally, Kostomarov told him his name. Shevchenko immediately burst into tears and hugged and kissed his long-lost friend. From that day on for the next two weeks, the friends saw each other every day. They met in the evenings in the Staropalinsky Inn, where Kostomarov went after finishing his daily work in the Public Library.[7]

At the end of August 1858, Prince Vladimir Shcherbatov, marshal of the nobility of the Province of Saratov, invited Kostomarov to participate in a committee to prepare for the emancipation of the serfs of the Saratov area. It was not the first time the historian's advice had been sought on the subject. During Kostomarov's European tour, he had been approached by Princess Elena Pavlovna with regard to the affairs of the peasants of the Poltava area, where she held a great estate. Their common friend K.D. Kavelin had put the princess in touch with the historian.[8] Now, Kostomarov was asked to join in the work in Saratov, and he gladly agreed. He spent the next several months back in the Volga town dealing with the serf question at first hand. He found the serf committee clearly divided into pro-noble, moderate liberal, and pro-peasant factions, and the last group the weakest. Kostomarov, certainly, must have had doubts about some aspects of the great emancipation project, most probably about compensation payments by serfs to their former owners, for in one of his letters he quoted the country folk as saying, 'This freedom, Father, is worse than slavery!'[9]

While Kostomarov was thus occupied in Saratov, his friends in the capital city were working to obtain for him a position at St Petersburg University. Indeed, he had good relations with many faculty members there, including Sreznevsky, Kavelin, P.A. Pletnev, and N.M. Blagoveshchensky. Their opportunity came when Kostomarov's old critic from the time of his first dissertation, Professor Ustrialov, retired from his post in Russian history. Kostomarov was quickly chosen to replace him. The historian received the good news in Saratov and quickly forgot his former project of teaching in Kazan. Prior to his departure from Saratov, Arkhimandrite Nikanor held a farewell dinner in Kostomarov's honour at the monastery in which he had spent many long hours in contemplative reading during his exile. Several of his Saratov acquaintances came. 'We spent a beautiful moonlit spring night together,' the delighted historian later recalled.[10]

Having said his farewells in Saratov, Kostomarov set off for St Petersburg via Kolomna and Moscow. He tarried a while at the archives of the Ministry of Foreign Affairs in Moscow before leaving for the capital. Once in St Petersburg, however, he immediately went to see the minister of education, Kovalevsky, who was familiar with his case as a result of his previous application to the University of Kazan. Kovalevsky received the historian warmly and told him that he had already approached the tsar with a view to having the long-standing teaching prohibition lifted. The tsar, however, had told him that he had heard negative reports about Kostomarov's work on Stenka Razin. When Kovalevsky had said that the book was a respectable work of scholarship, the tsar had replied that he would read the work through and decide the matter for himself.[11]

While the tsar took his time over *Stenka Razin* – the first edition of the study had appeared in *Notes of the Fatherland* the year before – Kostomarov settled down to his new life in St Petersburg. He took a room in a hotel close to the Public Library, where he spent most of the time working and preparing for his teaching at the university. The director of the library, Baron Modest Korf, smoothed the historian's way, and he made rapid progress in his work. He spent little time in his living quarters, which, unfortunately for the historian's peace of mind, were rocked by loud Italian opera music from an adjoining tavern. Shevchenko often visited him at his home, and on one occassion he teased him about his sensitivity to the loud music.[12] Other close friends of this period included the bookseller Dmitri Kozhanchikov, to whom he sold the rights for a book version of his work on Stenka Razin, the young Slavist and ethnographer Aleksander Kotliarevsky, who was later appointed professor at the University of Dorpat, and the Pole Wiktor Kalinowski, a true intellectual who buried himself in ancient manuscripts dealing with Lithuanian history but paid little attention to the hot political debates surrounding the contemporary Polish question. Kalinowski's brother was later executed for his participation in the Polish insurrection of 1863.

At about the same time, Kostomarov's friend Mordovets finally succeeded in publishing a Ukrainian literary almanac which the two men had completed a few years earlier but had been unable to get past the censors. Kostomarov had contributed some literary material and the large collection of historical songs he had gathered in Volhynia in 1844. The censor had done his work, however: much of the material was distorted or altogether omitted. 'Unfortunately,' Kostomarov later wrote, 'Matskevich, the censor to whom Mordovets had sent the manuscript, dealt with the songs in a truly barbaric way.'

He threw out everything he did not like without the slightest hesitation, not considering that the songs sometimes lost their meaning because of it. It seems that the affair of my Saratov folk-songs was known to him and served him as a moral example on the strength of which he used his red pencil. He did so most especially in those places where young maidens might be offended by the text. Although they were printed, the songs suffered horribly. I remained extremely dissatisfied with this manner of publishing the folk material I had gathered.[13]

The fact that the volume dealt with Ukrainian literature and ethnography also accounts for the severity of the censor. Two plays dealing with Ukrainian history and serfdom were completely suppressed because the censor objected to what he called their 'local patriotism.'[14]

But Kostomarov never limited himself entirely to Ukrainian history. During his long stay in Saratov, he developed a very real interest in the history of the Volga region and considered writing a general history of the Volga in addition to the work on Stenka Razin. On 28 July 1859, he wrote a letter to Mordovets in which he told him of his idea, but thereafter he became involved in other projects and his 'History of the Volga River' was never written.[15]

Kostomarov remained in close contact with his old Ukrainian friends from Kiev, including Bilozersky and Kulish. By this time, St Petersburg had become a centre of Ukrainian cultural and literary activity. In 1856, Kulish had founded a printing house in the city and had published his *Notes on Southern Rus'*, the novel entitled *The Black Council* (*Chorna Rada*), and new editions of the works of Ivan Kotliarevsky, Kvitka-Osnovianenko, and others. He had also published some smaller booklets meant to be read by the common people. At the same time, moreover, the Russian-born wife of Panas Markovych, who wrote under the masculine name Marko Vovchok, was beginning her literary activity; her *Popular Tales* (*Narodni opovidannia*) were first published in St Petersburg in 1857. Kostomarov eagerly joined this circle, in which he was revered as the leading Ukrainian historian whose recently published *Bohdan Khmelnytsky* had made known the history of Southern Rus' throughout Russia. Members of the Ukrainian circle would later recall Kostomarov's pride in his native land and his respect for the simple Ukrainian country folk, against whom he would brook no slight on the part of the elitist St Petersburg intelligentsia.[16]

Soon after he established himself in St Petersburg, Kostomarov's home became the regular gathering place for a wide circle of friends with intellectual and cultural interests. His evening parties, held regularly on Tuesdays (they had begun on Thursdays) soon became famous. Ukrainian, Russian, and Polish friends attended; in addition to Shevchenko and Bilozersky, radicals such as Chernyshevsky and Dobroliubov and Poles such as E.V. Żelegowski and Zygmunt Sierakowski were among the guests. Many years later, Bilozersky's wife recalled how very stimulating the atmosphere was:

It was interesting in the extreme. One could meet there outstanding representatives of scholarship and literature, some of them called from the farthest corners of Russia for the resolution of the peasant question. And, finally, there were the exiles who had just returned with the beginning of the new reign. The broad general question – the future liberation of the serfs – occupied all of them. Russians, Little Russians, and Poles constituted a single, indivisible society. Everyone dreamed together about the good of the Russian people and all humanity. Political, philosophical, and ethical questions were discussed, as was the idea of moral perfection.[17]

The Ukrainian circle in St Petersburg – the St Petersburg *Hromada*, or society, as it came to be called – quickly revived the idea of publishing a journal devoted to Ukrainian history and literature. This idea, which had been mooted in Kiev more than a decade before, took on a firmer shape after the publication of Kulish's *Notes on Southern Rus'*, and in 1858 Kulish approached the authorities for permission to publish such a non-political magazine under the title *The Cottage* (*Khata*). When the proposal was turned down, the Ukrainians tried again, this time listing the less politically undesirable Bilozersky as the formal publisher and editor. Such cautious duplicity, they were confident, would work. On 28 July 1859, Kostomarov wrote to Mordovets in Saratov: 'Bilozersky has delegated to me the task of inviting you to paricipate in a journal which he will publish next year and which will be devoted to the history, geography, ethnography, economy, literature, and, in short, everything that touches upon man's knowledge of Southern Rus' ... Perhaps you could write something about the Little Russian colonies along the Volga?'[18] By the end of 1860, the St Petersburg circle had received official permission to publish the journal. The chief promoters, Kulish and Kostomarov, were delighted.[19]

By October 1859, the tsar had read *The Revolt of Stenka Razin* and decided to confirm Kostomarov's position as professor of history at the university. The historian learned of the favourable decision from Shevchenko, who had found out from Kavelin. Kostomarov immediately went to see the minister of education, Kovalevsky, who welcomed him warmly and informed him that the tsar had said: 'There is nothing wrong with *Stenka Razin*. You can confirm Kostomarov as a professor. Only do not allow him to teach in Kiev.' The support of Tsar Alexander's close advisers the Miliutin brothers, who at that time were playing an influential role in the enactment of the Great Reforms, seems to have had some effect on the tsar's final decision.[20]

About a month later, Kostomarov delivered his inaugural lecture in old Russian history in the revered halls of St Petersburg University. His reputation preceded him. 'To speak the truth,' P.N. Polevoi, one of his St Petersburg students, later wrote, 'rumours about his punitive exile, about his suffering and the persecution he had undergone for his political offences, and also the romantic circumstances in which he had been arrested ... created a halo around the person of this new professor, about whom we did not know much.' Polevoi continued, 'Long before his appearance at the university, we loved and respected him and associated him with that group of professors of the liberal camp which at that time reigned supreme at the university.'[21] Indeed, so popular was Kostomarov expected to be that Kavelin felt compelled to warn the students against too enthusiastic a reception during the inaugural lecture; he told them that their adulation could seriously hurt Kostomarov in the eyes of the authorities.[22]

But reputation alone could not create a popular professor. Once again, Kostomarov worked his magic as he read his lecture. He would not deal primarily with the state but rather with 'the people' and with 'the development of the national spirit'; with the early *udel* period, when he believed liberty and local control were prominent, and with the later period of *edinoderzhavie*, or central rule, when statehood gained ascendency. Kostomarov spoke of the primary role of the common people in history, of local history and ethnography, and of the value of 'internal' history over 'externals': 'We will not wear ourselves out studying a tiresome row of princely personalities and wars with foreigners, but will select from them only that which shows us the degree of popular participation in them, the popular view of them, and their influence on the life of the nation.' He continued: 'We will not even tarry with any example of the noisy affairs of state more than for the sake of what is necessary for understanding its relationship to the national way of life and popular education ... No law, no institution will be important in and of itself, but only in its application to the national way of life. We will not deal with any literary monument if we do not see in it an expression of national thought or those powers which call forth this thought. In such a case, folk-songs become enormously more important ...'[23]

In spite of Kavelin's warning, the response was overwhelming. 'There was no end to the applause,' the delighted historian later recalled. 'The students praised me and lifted me up on their hands. It was as if I was a child. I had not expected such a reception.' That evening he went to the opera with a friend to hear *William Tell*, and the next morning the feeling of satisfaction had still not departed. 'When I was under police supervision at Saratov,' he asked himself, 'did I ever expect such a victory as I have experienced today?'[24]

Kostomarov thereafter lectured regularly at the university, and his brilliant style continued to enrapture the student body. On the one hand, he liberally spiced his lectures with citations of and long quotations from chronicles and old documents, and he spoke freely, ignoring the restrictions of contemporary censorship. On the other hand, he avoided the liberal phraseology then in fashion and limited himself to daring hypotheses about the past.[25] The hypotheses concerned such subjects as the ancient Ilmen Slavs, who, Kostomarov thought, breathed an ancient Slavic spirit of liberty; the 'South Russians' or Ukrainians, who, he thought, had preserved this spirit of freedom; and the Varangians, who he believed were not of Scandinavian but of Baltic or Lithuanian origin. His artistry as a lecturer was clearly described by one member of his audience:

He lectured remarkably well in spite of standing perfectly still, speaking quietly and with a slightly unclear, lisping expression that betrayed a strongly Little Russian manner of speech. Whether he was depicting the Novgorod popular assembly, or *veche*, or the turmoil of the battle of Lipets, he would stand with eyes closed. And after a few seconds, as if he himself had been transported into the centre of the events he was depicting, you would see and hear everything that Kostomarov was talking about while he was standing there motionless at the podium. His gaze would be fixed not on the audience but somewhere in the distance as if he were actually seeing that very moment in the distant past. The lecturer would seem to be someone from a different world, someone who had come from another world in order to tell us about the past in specific terms, in order to tell us something that was mysterious for others but well known to him.[26]

If Kostomarov's style and delivery were original and stimulating, so were the contents and message of his lectures. Unlike most of his predecessors and contemporaries, who were enamoured of the central institutions of the Muscovite and Russian state including the autocracy and its centralized administrative system, Kostomarov, who was not from the Great Russian heartland and had no affection for autocracy, was primarily interested in the various peoples who were ruled by that state. Many years later, when summarizing the content of his university lectures, he wrote that in general he saw in 'states' more the product of accidental conquests than the natural result of geographical and ethnographical peculiarities. The strong conquered the weak and tried to assimilate them; the weak resisted and strove to preserve their national characteristics. Where one people was not obviously stronger than its neighbours, free societies were formed, and those free societies strove to join together in federations. That was the case in ancient Greece, medieval Western Europe, and the Slavic lands which elected their own princes. The Russian state, he thought, was composed of parts which had previously lived an independent life and which continued to try to preserve that life even within the Russian state structure. 'The goal of my preoccupation with history.' he concluded, 'was to find and catch these peculiarities of the national life of the parts of the Russian state.'[27]

A good example of Kostomarov's preoccupation with regional ethnography and the life of the people is the attention he paid to the non-Slavic 'natives' (*inorodtsi*) who had been absorbed into the Russian state. Those peoples had been ignored completely by Russian political-administrative historians even though they made up a significant portion of the population. Kostomarov lectured on the non-Russian natives, beginning with the Lithuanians; he related their ancient history, described their social life, and ended with a discussion of their folk-songs. His treatment of the Lithuanians was complete enough to be printed later in one of the scholarly journals.[28]

During the same period, Kostomarov took an active interest in the publishing industry. He was especially interested in the journal entitled *The Russian Word* (*Russkoe slovo*), in which he published his inaugural lecture and his piece on the Lithuanians. The journal was owned by Count Kushelev-Bezborodko, who had published some of the historian's other works. But *The Russian Word* was foundering since the count spent most of his time in Paris and left management of the periodical in the hands of an all-powerful but not very capable assistant, whom Kostomarov jokingly referred to as 'the Grand Vizier of the eastern Calif.' The historian contributed a significant amount of material to the journal, however, and even tried to recruit his friend Mordovets as a permanent collaborator before moving on to other projects.[29]

In addition to lecturing at the university and writing for various scholarly journals, Kostomarov continued to lead an active social life and to increase his contacts in the capital. During the last month of 1859, for example, Shevchenko introduced him to his close friend and patron Count Fedor Tolstoi. This elderly gentleman was a sculptor and graphic artist and the vice-president of the St Petersburg Academy of Arts. Together with his friends and colleagues, he had personally intervened with the authorities to obtain Shevchenko's freedom. At Tolstoi's home, Kostomarov mixed with circles of artists and literati with whom he would certainly not otherwise have come into contact. He also met and was befriended by Count Dmitri Bludov, the president of the State Council. This well-educated aristocrat was fully devoted to the reform process then taking place in Russia and frequently invited Kostomarov to dine with him at home. His hospitality gave the historian an opportunity to meet state officials and learned men of a different sort. Moreover, Kostomarov found the count's daughter, Antonia, who was an exciting conversationalist, especially attractive.

But in spite of these pleasant contacts with the elite of Russian society, the unflagging historian never abandoned the cause of the common people to which he had devoted so much of his professional and personal life. The 'South Russians' or Ukrainians, of course lay closest to his heart, and he rose to their defence whenever he thought their past was being distorted or their good name besmirched. Thus, when the conservative political-administrative historian Sergei Soloviev, a kind of semi-official court historiographer, criticized the Ukrainian

Cossacks as an unproductive, anarchical force which had set back the development of the organized state and its civilization, Kostomarov replied with a spirited rejoinder supporting the Cossacks as representatives of popular liberty and defenders of the South Russian people against Polish oppression and Turko-Tatar raids; not only did they represent the South Russian people, they *were* the South Russian people. 'In contradiction of the honourable professor,' he concluded, 'let us be permitted to say' that

if the consciousness of these people [the Ukrainian Cossacks] was weak for the purpose of the creation of a new society, then all the same it stood higher than that system which existed under the leadership of the Polish aristocracy. If there were no constructive elements among the Cossacks, they still stood higher than those who wished to destroy that which already existed. They wanted to preserve their ancestral faith, which had been deluged with Jesuit trickery, the arbitrariness of [King] Sigismund, and the anarchy of the lords. They wanted to free themselves from the jurisdiction of the lords and their frightful laws. These lords could judge their underlings and punish them with death, and to some extent they passed on this function to their officials and to Jewish leaseholders. Therefore, the demands of the people were expressed in the popular uprisings which have been called the Cossack revolts ... Mr Soloviev considers the Cossacks to have been thieves and parasites, but are not those landowners who spent their days in drunkenness, in luxury, and as absentee landlords, from which the simple people suffered most grievously, are not those people more deserving of such names? After all, it was such behaviour which drove tolerance from the common people, was it not? One Englishman who visited Poland in the seventeenth century was surprised not so much at the thievery and evil deeds of the [South] Russian people as at its patience, which seemed strange to him. The true atmosphere of that society was quite apparent to the outsider, but Mr Soloviev wants to place the lords above those who wanted to organize themselves into Cossack detachments.[30]

A centralist historian and admirer of the Russian state, Soloviev had initiated the debate, but he did not carry it on. Instead, it was the partisans of the old Polish-Lithuanian Commonwealth, the men from whom, in fact, Soloviev had gotten his ideas, who replied to Kostomarov. The Polish publicist Zenon Fisz, who wrote under the pseudonym Tadeusz Padalica, led the attack. Padalica accused Kostomarov of being prejudiced against the Poles and predisposed to the Cossacks, of misunderstanding the facts, and of distorting the religious history of the Commonwealth. Padalica maintained that the Poles had tried to civilize and 'ennoble' the Cossacks and integrate them into the Commonwealth, and that the famous Union of Hadiach (1659) was a good example of that policy. But Kostomarov immediately rejected such 'presumptuous' claims and defended the various leaders of the Cossack revolts as popular heroes whose terrible actions were nevertheless justified by circumstances. The anarchy and oppression of the Polish landlord system, he believed, had been the ultimate cause of all the troubles. Moreover, only a few Cossack leaders had accepted the Union of Hadiach, and the masses of the common people instinctively had known that the alliance with the aristocratic Commonwealth would eventually return them to slavery. Thus, the Union had had no chance of success, and the Polish civilizing mission had been a fraud.[31]

In further articles, Padalica argued that oppression in the old Commonwealth was sporadic, and Kostomarov argued that it was pervasive. Kostomarov further quoted the old Polish chronicles on the extent of the oppression under the Commonwealth, arguing that the Polish nobles had even handed the keys of the Orthodox churches over to Jewish leaseholders, whom the poor Orthodox population consequently had had to pay to be allowed the use of their churches.[32] Padalica and Kostomarov were obviously divided by very different interpretations of the role of the old Commonwealth in the history of Eastern Europe.

That did not mean, of course, that Kostomarov had no admiration for Polish culture. He had studied the Polish language and read Polish literature for many years, and his love for the poetry of Adam Mickiewicz was well known. In St Petersburg, he befriended many Poles, who thereafter frequented the discussion circles in which Kostomarov moved. In addition to the 'Slavic' poet Żelegowski and the oppositional activist Sierakowski, many prominent Poles such as the literary historian W.D. Spasowicz were counted among his friends and acquaintances. Nevertheless, Kostomarov's love for Polish culture was circumscribed by his firm disagreement with the widely held theory that the Poles had 'civilized' Southern Rus', and his words favouring Poland were muted by contemporary Polish efforts to resurrect the Polish-Lithuanian Commonwealth 'within the borders of 1772,' a plan which would have brought more than half the Ukrainian ethnolinguistic territories under Polish rule. Kostomarov was exasperated by Polish political propaganda in Western Europe, which preached liberty and national freedom for Poland and at the same time denied the right to independent existence to Southern Rus'. On 22 January 1860, he wrote to his liberal friend Kavelin, who was inclined to sympathize with Polish political grievances, and warned him against the Polish national movement. 'The Poles can deceive the European public with their proclamations about liberty and nationality,' he explained, 'but they will find it difficult to fool us South Russians ... It might be all the same to you Muscovites if Poland were liberated and set up the boundaries of its state on the Dnieper ... but that does not appeal to us. We do not want to be enslaved for the sake of certain European ideas. We especially do not want that kind of rule from which we once liberated ourselves with such losses.'[33]

It was not only in private letters to Kavelin that Kostomarov expressed such thoughts. In January 1859, Alexander Herzen, the most famous of Russian political émigrés, had tackled the difficult question of Polish indpendence and the eastern borders of a resurrected Polish state in a major article in his London-based free Russian newspaper *The Bell* (*Kolokol*). In that article, Herzen promoted the idea of a Panslavic federal state encompassing both Poland and Russia, but he admitted Poland's right to complete independence if that was truly what the Polish people desired. He went on to extend the same principle to the Polish-Russian borderlands and to Ukraine in particular, which he offered to recognize as a separate and independent state if that was how its population saw the matter.[34] Herzen's illegal paper was widely circulated in Russia, and Kostomarov, it seems, was immediately struck by the concordance of Herzen's views with his own. He sat down, penned a reply, and sent it off to London.

Exactly one year later, on 15 January 1860, Herzen published this reply in *The Bell*. Though Kostomarov's piece took the form of an anonymous letter to the editor, the identity of its author was clear from the content and style. Its main argument also was clear, and it seems Herzen himself added the title 'Ukraine' when he published it.[35]

In his public 'Letter to Herzen,' Kostomarov summarized his views on the existence of a separate Ukrainian people and the history of Ukraine from ancient times to the present, and briefly outlined the political desiderata of the Ukrainian intelligentsia.

Kostomarov began by offering his sincere thanks to Herzen for his article, which admitted the possibility of Ukrainian indpendence and the desirability of a democratic Slavic federation. He saw that most Great Russians did not consider 'Little Russians' a separate people and that the Polish nobility similarly claimed the Ukrainian land for their own.

Both those views, however, were mistaken. Although the nobility of eastern Ukraine was largely Russified and the nobility of western Ukraine predominantly Polish, the Little Russian nationality still existed in the common people. Therefore, the disputed land belonged neither to Russian nor to Pole but, in Kostomarov's words, 'to that people which has been settled there from ancient times, which now lives there, and which works the land.'

Kostomarov then recounted the history of 'Ukraine or Southern Rus'.' He mentioned what he believed were the federal inclinations of ancient times and the freedom-loving character of the Ukrainian people, which contrasted with the aristocracy of the Poles and the formal religiosity of the Great Russians. During the revolt led by Bohdan Khmelnytsky (1648), the Ukrainian people had shown its desire for freedom; in rejecting the subsequent Union of Hadiach (1659), it had clearly scorned the aristocracy of the Poles. However, Ukraine had passed under Russia, and the Russian empress Catherine II had quickly reintroduced serfdom. 'Ukraine fell silent,' its citizens were despised, and its language mocked. But with the awakening of the Slavic peoples Ukraine too awoke. Moreover, unlike in Moscow, where the expression of Panslavism had become simply a ritual in praise of old Muscovy, in Ukraine the idea had taken hold as expressing commitment to a Slavic federation in which each member would preserve its individual freedom. Kostomarov then mentioned Shevchenko and himself by name, described the destruction of the 'Ukraino-Slavic Society,' and outlined the punishment meted out to Shevchenko and himself. Afterwards, he continued, the authorities had persecuted Little Russia: they forbade the publication of Little Russian books and stifled Little Russian material appearing in the Great Russian language; even the mention of the names 'Ukraine,' 'Little Russia,' and 'the Hetmanate' was enough to provoke persecution. But with the reforms of Alexander II, Little Russia had awoken once again. Some fine Ukrainian-language books had appeared, and hopes were raised for the liberation of the common people from serfdom.

But what, according to Kostomarov's anonymous letter to Herzen, did the Ukrainian people want for the future? First, it wanted full civil rights for all, with no special privileges for the nobility. Second, it wanted the government to permit and even to support the establishment of Ukrainian-language schools. Kostomarov concluded:

Aside from that we do not desire or demand anything for ourselves that is different from the general demands of all Russia. None of us thinks of tearing up the bonds between Southern Rus' and the rest of Russia. On the contrary, we would like all the other Slavs to unite with us into a single union, even under the sceptre of the Russian tsar, if that tsar transforms himself into the ruler of free peoples rather than the voracious lord of a Tatar-German Muscovy. In the future Slavic union ... our Southern Rus' must be consolidated into a separate civic polity. It must comprise all the lands where the people speak the Southern Russian language. It should preserve its unity not through a pernicious deadly centralization, but rather through a recognition of equality of rights and personal advantage ... Let neither the Great Russians nor the Poles claim as their own the lands which are populated by our people.[36]

Such was the political program of Mykola Kostomarov in 1860.

Its closeness to the political program of the Cyril-Methodian Brotherhood of 1847 is immediately apparent. However, in his writings legally published in the Russian Empire during the period after his release from exile, Kostomarov had always to take into consideration the attitudes of the Russian authorities and the power of the censors. Accordingly, he only indirectly touched upon politics and seldom used the politically provocative name 'Ukraine.' He restricted himself to history and to ethnography and talked about 'Southern Rus'' and the 'Southern Russians.' Nevertheless, in almost all his writings during the period he remained at odds with the conservative state traditions of Russian historiography and, whenever he found them, did not hesitate to debunk old Muscovite myths and official Petrine legends. His views on the origins of the Russian state and the lineage of the ancient Rus' princes were outstanding cases in point.

In January 1860, Kostomarov published his thoughts on the origins of the Varangian Rus' princes in the progressive journal *The Contemporary*. In his article, entitled 'On the Beginnings of Rus',' he argued that the officially sponsored theory – first elaborated by G.S. Bayer (1694–1738), a German historian working in the Russian service – that the Varangians were descended from Scandinavian Vikings, and the nativist theory – first proposed by M.V. Lomonosov (1711–62), a Russian natural philosopher – that the original Rus' princes were actually Slavs, were both false conceptions originating in misguided patriotism. If Lomonosov was too much the impassioned Slavist, then those who wished to trace Prince Riurik to Scandinavia were also impassioned patriots. The so-called Norman theory, wrote Kostomarov, 'was an invention of German scholars.' He continued: 'It is well known that our Germans from the smallest to the biggest, both scholars and non-scholars are more or less inflated with their belief in the excellence of their race as compared to the Slavic ... German scholars ... wanted to show that the Slavs were incapable of building a state and civic life without the influence of the German element.' Kostomarov followed that point with the assertion, that neither the noble Teutons nor the glorious Slavs were the forefathers of the ancient Rus' princes, and that those princes traced their origins to the swamps and forests of early Lithuania. In his opinion, the ancient Lithuanians, or 'Zhmuds,' were the original Rus', and there was no historical basis for speculating about an influx of Varangian Normans.[37]

In the same issue of *The Contemporary*, moreover, in a separate section entitled 'The Whistle,' the famous literary critic Nikolai Dobroliubov published a caustic review of the pro-Normanist work of the distinguished Moscow historian Mikhail Pogodin, who had spent most of his scholarly career studying ancient Russian history. Dobroliubov attacked Pogodin, who was closely associated with the conservative cultural policies of the regime of Nicholas I, for merely repeating old stories. He said that Pogodin had dealt respectfully with other historians such as Mykhailo Maksymovych who rejected the Norman theory, because they at least defended the Slavic origins of the Varangians and thus held a patriotic enough position. 'But suddenly,' Dobroliubov concluded, 'an attack has come from a complete different side: Kostomarov traces Rus' from the Zhmuds ... What is there to be done about this?'[38]

Pogodin was furious when he read the pieces by Kostomarov and Dobroliubov. It seemed to him that the editors of *The Contemporary* were out to get him and that the two articles had been coordinated. He read and reread Kostomarov's essay and composed a reply. Then he read and reread his reply and decided to take it to Kostomarov in person and demand personal satisfaction by challenging him to an academic duel, a public debate. Pogodin took the train to St Petersburg and confronted Kostomarov in the Public Library with a letter criticizing his Zhmud theory and challenging him to debate: 'I throw down the glove and challenge you to a duel ... I have no need of seconds, for the shades of Bayer, Schlotzer, and Krug stand before me ... While you, for your amusement, can invite as a second your beloved kings of The Whistle!'[39]

Kostomarov accepted the challenge without hesitation. Arrangements for the debate were taken in hand immediately, and Kovalevsky, the minister of education, instructed that the matter was of such grave import that it should be held in the Great Hall of St Petersburg University. Kostomarov suggested that Kalachev, F.I. Buslaev, and Kavelin act as judges. Pogodin preferred to leave judgment to the public. He replied: 'This is a matter of internal, personal conviction which we would be better off leaving to the audience. Our main goal is to awaken in youth an interest in the question of the origins of Rus'. This is very important in our time since the millennium of the foundation of our state by the Rus' will shortly take place.' The debate was set for 19 March, and Pogodin's letter and a reply by Kostomarov were published in the press.

Soon, all St Petersburg was talking about the event. Tickets for the 'duel,' which were sold with the proceeds going to poor students, became prized commodities, and the distinguished literary figure Prince Viazemsky soon found that they could not be bought at any price.

On the evening of 19 March, the Great Hall, which held fifteen hundred people, was filled to overflowing. All seats were taken, and the aisles were crammed. At eight o'clock, Pogodin and Kostomarov entered the room and with great difficulty made their way to the front. Pletnev, the university rector, introduced the protagonists, and a hush fell over the crowd. Pogodin spoke first and set forth his position. He seemed, however, rather irritated. Kostomarov responded by calmly setting forth his position. He occasionally spiced his comments with some humour, and for the next two hours the two historians engaged in a lively debate. The atmosphere was tense and the hall hot and stuffy, and towards the end Kostomarov fainted from exhaustion. He was soon revived, however, and at the conclusion the two men were carried from the hall on the shoulders of an enthusiastic throng of students.

There was never any doubt, however, which side the young people favoured. Pogodin represented the conservative establishment; Kostomarov, innovative youth. The audience supported the latter with frequent and enthusiastic applause. Pogodin, 'the old man' as he was called, was treated with respect, but Kostomarov had captured the hearts of the throngs of young people who had filled the hall.[40]

More serious observers of course were more circumspect. Several newspapers and journals criticized the form the debate had taken, and one even concluded that Russia was not yet mature enough to hold public debates on such questions. Prince Viazemsky concluded: 'Previously we did not know where we were heading to. Now we do not know where we are coming from.'[41]

Kostomarov, however, clearly felt himself the victor, while Pogodin could only complain about the behaviour of the students. In a long letter to Pogodin, Kostomarov replied to the latter's grievances and claimed a clear victory. 'If the students were more inclined to share my opinion than yours,' he wrote, 'that was not because I was their professor but rather, as they say, because my theory seemed more believable than the Norman theory.'

In so far as our personalities go, there can be no talk of victory or defeat. But there must be a discussion of whether one or the other learned opinion has prevailed – otherwise why did we debate each other in public? My opinion has clearly won over yours. I speak now with full and inexpressible satisfaction. I did not hear about this from the students. On the day after the 'battle,' while I was at a concert I received victory greetings over you from both acquaintances and strangers. The general opinion is that if I could not fully confirm my own theory, then all the same it is more credible than the Norman theory and that the proofs with which you went into battle were insufficient ... that progress is on my side and stagnation is on yours.[42]

Others too felt that Kostomarov had triumphed over Pogodin. Even many of Pogodin's close friends, Moscow Slavophiles such as A.S. Khomiakov, felt that he had not properly upheld the honour of his native city. Pogodin tried to satisfy such concerns by criticizing Kostomarov's views again, in an article published in the conservative Moscow Slavophile organ *Russian Conversation* (*Russkaia beseda*); Kostomarov replied only with 'A Final Word to Mr Pogodin,' which he published in *The Contemporary*. A few satirical words by Dobroliubov, which Kostomarov thoroughly enjoyed, brought the exchange to a swift conclusion.[43]

During the following months, however, it became clear that although Kostomarov may have won the principal battle, he had not won the war. A number of scholars and journalists fiercely criticized his Zhmud theory, and they tended to treat him more as a sensational publicist than a serious researcher. His enemies closed in on all sides, and attacks on him appeared in the *St Petersburg News* (*Sankt Peterburgskie Vedomosti*), *Notes of the Fatherland*, and elsewhere. To Kostomarov, Russian subjects of German origin seemed especially active in the criticism, and on 6 July 1860 he passed on to his friend Mordovets a report that as far away as Berlin the Russian public was being accused of ignorance for accepting his theories.[44]

Whether from German or from Slavic sources, many of the criticisms directed at Kostomarov's Zhmud theory were sound. The theory was never to attract a wide following. But the criticism that Kostomarov was not a serious scholar was clearly wide of the mark. It was true that his style was romantic, his hypotheses daring, and his presentation masterful, but that did not mean his content was contrived. He invariably displayed a thorough mastery of the sources, and in scholarly fashion he did primary research in the archives and published his findings. That was, as Mordovets later put it, where he felt himself 'a real warhorse.'[45]

Kostomarov's professional colleagues were well aware of his enthusiasm, his great love, for archival research. His talent in that area was implicitly acknowledged by an appointment in April 1860 to the Archeographic Commission. (He was simultaneously elected a member of the Russian Geographical Society.) During the following months, he made two trips to Novgorod and, in the company of Count Tolstoi, one trip to Pskov to see the architecture and gather material for a course of lectures on those medieval Russian cities, which were unique in their commercial and freedom-loving traditions. By summertime, he was in Moscow and at the Saint Sergius Monastery complex, near the old capital, where he continued his search for ancient manuscripts. At this time, he made the acquaintance of the famous paleographer R.V. Gorsky and discovered a thirteenth-century manuscript of the 'Life of the Blessed Nifont,' a kind of medieval psychological novel portraying the struggle of good and evil. Kostomarov copied some passages and later had them published in Count Kushelev-Bezborodko's *The Russian Word*.[46] In Moscow, he spent some time at the Synodal Library and in the archives of the Ministry of Foreign Affairs, where he gathered new material on the history of Ukraine after Khmelnytsky.

Kostomarov was able to discover great masses of new material in spite of the unhelpful attitude of certain archivists, who preferred to bestow their favour on historians who were on better terms with the regime. His intellectual adversary, Sergei Soloviev, was the most famous of those historians. 'Lord, when will all this be published!' Kostomarov complained to his friend Mordovets. 'Only Soloviev is able to work well. They give things to him to take home to work on, while they allow me to work only three hours a day and, on top of that, in the midst of terrible noise.'[47]

The conflicts with archivists and other government officials as well as the time spent away from friends and supporters in St Petersburg seem to have taken a heavy toll on the historian. His psychological state was as delicate as ever. In Moscow, he suddenly fell into a deep depression, and on 17 August 1860 he wrote to Mordovets, who had tried to console him:

You write to me that we are all unfortunate. Understandably so, and no political or social speculations can correct that because we are created so that our lives are unhappy, others less so. But our physical attributes include within themselves the conditions of unhappiness. And what concerns the unhappiness that flows from our moral illnesses, that too is in our nature. The fault here is the incompleteness of our knowledge and the inconsistency of our abilities. Is it possible that you still believe in some kind of utopia? Is it possible that you imagine that human society will transform itself into some kind of happy community? ... That is all a dream. Man essentially suffers, just as he has suffered and will suffer. Freedom is pure nonsense. If you destroy the monarchy, the aristocracy, and the police, weaker spirits and bodies will always become slaves of stronger ones. I confess to you that I long ago lost faith in any sort of progress, and now I have lost faith in love itself ... Speaking of myself personally, I am very unhappy. I feel that I am growing old and there is nothing to replace youth. Life is boring, and I see emptiness in the future.[48]

What startling words from a prominent intellectual at the height of his career! What a shocking confession from the impassioned patriot who had so recently written to Herzen about the nobility of the ideals of an independent Ukraine and a free Slavic federation!

Such fits of depression did not last long, however, and the highly strung historian quickly returned to his 'normal' ways. His friends and colleagues were aware of his unstable psychology and took it into account in their dealings with him. Upon his return to St Petersburg, Kostomarov was his normal self. He continued to teach at the university, participate in the social life of the capital, and attend church regularly.

Shortly before his travels to Novgorod, Pskov, and Moscow, Kostomarov's mother had arrived from Saratov to live with him. He had rented a larger and more comfortable apartment on Vasiliev Island. His life became better ordered. He settled in to his new quarters and analysed the manuscripts he had collected over the previous months. Moreover, he continued his search for unpublished material on Russian history. Through the autumn and winter of 1860–1, for example, he went through the collections of the St Petersburg Theological Academy, located at the Alexander Nevsky Monastery complex. From those ecclesiastical sources, the historian was able to gather much new material concerning Russian social history, some of which he incorporated into his bulky *History of the Domestic Life and Manners of the Great Russian People.*[49]

At about the same time, Kostomarov incorporated some of the material on Southern Rus' that he had found in Moscow in a series of lectures on Ukrainian history after Bohdan Khmelnytsky, specifically the hetmanate of Ivan Vyhovsky (1657–9). In January 1861, he delivered the lectures at the Great Hall of the university, with the proceeds going to the benefit of poor students. In spite of a severe cold spell – temperatures dipped to 30°F below zero – Kostomarov's reputation as a lecturer drew large crowds. The historian later reworked and published his material on Vyhovsky as a major essay. It was the first significant scholarly investigation of that important era of Ukrainian history and one which required a thorough mastery of Polish as well as Russian and Cossack sources. Moreover, unlike earlier Russian historians, Kostomarov did not treat the rebellious Cossack hetman as a simple Polonophile 'traitor' to Russia but colourfully and skilfully depicted his difficult geopolitical situation in a Ukraine stuck between Muscovy and Poland.[50]

Also at that time, Kostomarov began the laborious task of publishing material on Ukrainian and Belorussian history for the Archeographic Commission. For a while, he conscripted his friend Panteleimon Kulish into the enterprise. Kostomarov began by publishing material from the Moscow archives on the era of Bohdan Khmelnytsky and then continued with material on the various Cossack hetmans who succeeded him. All this material appeared in the large-format *Documents Relating to the History of Southern and Western Russia* (*Akty otnosiashchiesia k istorii iuzhnoi i zapadnoi Rossii*) initiated by the Archeographic Commission. Over the course of the following years, Kostomarov edited twelve of these bulky volumes. They contained the charters of the various Rus' and Lithuanian princes, documents dealing with the religious conflicts in Ukraine in the sixteenth century, material on Khmelnytsky, and sources for the history of the so-called period of ruin which followed. So important was Kostomarov's contribution to the collection and publication of the sources of Ukrainian history that half a century later the Ukrainian historian Ivan Krypiakevych wrote that no project in modern Ukrainian history could be undertaken without substantial use being made of them.[51] Kostomarov's great love for original work in the archives, which had long been observed by friends and admirers such as Danylo Mordovets and Aleksandr Pypin, was certainly not without positive results.

The period extending from the time of his liberation from exile in Saratov to the winter of 1860–1 was one of great change for Kostomarov. During that period, he made his first trip abroad, was elected to the faculty of the University of St Petersburg, was reunited with his friends from the 1840s in Kiev, became a popular lecturer in the capital, entered the world of scholarly polemics over the most important questions of Russian and Ukrainian political history, offered the world a new political program on the pages of Herzen's free Russian newspaper, defeated in public debate one of the pillars of the conservative scholarly establishment, and began the task of gathering the source material for a modern history of his native Ukraine. All the while, he continued to write extensively and publish prolifically. His works on Bohdan Khmelnytsky and Stenka Razin established his reputation as a major Russian historian; his subsequent activities splendidly confirmed that reputation.

Through all these achievements, Kostomarov's character remained the same. He was still the intense, self-centred, nervous, hypochondriac, poetic, yet jocular visionary he had been twenty years before. He continued to be subject to sudden bursts of enthusiasm and to unexpected fits of depression; and he continued to be comforted and steadied by the quiet support of his mother and his best friends. At the zenith of his career, he privately confided to Mordovets that he had given up hope in progress and freedom and was bored with life. But his restless scholarly and public activities told an entirely different tale. His letter to Herzen not only confirmed that he held fast to the political beliefs of an earlier era, but also made those beliefs public for all the world to know. Though he complained constantly to Mordovets, he later confessed that the period from 1859 to 1861 had been made up of 'the brightest and most poetic years of my life.'[52] And they were not over yet.

6

The *Foundation* Years

Great was the rejoicing among Kostomarov and his friends, the Ukrainian circle in St Petersburg, when in the last months of 1860 Vasyl Bilozersky finally succeeded in getting official permission to publish a journal devoted to Ukrainian subjects under the title *The Foundation* (*Osnova*). Although Panteleimon Kulish's earlier proposal for a journal entitled *The Cottage* had been unceremoniously turned down, he had managed to bring out a literary almanac of the same name which had proved interesting and popular. There was much hope that *The Foundation* would be equally successful.

The St Petersburg *Hromada* was entirely wrapped up in the project, and its members even began to call themselves 'Osnovans,' or 'Foundation Layers,' after the title of the journal. They would gather every week at the home of one or another member to discuss cultural and literary affairs. In addition to Kostomarov, Kulish, Bilozersky, and, of course, Shevchenko, another former Cyril-Methodian, Markovych, and the writers Oleksander Afanasiev-Chuzhbynsky and Oleksa Storozhenko attended regularly. Artists, poets, and writers mixed freely at these evening parties, and the circle never failed to attract new faces. One young Russian student, an admirer of Kostomarov who had seen Shevchenko briefly during Kostomarov's lectures, was especially attracted to the poet, who invariably had a sparkle in his eye. This student was particularly struck on one occasion, when a young Ukrainian girl, not exceptionally beautiful but dressed in full peasant costume, appeared for the purpose of serving as a model for the assembled artists. Such was the captivation of Kostomarov's circle with the common people, and such were the expectations of the 'Osnovans' of their national poet, Shevchenko, who had arisen from the common people.[1]

By the last months of 1860, however, life was once again delivering Shevchenko some very hard blows, and Kostomarov too was affected. In early October 1860, the poet met Kostomarov at a performance of *William Tell*. Shevchenko had been deeply hurt by an unhappy love affair and mentioned it in his conversation with Kostomarov. Shevchenko told Kostomarov that they would both remain unmarried 'vagabonds,'[2] a remark which could not have been very encouraging to the over-sensitive historian. By the end of the year, Kostomarov was seeing the poet infrequently, since Shevchenko had become very ill and was staying indoors. On 2 January 1861, Bilozersky wrote to Shevchenko, 'We are all very sad that you are ill, but we expect that if all goes well, you will get somewhat better and will not deprive us of the joy of seeing you among the "Osnovans," since you are the instigator of our general cause.'[3] From that time on, however, the unfortunate Shevchenko ceased to attend the meetings of the editorial board of *The Foundation*.

Nevertheless, the project went ahead, and the first issue was published in January 1861. It was bilingual. In general, poetry and belles-lettres were printed in the Ukrainian language, and scholarly prose, memoirs, and other kinds of material were printed in Russian. Following the original plans that Kostomarov and his colleagues had made in Kiev during the 1840s, the journal contained not only poetry and historical material but also literary criticism, journalistic articles, ethnographic pieces, and works dealing with economics and pedagogy. Memoiristic material, letters, excerpts from diaries, bibliographies, reviews, and smaller notes and comments filled out each number. The cover of every issue bore a motto from Volodymyr Monomakh, I Wish Good Things to You, Brothers, and to the Land of Rus' (*Dobra khochu brat'i i Rus'koi Zemli*). From the contents of every issue, it was clear that the thrust of *The Foundation* was to promote, indeed to lay a foundation for, the development of a Ukrainian national movement of sorts and to encourage national consciousness. Moreover, it was evident that *The Foundation* sympathized with the enserfed peasant masses and favoured their complete emancipation.

Kostomarov's contributions were significant beginning with the very first number. He supplied some of his Ukrainian-language poetry, written in the 1840s, and also a number of lengthy articles in Russian on various historical subjects of interest to Ukrainian readers. The articles, usually summaries of his university lectures, were original contributions to Russian and Ukrainian historical thought that expressed in more restrained form the philosophical and political ideals which the historian had adopted during his younger days in Kharkiv and Kiev.

The first of the historical tracts, published in the opening issue of *The Foundation* and entitled 'Thoughts on the Federal Principle in Ancient Rus',' directly challenged the official view of the Russian state as originally a unitary polity. The unitary theory had been formulated many years previously by Karamzin and, like the idea that all the East Slavs formed a single Russian nationality, was still generally accepted. Breaking with Karamzin, Kostomarov stressed that Russian civil life from its very origins had two different sides. On the one hand, there was a tendency to consolidate in a unified state (*edinoderzhavnoe telo*), and on the other, a tendency to form political entities which preserved their individuality and traditions within the general state structure; the principle of unification worked in tandem with the principle of diversity. In other words, Kostomarov maintained, the 'federal principle' was at work here and was free to operate because there existed no overwhelming force – and naked force was the real creator of unitary states – to destroy the various autonomous entities.

Kostomarov then proceeded to list the factors which promoted and maintained this internal diversity. First, there was the varied origins of the East Slavic tribes which had formed Rus'. Although these Slavs were closely related, Kostomarov argued, the vastness of the Russian land and geographic and climatic conditions – some of the Russian tribes lived in deep forests, others by the sea, still others near the open steppe – made for a variety of customs and traditions. Moreover, outside influences were not uniform: in one area Norman influences were felt, in another Bulgar, in still another Turko-Khazar. Sometimes this diversity even resulted in warfare among the various Slavs of Rus'. 'Thus,' Kostomarov concluded, 'minor folk distinctions in a certain way acquired the form of varied nationalities,' and those nationalities were preserved even after the acceptance of Christianity. As time passed, the various Russian nationalities made their homes in one or another of the Russian principalities. Ethnic and state structures thus coincided. By the end of the Kievan period, Kostomarov thought, the early Slavic tribes of Rus' had come to form six principal nationalities: the South Russian or Ukrainian, the Northern, the Great Russian, the Belorussian, the Pskov, and the Novgorod.[4]

Having thus explained the ethnic and political diversity of the old Rus' state, Kostomarov turned to the factors which held it together and which distinguished the 'Russian' Slavs from the other Slavic peoples.

First, all the Slavic peoples of Rus' were united by their common origin, their similar ways of life, and the similarities among their language. Thus, they shared certain folk beliefs, domestic customs, and historical institutions such as the *veche*, or popular assembly, and a general consciousness of their ethnic unity as transcending their linguistic differences. (Those differences, however, Kostomarov believed to be very ancient, dating from prehistoric tribal times. Accordingly, modern Belorussian was an ancient Russian language, a language descended from that of the Krivichi, and not simply, as was often said, a corruption of pure Russian speech by Polish and Lithuanian influences.) Moreover, Kostomarov pointed out that all Rus' was united by a common written language, a 'book Russian,' revered in all parts of the land of Rus'. Second, a common princely house united all of Rus'. All Russian princes traced their origin to the legendary Prince Riurik, and that genealogical unity was later followed by political unity. Foreign pressures like those exercised by the Tatars and Germans only increased the tendency towards unity. (The domestic rivalry with the house of Gedimin, however, fell into a different category.) Third, a common Christian faith and a common Orthodox church united all the 'Russian Slavs.' All the Russian nationalities shared the same liturgy and rituals, the same church law, which in turn influenced civil law, and the same hierarchy, which consciously propagated the idea of unity. Thus, Kostomarov concluded, old Rus' inclined towards a sort of 'federation,' and the federal principle lasted until the Mongol conquest, when the basic state structure underwent a complete change.[5] In general, this first historical tract was a sophisticated critique of Karamzin's unitary and unilinear scheme of Russian history and introduced a new element of variety and complexity into the pre-Mongol period.

It was followed by an even more challenging contribution to *The Foundation*, which extended the same arguments into later times and, in fact, postulated that contemporary Russia was made up not of a single Russian nationality but of what Kostomarov called the 'two Russian nationalities' (*dve russkie narodnosti*). Entitled 'Two Russian Nationalities,' the essay represents a crystallization of Kostomarov's thinking about nationality and Russian history.

In Kostomarov's view as stated in the essay, historical research and personal observation confirmed that two separate peoples did indeed exist within the context of the Russian matrix and, moreover, had existed since ancient times. Kostomarov considered geography and historical circumstances the creators of nationalities, and like so many others, he believed that the 'Great Russian' and 'South Russian' nationalities had been formed at the dawn of history in their part of the world. Though the respective names for the two peoples had changed, indeed, had been reversed over time – he was referring to the specific geographical sense of the name Rus', which had originally designated the lands of the Dnieper basin – their national traits, moulded in ancient days, had endured uninterrupted through the centuries. This notion reflected Kostomarov's view, based on his Herderian-derived philosophical idealism, of the importance of 'national spirit' in the definition of nations. In other words, Kostomarov believed that each ethnic group or nationality had a spirit of its own which was reflected in concrete national traits and that these could be discovered by historical research and personal observation.

On the basis of his own inquiries, according to the essay, Kostomarov believed that Russian history showed the Great Russian people as practical, materialistic, communal, and possessed of a strong sense of family. All those qualities led them to be successful state builders who emphasized centralization and absolute authority. By contrast, Kostomarov believed, the 'South Russian' or Ukrainian people were impractical, poetic, and individualistic, with weak family bonds. Such qualities were not conducive to state-building but had produced egalitarian and freedom-loving societies, from that of old Kievan Rus' to the early modern Cossack brotherhoods. Kostomarov further believed that, as manifest in their petty religious schisms, their autocracy, and their village commune, the Russian people had retained their fundamental traits up to the present and that, as manifest in their religious flexibility, their Cossack traditions, and their individual land-holding, the 'South Russians' or Ukrainians also had retained theirs. In a concluding statement, Kostomarov speculated that in their spirit of democracy the Ukrainians were closer to the Poles – who he also thought had a spirit of democracy – than to the Russians, who were inveterate autocrats. At the same time, however, Kostomarov thought the Poles were more aristocratic than the Ukrainians. The essay ends rather abruptly with a rejection of Polish political overtures towards the Ukrainians as a mere cover for their traditional assimilationist tendencies. The absence of a summarizing conclusion is a real weakness in this otherwise impressive ideological tract.[6]

There can be no doubt that the publication of Kostomarov's 'Two Russian Nationalities' marked the high point of the historian's ideological leadership of the Ukrainian national movement in Russia. For not only did Kostomarov clearly define Ukrainian and Russian nationality in terms easily understood by his contemporaries, the readers of *The Foundation*, but he also pointed directly to their political implications. In what is certainly one of the most memorable passages in the essay, he writes that 'the South Russian group had in its specific character a preponderance of personal liberty while the Great Russian had a preponderance of communality.'

The root idea of the South Russians was mutual agreement, which could fall apart if disagreements arose; meanwhile, the Great Russians strove for a determined form which could not be abolished once it had been set up. They credited the very establishment of such forms to God, and the forms were consequently above human criticism. In various specific public institutions, the South Russians stressed the spirit while the Great Russians tried to create forms.

He then concludes:

In the political sphere, the South Russians were able to form a voluntary association which was tied together only in so far as was absolutely necessary and which lasted as long as it did not disturb certain inalienable rights and personal freedoms. The Great Russians tried to form a durable common body which would last forever and was permeated by a single spirit. The South Russians approached federation but were unable actually to form one; the Great Russians actually produced autocracy and a strong state.[7]

The contrast was clear: Ukrainian freedom and Ukrainian statelessness versus Russian autocracy and Russian statehood.

Kostomarov published one more major historical tract in *The Foundation*, which completed what can be seen as a kind of cycle of historical discourses. In this final tract, entitled 'The Characteristics of South Russian National History,' the historian returned to his theme of the distinctiveness of Ukrainian national history and concentrated his attention on Kievan Rus' prior to the Mongol invasions. He described that period as a truly brilliant historical era in which all the national traits which he had earlier attributed to the Ukrainians showed themselves very clearly. Kievan Rus' valued liberty and was prosperous, commercial, agricultural, and cosmopolitan. The city was fabulously rich, its citizens gentle yet strong. Greeks, Varangians, Poles, Germans, Jews, Pechenegs, and Bulgars mingled freely on the streets. There was political control without centralization, and the popular sense of equality was formidable. The richness of the era's intellectual and artistic culture stood in stark contrast to the poverty of later times. There existed an easy mix of paganism and Christianity, and a tolerant kind of secularism prevailed. The great monuments of this age, the *Chronicle of Nestor* and the anonymous *Lay of Igor's Campaign*, encapsulated its spirit. There were many parallels with later Ukrainian history, but the contrast with dark, Byzantine, and Tatar-oriented Muscovy was clear enough for all to see. Kievan Rus' belonged to 'South Russian,' that is, to Ukrainian, history.[8]

'The Characteristics of South Russian National History' brought to a close Kostomarov's series of articles on nationality in Russian history. He had argued cogently therein against Karamzin's uninational and unilinear scheme of Russian history and had offered an alternate view. Kostomarov postulated a diverse and complex view of Russian antiquity, stating the existence of two and more Russian nationalities and claiming Kievan Rus' for the 'South Russians.' Kievan Rus' was rich, cosmopolitan, and freedom-loving. Great Russian history began several centuries after that of Kievan Rus' and was marked by the Tatar conquest and by autocracy. Those were points Kostomarov would continue to develop in his writings.

The appearance of *The Foundation*, with Kostomarov's leading articles on Russian and Ukrainian history, made an immediate impact on the 'Little Russian' reading public. The reaction was one of delight and enthusiasm. After many years of silence, the voice of the Ukrainian intelligentsia was finally ringing out loud and clear. 'Little Russia' existed; 'Ukraine' existed. The editors received enthusiastic letters from all parts of Ukraine, from the Crimea, the Caucasus, Moscow, Kazan, and many other places in the empire where Ukrainians made their home. Several of the letters were later published in the pages of the journal.[9] There is no doubt that Kostomarov was deeply gratified by the response.

Shevchenko, however, could not share in the general satisfaction. He died on 26 February 1861. Kostomarov, who had been well aware of the seriousness of his close friend's sickness, had visited him twice since the beginning of the year. On the second occasion, just a few days before his death, Shevchenko had told him that he felt a little better and had proudly shown him a gold watch he had purchased a few days before, the first watch he had ever owned. He promised to come to see the historian in the near future. But on the morning of 26 February, a common friend brought Kostomarov the news of his comrade's untimely death.

The funeral, at which Kulish, Bilozersky, and Kostomarov all gave orations, took place two days later at the Smolensk Cemetery in St Petersburg. Kostomarov, in particular, was deeply distraught. He spoke with a quivering voice and in the end broke down, unable to finish his speech – he simply fell silent and left. The speech was printed in full in the next issue of *The Foundation* and gave a good picture of the thoughts that were disturbing the historian.

In the oration, Kostomarov quoted from a Ukrainian folk-song and noted the Cossack poet's lonely death – 'without a family dear, without a wife true' – but also the power of his poetry, the poetry not only of Ukraine but of all village folk, which had brought the throngs to honour his coffin. Kostomarov ended with the inspiring words of the old Cossack duma:

> Your glory will not die and will not perish.
> There will be an illustrious glory
> Among the Cossacks,
> Among friends,
> Among the knights,
> Among good young men!
>
> Oh God, sustain the people of Rus',
> The Christian people,
> From the lower Dnieper basin,
> For many years,
> To the end of time![10]

Those were the historian's final words of farewell to his old friend, the Ukrainian poet. But they were not his last words about him. At around the same time, for example, he spoke of the funeral in a letter to Mordovets in Saratov. 'He wrote to me,' the latter recalled many years later, 'about the funeral of his best friend as if he were speaking about the funeral of some Kievan or Tverian grand prince.'[11]

Moreover, in the next issue of *The Foundation* Kostomarov published a spirited and profound essay on Shevchenko entitled 'Memories of Two Painters.' He compared Shevchenko to one of his younger contemporaries, shared some of his personal reminiscences of the man, and examined his place as a poet in relation to the question of Ukrainian

and Russian nationality. Once again, he stressed Shevchenko's importance as a national bard of Ukraine and a true poet of the people. For
Kostomarov, however, Shevchenko did not simply imitate the folk-songs
of the people or record their lives and manners. Instead, he continued
old national traditions and extended them into the future. The historian
wrote:

Shevchenko's poetry is an immediate continuation of folk poetry. And it is
no coincidence that it appeared exactly at that moment when the folk-song
began to pass from memory. Shevchenko's poetry is both the legitimate and
the beloved daughter of old Ukrainian poetry as it was organized in the
sixteenth and the seventeenth centuries, just as the latter was in exactly the
same way the daughter of ancient South Russian poetry, that poetry which is
so distant from us and which we judge by the bard of Igor.

Kostomarov also argued, however, that Shevchenko, who had elevated
the thought of the people, who had represented its freedom and
expressed its feelings, that same Shevchenko was more than just a 'Little
Russian poet'; he was a poet for all Russians. Translations were not
necessary for the Great Russians, and one did not have to be a Ukrainian ethnographer to appreciate his poetry, as was the case with some
other Ukrainian poets. Shevchenko was a poet with a universal message, a poet for all Russians, 'Great' and 'Little,' north and south. And
that was particularly true given the special relationship between Little
Russia and Great Russia. Kostomarov then proceeded to explain that
relationship.

Indeed, in his informal 'Memories of Two Painters' Kostomarov made
one of his clearest statements on the nature of national identity among
the East Slavs of the Russian Empire. He began by asserting once again
that the Russian people was composed of two distinct nationalities. But
he immediately went on to say that there was a close, unbreakable
spiritual and blood relationship between the two nationalities, and that
so deep was the relationship that no political or social disturbance could
disrupt it. The two nationalities, moreover, were complementary: 'The
Great Russians,' he wrote, 'cannot complete their development without
the Little Russians, nor can the latter complete their development without the former. They are necessary to each other. One nationality com-
plements the other.' And for that reason alone, Shevchenko, who had
been severely criticized by some for his deep hostility to Ukraine's
oppressors, could never hate the Russians.[12]

During the same period, Kostomarov also addressed the question of relations between the Ukrainians and the Poles. Just as he was greatly disturbed by Great Russian attempts to deny the existence of a 'Little Russian' or Ukrainian identity in Southern Rus', so too was he agitated by the attempts of the Polish émigrés in Western Europe and in Habsburg Galicia to portray the Ukrainians as an exotic variety of the Polish ethnic group. The rationale behind that portrayal was the Polish claim that a resurrected Polish state should be bounded by the frontiers of 1772, those of the old Polish-Lithuanian Commonwealth, which had covered much of Eastern Europe and included Ukrainian-populated territories such as Eastern Galicia, Volhynia, and most of Ukraine as far as the Dnieper River. Though almost all Polish political groups ascribed to such views, Polish émigrés from the Ukrainian lands, especially Franciszek Duchiński, the émigré from Kiev, were particularly vocal. In a number of books and articles, moreover, Duchiński elaborated the theory that both Poles and Ukrainians were Slavs and therefore European by race, while the Muscovites, who had never been included in the Polish-Lithuanian Commonwealth, were not really Slavs but of Finnish or 'Turanian' ancestry and therefore, in spite of their Slavonized speech, not true Europeans. Duchiński further argued that the true Rus' of old lay in the Dnieper basin and not in Muscovy or Russia; according to that logic, Rus' belonged to historical Poland, not to historical Russia, or, as one of Duchiński's followers put it: 'Rus' is not Russia, but Poland, and Russia is not Slavic, and the Russians themselves do not know what is and what is not Rus'!'[13]

Kostomarov wasted no time in replying to those assertions. In one of his first articles in *The Foundation*, he criticized Duchiński's ideas, which were being widely disseminated by the Polish press outside the Russian Empire. In a critique of the Cracow paper *Czas* (Time) and the Paris-based *Revue contemporaine*, he reasserted the existence and the independence of the South Russian or Ukrainian nationality and stated that Rus' indeed still existed as an entity independent of the Polish nationality. Moreover, Kostomarov maintained, the Ukrainian nationality still existed in Galicia itself – in *Chervona*, or Red Rus' – which was then controlled by a Polish administration under the Habsburgs. He then proceeded to destroy Duchiński's argument concerning the Finnish or Turanian ancestry of the Russians.

Kostomarov conceded that the modern Russians, unlike the Poles or Ukrainians, might have a great deal of Finnish blood flowing in their veins, but he argued that that did not make them any less Slavic. Over the course of many centuries, he believed, the Finnish tribes of central Muscovy had been completely Slavonized. The modern Russians, who might be partly of Finnish origin, were just as Slavic as the Mecklenburgers of modern Germany, though partly of Slavic origin, were German. Just as no one denied the Mecklenburgers their German character, so no one should deny the Russians their Slavic character. Moreover, the whole idea that the 'Asiatic' or 'Turanian' Finns were somehow inferior to the 'European' Slavs seemed to bother Kostomarov. 'It is absurd and inhuman,' he wrote, 'to react with contempt to any kind of nation. There would not be the slightest shame for the Great Russians in being Finn, Tatar, even Kalmuk, if they really were so, and the whole question could be reviewed without any premise of Don Quixote national pride.'[14]

Several months later, Kostomarov returned to his argument with the Poles. In an article entitled 'The Truth to the Poles about Rus',' he again criticized Polish polemicists who followed Duchiński for trying to exclude Muscovy and the Great Russians from the family of Rus' peoples. He pointed out that Duchiński was wrong in claiming that the Muscovites of old had not called themselves 'Russians' and that he was wrong in saying that the name 'Russia' was a neologism invented by Peter the Great. Kostomarov stated that Peter's own father, Tsar Alexis, had called himself 'Tsar of all Great, Little, and White Russia,' and earlier rulers had spoken of 'all Russia' (*vseia Rossii; vseia Rusi*) in various other forms. Similarly, he clarified certain questions of East Slavic ecclesiastical and linguistic history and argued that the Ukrainian language was an independent language closer to Russian than to Polish, from which it had only borrowed some words and expressions during the centuries that the Ukrainians had lived within the Polish-Lithuanian Commonwealth. Moreover, he maintained, Polish polemicists were dead wrong when they claimed that the Ukrainians were sympathetically drawn to Polish rule; the numerous peasant and Cossack uprisings against Polish rule revealed the exact opposite. In general, it was incumbent upon the Poles, as Kostomarov put it, 'to recognize that at the present time the Polish nationality has no rights to our South Russian land.'[15]

These polemics with the partisans of Polish claims to Ukraine did not occur in isolation. Simultaneously with his article 'The Truth to the Poles about Rus',' Kostomarov published a second article, entitled 'The Truth to the Muscovites about Rus',' in which he defended the 'South Russian' or Ukrainian nationality against what he considered the unwarranted claims of the Great Russians, in particular the claims of the so-called Moscow Slavophiles.

Kostomarov's dispute with the Slavophiles took the form of a reply to the Moscow journal *The Day* (*Den*), which had criticized his essay 'Two Russian Nationalities.' *The Day* maintained that the 'South Russians' did not form a separate nationality and that they had gotten their civilization from the north, from Novgorod, which had colonized almost all of old Rus'. In Kostomarov's opinion, of course, that was pure nonsense. The reverse was true: Novgorod had been formed by a branch of the South Russian people, and its people never even called their land 'Rus'' except in a general sense, in so far as it belonged to the Kievan state. Kostomarov thought the Slavophile harping at a special 'civilizing mission' for the 'north' just another manifestation of old Muscovite chauvinism and disdain for the smaller Slavic nationalities; the promulgators were not true 'Slavophiles,' he suggested, but 'glory lovers' who would retain all good deeds for themselves. Even their disdain of the Poles was misplaced.[16]

That did not mean, however, that Kostomarov was opposed to all Slavophile ideas. On 8 February 1861, he had delivered his inaugural lecture as full professor of Russian history at St Petersburg University, and the lecture, after a certain amount of trouble with the censor,[17] eventually was printed. Entitled 'On the Significance of the Critical Works of Konstantin Aksakov on Russian History,' it was devoted to an analysis of one of the more important Slavophile historians, who had recently died, and it gave him considerable credit for his various achievements. In particular, Kostomarov praised Aksakov for his criticism of Karamzin, Soloviev, and the 'state school' of Russian history, which focused on rulers, government, and international relations but gave little or no attention to social or 'internal' history and the history of the Russian people. Kostomarov believed that Aksakov was right on the mark when he claimed that Russian scholars of the statist trend were blindly following in the footsteps of Western European, especially German, practitioners of historical 'science.' That so-called science was full of ethereal ideas and artificial constructs which bore no true relation to actual Russian national life. Before the Slavophiles, argued Kostomarov, the Russian people had been ignored by 'Russian' historians. In particular, Sergei Soloviev, the leading light of the state school, had paid little or no attention to 'the people' in his multi-volume history of Russia; his theoretical framework, the 'clan principle' (*rodovoi byt'*), which he had borrowed from Evers, a Baltic German, had absolutely no factual basis in Russian history and was merely a misleading theoretical construct. Aksakov, said Kostomarov, was right to replace the 'clan principle' with the family, the commune, and the *veche*, or popular assembly, as major institutions which did play a role in Russian history. Moreover, Aksakov was right to point to the 'land' (*zemlia*), a loose union of cities and towns of the same ethnicity, as another major factor in Russian history. The peoples of the old Russian lands, Kostomarov continued, had never had the slightest conception of a centralized state; they understood only a 'union of the lands.' In addition, the acceptance of Orthodoxy strengthened family ties, added a 'nobility,' and created the concept of aristocracy, and that trend was strongest in Muscovy. The special place of Muscovy lay in the fact that it alone took up the cause of all Rus', not Moscow but all Rus', in the senses both of the 'land' and of the 'state.'

At the same time, however, Kostomarov saw many problems with the Slavophile approach to Russian history. In particular, the narrow and extreme Moscow patriotism of the Slavophiles led them into several fundamental errors. The worst, of course, was their inveterate praise of autocracy, which they saw as a native characteristic of Russia. Kostomarov could hardly criticize autocracy under the conditions of tsarist censorship in which he was writing, but he did criticize the Slavophile notion of popular freedom in old Muscovy. Aksakov was wrong, Kostomarov contended, when he said that there was commercial and religious freedom in old Muscovy. Traders could not travel freely, especially abroad, and religious dissent was severely punished; Catholics could not build a church, and Jews were not permitted even to enter the country. Moreover, Kostomarov continued, Aksakov attributed too much significance to the Muscovite popular assembly (*Zemskii sobor*) and separated the princes from the people by a 'Chinese wall' which never really existed. Aksakov and the Slavophiles were a valuable antidote to the distortions of Soloviev and the state school, but they too were not without serious faults.[18]

Just how serious Kostomarov thought those faults was revealed in the historian's private correspondence with Konstantin Aksakov's brother and fellow Slavophile, Ivan Aksakov. The latter, who apparently appreciated the historian's kind words in honour of his late brother, nevertheless wrote to Kostomarov that he thought the absorption of Little Russia into Russia a historical necessity, that the two were the head and heart of the same organism, that the Little Russian people loved the tsar as much as did any inhabitant of Riazan or Vladimir, that they viewed their Little Russian landlords just as they did Russian landlords, that the Little Russian language could not be developed into a full literary language, but that he, Aksakov, shared Kostomarov's concern for the Russian people living under the Poles, especially in Galicia, and that while he was willing to let Congress Poland go its own way, he would not give up a single inch of 'Russian' soil to the Poles. Kostomarov immediately replied with a personal letter that was far more sharply worded than any of his public critiques of the Slavophiles. He privately accused Ivan Aksakov of preaching a 'cheap' or false freedom yet simultaneously ordering the Ukrainian 'Khokhol' to become a Muscovite. His gracious condescension to the Congress Kingdom was nothing less than a new Treaty of Andrusovo which would divide Ukraine between the Russians and the Poles. 'You hardly know the depths of the [Little Russian] national spirit,' Kostomarov admonished his correspondent.

... You would write: *This is yours, Pole; this is ours.* But perhaps [the people] will cry out: *Hold on, sir, we are not yours and we do not want to belong* [*to them*]. *We want to live on our own* ... Do you not suspect that in the subconscious of every thinking and intelligent South Russian there sleeps a Vyhovsky, a Doroshenko, and a Mazepa [who fought against Russian rule] and that they will awaken when the opportunity arises?

Kostomarov continued by saying that Little Russian literature had the right to develop freely and that on that score he stood closer to the Westernizing and atheistic journal *The Contemporary*, which had even suggested that Ruthenian newspapers in Galicia use 'Little Russian' rather than Russian, than he did to Aksakov and the Slavophiles, who constantly preached unreal theories of 'internal freedom.' Kostomarov concluded by implying that such freedom was nothing but a lie.[19]

These criticisms of the Slavophiles, both public and private, like his earlier criticisms of Polish polemicists, formed an important part of Kostomarov's major statements on the relationships among nationalities during 1861. But they were not quite complete. Together with the Poles and the Russians, the Ukrainians lived in contact with a third major nationality, the Jews, and Kostomarov had not yet addressed the question of Jewish-Ukrainian relations. He did so in the first issue of *The Foundation* for 1862.

The occasion of Kostomarov's statement on Jewish-Ukrainian relations was a controversy between certain Jewish writers and *The Foundation* concerning the use of the traditional Ukrainian name for Jews, *Zhyd*, on the pages of *The Foundation*. A Jewish activist in Ukraine named Venianin Portugalov, who was seemingly otherwise sympathetic to the Ukrainian national awakening, took exception to the use of the term, which he considered strongly pejorative. (The word was, indeed, a pejorative in Russian.) Portugalov suggested that Ukrainian writers should instead use the formal and polite Russian word *Evrei*, derived from 'Hebrews.' The editors of *The Foundation* printed Portugalov's letter together with a rejoinder by Kulish which maintained that the word *Zhyd* was, in fact, the proper national name for Jews in the Ukrainian language, that the common people knew no other, and that in and of itself the name was not pejorative. Kulish added, however, that the existence of a foreign group in Ukraine which was indifferent to its interests was harmful to the country and that the Jews should try to assimilate to the Ukrainians.

The Odessa Jewish journal *Sion* went on to comment on the matter. *Sion* accepted that the word *Zhyd* was the proper Ukrainian term for Jews but objected to Kulish's remark that Jews should assimilate to Ukrainians. *Sion* preferred high Russian culture to low Ukrainian culture and proposed that Jews assimilate to Great Russian culture. That recommendation infuriated Kulish, who recalled that three years before, he, Kostomarov, and Marko Vovchok had written a letter defending Jews from the attacks of Russian reactionaries, but now *Sion* was siding with those same reactionaries. *Sion* then appealed to the Russian public, and numerous periodicals entered the fray.[20]

At that point, Kostomarov finally stated his opinion in a wittily entitled article 'To the Judeans' (*Iudeiam*), a neologism which avoided both the traditional Ukrainian *Zhyd* and the polite Russian *Evrei*. Kostomarov used the occasion to investigate the history of Jewish-Ukrainian relations and the causes of Ukrainian animosity towards the Jews, the existence of which he did not deny. He explained the matter thus:

When the Judeans settled in Poland and in Little Russia, they occupied the place of the middle class, becoming willing servants and agents of the mighty nobility; they clung to the stronger side, and they fared well until the people, rising against the lords, brought under their judgment the helpers of the latter. Judeans, caring only about their own comforts and that of their kin, began to extract advantages from the relationship which then existed between the nobles and the serfs. In that way, the Judeans became the *factotum* of the lords; the lords entrusted to them their income, their taverns, their mills, their industry, their property, and their serfs; and sometimes even the faith of the latter; the lord entrusted their faith [that is, the keys to the Orthodox churches] to the Jews when, in his fanatical eyes, it had ceased to be a holy thing. The Jews considered that they were acting rightly and legally because the law favoured the strong class which was ruling the country. The Cossacks rose up against the lords and mercilessly destroyed the Judeans.[21]

Kostomarov concluded that Christian fanaticism played a minor but not a major role in anti-Jewish activity. After all, Orthodox Ukrainians had consorted with and tolerated Protestant Germans, Catholic Poles, Muslim Tatars, and others over the centuries. The key factor, he believed, was the negative Jewish economic role. Kostomarov concluded by once again urging the Jews to assimilate into Ukrainian society and explained that that would mean the destruction of their economic monopoly but also their attainment of full civil rights.[22]

But Kostomarov's final contribution to *The Foundation* primarily concerned the 'Little Russian' or Ukrainian community itself within the Russian Empire. It was addressed to the Ukrainian readers of *The Foundation* and dealt with the fundamental question of the Ukrainian national awakening of the nineteenth century: the growth of a national literature and the spread of literacy in the Ukrainian language across the countryside.

Kostomarov's approach to national literature was fundamentally egalitarian and populist. In 'Thoughts of a South Russian,' he called for the expansion of a literary production that would be useful to the common people. He invited his intellectual colleagues to help finance and to become involved in the publication of textbooks, translations of the Gospel, and other books that would be of interest to the common people. His approach was eminently practical, and he went to great lengths to stress that although romantic poetry and belles-lettres could inspire the hearts of the intellectual elite, they would be less beneficial to the villagers than texts relating to their everyday life. After all, he commented, 'nightingales do not eat songs!' The implication of Kostomarov's approach, of course, was that Ukrainian literature and the Ukrainian language had to conquer the village if they were to survive. If, however, Ukrainian literature was rejected by the villagers as useless, and the same villagers turned to education in Russian or other languages, then the national language and the national awakening would be doomed. That was a fate that no amount of brilliant but esoteric poetry could prevent. He wrote:

It is far easier to compose tales and write verses, often colourless and empty, with dark-haired maidens, stormy winds, burial mounds, steppes, and cuckoos, than it is to commit oneself to progressive studies, to the hard work of writing books that the people really need. Even our rich folk who make a show of their love for the people would rather have a bit of fun and, in pretend folk custom, say a few words or phrases in Ukrainian and argue about the significance of Shevchenko than give even a few rubles from their income for the cause of popular education.

Kostomarov then went into detail about what he thought really necessary:

Of course, we have to be intelligent about this. It would be comic if someone were to translate into Ukrainian Humbolt's *Cosmos* or Mommsen's *History of Rome*. The time has not yet come for such works. We must limit ourselves to an elementary exposition of scientific knowledge, that which is necessary for primary education. Therefore, at the present time, besides books of ABC's, the common people need short biblical and church histories, catechisms, excerpts of the teachings of the church fathers, lives of the saints whom they greatly love, and explanations of the Divine Liturgy. And if fashionable progressives consider it possible to submerge the people in materialism, we say that the people will turn with abhorrence from their science and will quickly recognize that under the cover of science they are trying to deprive them of things that are truly close to their hearts. The South Russian people will be able to accept education with love if it is given to them in the spirit of Orthodox Christianity.

He continued:

Beyond the sphere of religion, one must also deal with nature ... Together with this, it is necessary to compose grammars in the native language, grammars from which the people would be able to recognize the structure of ordinary speech. Finally, it is necessary to write the kind of booklets that would give the people the fundamentals of its position in the state and its legal rights. We can stop here; history, in spite of the ideas of some people, cannot be considered necessary in this plan for elementary education. History is that kind of science which requires a great deal of background knowledge and a significant level of development; history has no use without it. Books composed for the people must be written in such a way that they can be read and not in a way that will alienate people.[23]

Having thus set forth his plan of action, Kostomarov dealt with possible critics. To the Great Russians who controlled the state, he maintained that when Ukraine was first united with Muscovy, it retained its old privileges and customs, including its language; only the influence of Western European ideas – Kostomarov was probably referring to the centralizing reforms of Peter I and Catherine II – had deprived the South Russians of their language and rights. Those should now be restored, and, despite the criticism of those who said that their restoration would split the Russian people, the resultant harmony and understanding would only strengthen the Russian state.[24]

In spite of its loyalist decoration, Kostomarov's 'Thoughts of a South Russian' was a bold affirmation of the general direction of the Ukrainian literary movement and of the Ukrainian national awakening. It elicited an immediate and enthusiastic response from the Ukrainian reading public. Letters poured in to the editors of *The Foundation* from all parts of Ukraine, and many of them were printed in the journal. The authors all agreed on the immediate need for popular education in the native tongue and thanked the historian for his bold suggestions. They asked that he take upon himself the task of beginning publication of the kind of books and pamphlets about which he had spoken. In response, in his capacity as a member of *The Foundation*'s editorial board, Kostomarov printed a public appeal to Ukrainian society to send in money for the publication of Ukrainian books.[25] Moreover, he wrote privately to many of his friends in Ukraine, especially in the Kharkiv area, urging them to donate money and to collect money from wealthy benefactors in support of the cause.[26]

Once again, the public reaction was positive. Money began to flow in to Kostomarov from wealthy donors in various parts of Ukraine. The great bulk of the donations came from the Kharkiv area, where the nobility was largely of Ukrainian ancestry; nothing came from Right-Bank Ukraine, where the nobility was of Polish nationality. One particularly significant group of supporters was formed in Kiev among the students of the Kiev Theological Seminary. The seminarians collected some money and sent it off to Kostomarov together with a letter stating their willingness to help the cause of popular education in the native language by distributing Ukrainian books among the common people, with whom they would one day be in close contact.

Kostomarov was delighted by the letter from the Kiev seminarians, which seemed to fit in exactly with his plans. He immediately replied to them in Ukrainian, saying: 'When you do become pastors, let each of you have stamped upon his heart the love for your country and your people which you now have, and may you be a light to your people and may you become strong defenders of the national language and popular education. And if all seminarians were to have such a spirit as yours, our nationality would never be broken by any hostile force through the ages ... He who loves the people, loves its speech, but he who says that he loves the people but hates its speech is a liar.'[27]

All in all, Kostomarov was able to collect some five thousand rubles for the purpose of publishing books for the common people in the Ukrainian language. He printed announcements of the progress of his work in the St Petersburg newspapers and in *The Foundation*. Within a short period of time, he had also published a simple book of arithmetic for the common folk by his younger colleague, Oleksander Konysky, and a book of Bible stories composed by a close friend, the priest Stefan Opatovych. Kostomarov greatly valued the dedication of Konysky and Opatovych, and several months later, when Konysky was threatened with arrest and exile for his Ukrainian activities, Kostomarov cautioned him, 'You must preserve yourself, not for your own sake, but for Ukraine and the whole national cause.'[28] Other volumes too were prepared for the press, and the project seemed destined to change the course of general education in the Ukrainian-speaking regions of the Russian Empire.[29]

But serious problems prevented the realization of that change. Foremost among them were the pressures exerted by the government to prevent an increase in the use of the Ukrainian language in printed books. In 1863, the year of a general insurrection against the Russian government in the Polish regions of the empire, the authorities issued the infamous Valuev administration circular, instructing officials to block all publications destined for mass distribution in the Ukrainian language. As a result of the circular, Kostomarov was compelled to cease the publication of his popular textbooks and pamphlets – some of which were still in press – and to deposit the money in a bank for safe-keeping until political circumstances had changed. Eventually, he tired of waiting for more liberal policies from a government growing ever more reactionary and gave the money to the St Petersburg Academy of Sciences to be awarded as a prize to the compiler of the best Ukrainian-Russian dictionary, a project that perhaps could be undertaken even in the difficult political circumstances. Several times, Ukrainian activists appealed to Kostomarov to release the funds to support Ukrainian publishing ventures of various sorts, but he rejected all those proposals.

In the 1870s, Kostomarov's younger contemporary Mykhailo Drahomanov, who had been sent to Western Europe by his Kievan colleagues
to publicize the Ukrainian cause and to publish Ukrainian books in
freedom, appealed to Kostomarov to release the funds for the publication abroad of a new, uncensored edition of Shevchenko's poetry and
a Ukrainian translation by Kulish of parts of the Bible. On 8 January
1877, Kostomarov replied with a long letter to Drahomanov in which he
told the story of the funds and repeated his position that the money had
been collected for the sole purpose of publishing Ukrainian books
legally in the Russian Empire and that until the government permitted
such publication and the official Holy Synod allowed it, the money
would remain frozen. It was not until several years after the historian's
death that the money was finally put to practical use.[30]

The Ukrainian journal *The Foundation*, into which Kostomarov had put
so much effort, faced still other problems. Though the censorship had
not yet become unbearable in 1862, different obstacles began to present
themselves. There were great difficulties in getting the organ out on
time, correspondence with potential contributors was not maintained,
much valuable material remained unpublished, and, in general, Vasyl
Bilozersky proved a poor administrator. In addition, personal disputes
broke out among various members of the editorial board. The situation
became so bad that Mordovets in Saratov could detect the problems. He
later compared the chaos and declining state of *The Foundation* to the
time of the Cossack 'ruin' in old Ukraine. The various editors played
the role of various warring Cossack hetmans. Thus, Kulish was the
arrogant and wily Vyhovsky, Bilozersky the incompetent Yury Khmelnytsky, and Kostomarov the experienced Pavlo Teteria.[31] More serious
still, after the initial burst of enthusiasm, the high price of the journal
drove away many potential readers, and the number of subscribers fell
substantially. (They had never numbered much more than a thousand.)
Finally, the money which Bilozersky had originally invested in the
enterprise ran out, and in October 1862 *The Foundation* ceased publication. There were, of course, sporadic attempts to revive the journal, at
one point as a quarterly supplement to a more popular political magazine, but none succeeded. By late 1863, the changing political climate
made revival of the journal impossible.[32] The end of *The Foundation*
signified the end of an era in Kostomarov's own career.

There is no doubt that *The Foundation* period was one of the most significant in Kostomarov's public life. He was constantly writing, speak-

ing, and publishing. His books were being widely circulated, and his articles, which often summarized the major arguments of his books, appeared in *The Foundation* and *The Russian Word* and other influential journals. His contributions to *The Foundation* were particularly significant in the history of the Ukrainian national awakening.

Kostomarov contributed essentially three types of piece to *The Foundation*. First, he published his Ukrainian-language poetry and his evaluation of Shevchenko's poetry; second, his series of historical discourses; and third, his major statement on the question of literacy, literature, and the national awakening.

Kostomarov's evaluation of Shevchenko was notable in that the historian was able to see the significance of his poet friend not only as the most important Ukrainian bard of modern times but also as a poet who wrote in universal terms as intelligible to the Russians as to the Ukrainians. For Kostomarov, Shevchenko represented a national Ukraine which nevertheless was not exclusive and harboured no unjustified animosity towards Russian or Pole.

Kostomarov's historical tracts were similarly important. They completely dismantled the monolithic and unilinear scheme of Russian history which had been devised by Nikolai Karamzin at the beginning of the nineteenth century and had been accepted almost universally until the 1860s. Though Kostomarov worked within the context and used the vocabulary of 'the Russian people' and 'contemporary Russia,' he clearly divided all Russian history into the history of two or more independent 'Russian' nationalities and presented what he thought the most brilliant period, that of Kievan Rus', as belonging to the history of the South Russian nationality. That conceptualization was the direct forerunner of the thought of the later Ukrainian historian Mykhailo Hrushevsky (1866–1934), who accepted Kostomarov's premises but changed his vocabulary to one of 'Russian history' and 'Ukrainian history' within the context of the 'three East Slavic' nationalities. It is no wonder, therefore, that Hrushevsky, when reflecting on the significance of Kostomarov's historiographical contributions to *The Foundation*, saw them as representing 'a full revolution in the historical thought of Eastern Slavdom.'[33]

Finally, Kostomarov's contribution with respect to literature and the language question revealed his underlying assumptions about the course of the Ukrainian national awakening: he was fully convinced that the awakening had to proceed from the bottom, from practical literature for the country folk to high literature and sophisticated scholarship.

Furthermore, the literature had to take into account the morals and feelings, especially the religious values, of the common people. Kostomarov's public position on popular education explains in part why he himself, a leading light of the national awakening, notwithstanding his work and dreams of the 1840s continued to write and publish his major scholarly work in Russian rather than Ukrainian: in his opinion, not only was the Ukrainian language not yet sufficiently developed for sophisticated scholarly prose, but, as he put it, scholarly or scientific prose was not yet the stuff for the common people. In Kostomarov's plan, simple texts came first, high literature later. It was a good plan, but political changes and subsequent censorship restrictions delayed its implementation indefinitely.

Nevertheless, the very fact that Kostomarov advocated such a plan was significant. No longer was the national awakening the hazy dream of a few isolated intellectuals who busied themselves in writing esoteric verse for the eyes of one another, or in gathering the remnants of a folk heritage that was faced with sure destruction with the advent of the modern world. Instead, the awakening was passing into a stage which involved a wider audience and wider public participation; it was the beginning of the stage of mass mobilization. The fact that the transformation was cut short by the censorship restrictions of a Russian government panicked into repression by a serious political revolt in the Polish lands did not negate its importance. The direction was now clearly marked, and others would proceed in the not too distant future.

Kostomarov's achievements during the *The Foundation* period did not go unnoticed by his countrymen in the south. Nationally conscious Ukrainians everywhere took pride in his fame as a distinguished historian and revelled in his sharp polemics in defence of his native land. 'At that time,' his close friend Mordovets wrote, 'his popularity was finally confirmed throughout all of Russia, and Little Russia was just as proud of him as it was of his recently departed friend Shevchenko. Enamelled plates painted with the portraits of Shevchenko, Kostomarov, and Kulish appeared in the public markets in Kiev, Kharkiv, Voronezh, Odessa, and everywhere along the Don. Those plates have now become a rarity.'[34] Kostomarov was becoming something of a national hero.

7

After *The Foundation*

Kostomarov was deeply involved in the publication of *The Foundation* in 1861 and 1862, but the journal did not consume all his energies. He continued to teach and to contribute to other journals. During his second year at St Petersburg University, he lectured on the history of Novgorod and Pskov, two commercial cities which he thought displayed marked 'democratic' tendencies during the late medieval period. The lectures were even more popular than the previous ones on early Russian history. The historian was so overwhelmed by the number of students who came to see him that he had to limit their access to him fairly strictly.

An example of his continuing popularity occurred at the time of his lecture on Konstantin Aksakov. The university authorities, at the request of the minister of education, asked him to postpone his lecture, but the students objected so clamorously that the rector was called in to quiet them down. The lecture, when finally read, was a great success. The minister himself was present, and again Kostomarov was carried out in triumph by crowds of enthusiastic students.[1]

But the uncontrolled enthusiasm of the St Petersburg students was not without negative consequences. The authorities thereafter tightened control over the students, and Kostomarov himself again came under suspicion. When, a short while later, he was caught at a church in which Polish students suddenly began singing revolutionary songs and which he had entered by mistake, he had some explaining to do to I.D. Delianov, the superintendent of the St Petersburg school district.

When Shevchenko died, the historian was filled with mixed emotions. He was deeply disturbed by the loss of a close friend, but it was also the time when the tsar's decree emancipating the serfs was being read out from church pulpits across the Russian Empire. Many years later, Kostomarov recalled that all Russian society was at that moment buoyed up with joy and great hope for the future. 'It was felt,' he wrote, 'that Russia had thrown off the shameful burden it had born through the centuries and had entered upon a new life as a free Christian nation. It seemed as if the Russian people had not lived through such an important moment since that distant time when Vladimir had introduced Christianity.'[2]

At the end of the academic term, Kostomarov received an invitation to deliver a special lecture at Novgorod for the benefit of a local school. He gladly accepted, and on 30 April 1861 he addressed the proud citizens of modern Novgorod in the hall of the same building which had once housed its great bell of assembly. In his lecture, entitled 'The Significance of Novgorod the Great in Russian History,' the historian made it clear that he deeply identified with the principles of popular rule, personal freedom, and local autonomy and federalism which he thought were embodied in old Novgorod before its conquest by autocratic Muscovy. Kostomarov argued that there had always been two sides to Russian history, a side which stressed popular rule as institutionalized in the *veche*, or popular assembly, and a side which stressed *edinoderzhavie*, or central rule. Novgorod produced the first, and Muscovy, especially after its conquest by the Mongols, developed the second. Between the two, there emerged 'an inevitable fight to the death,' and, of course, *edinoderzhavie* conquered. Moreover, after the conquest of Novgorod this principle, the principle of 'statehood,' grew stronger than before, until finally, at the time of Peter the Great, it reached its apotheosis, and two separate 'nationalities' were created, a state or ruling nationality and a mass or ruled nationality. The historian then asserted that the institution of serfdom was the highest expression of the prevalence of the state principle over the popular or national principle. He concluded that only with the emancipation of the serfs was a new era at last beginning.[3]

After his public lecture in Novgorod, which had been warmly received, Kostomarov set off with Kulish on his second great voyage across Western Europe. The two friends travelled through Germany, chatting away in Church Slavonic, to the certain amazement of their various travelling companions. The historian was particularly impressed by the old German city of Nuremberg, which dated from medieval times. Thence to Switzerland, Italy, Switzerland again, and southern France, where Kostomarov took some time to bathe in the Mediterranean. In Italy again, Kostomarov and Kulish parted company, and the historian went on to Florence without his friend. Italy was going through turbulent times and was in the course of being united under the native crown of Sardinia, a process of which it seems the historian approved. Back in Berlin, Kostomarov consulted a famous oculist about his eye problem and was pleased to learn that he did not have cataracts. His eyes continued to hurt him, however, and the doctor was not able to relieve the pain. By August, he was back in St Petersburg.

Kostomarov found his university radically changed. Kovalevsky, the minister of education, Delianov, the superintendent of the St Petersburg school district, and Pletnev, the university rector, had all retired, and a new administration was in place. The new administrators, who were determined not to tolerate the disturbances of the previous year, drew up a series of stiff rules for student behaviour. In reaction, the students demonstrated; many were arrested, and the university was closed. More disturbances followed, and a rumour spread that certain popular professors, Kostomarov in particular, had instigated the trouble.[4] Eventually, the disorder spread to other Russian universities, and in Moscow it even descended to the level of street fighting. In Kiev, the disturbances had an effect on the national question whereby Russian-Polish animosities were deepened.

By December, the problem had not been solved, and another administration, this one more reformist, was appointed. A.V. Golovnin was appointed minister of education, and Prince Suvorov was named governor-general of St Petersburg. The university was closed indefinitely, but the authorities simultaneously released the students who had been arrested and set about drawing up new legislation which would give the university more autonomy. Golovnin even wanted to meet Kostomarov and invited him to dinner. The historian found the minister 'a very well educated and well intentioned man.' Wishing to help the scholar while the university was closed, Golovnin made Kostomarov an editor at the Archeographic Commission with full salary for three years. The historian also met Prince Suvorov and was similarly pleased with him, judging that he 'looked kindly upon the university question.'[5]

Kostomarov's relations with the authorities were certainly helped by his public position on the wave of the liberal and oppositional protest that was sweeping through the Russian university system. In January 1862, for example, the scholar published an article entitled 'The Millennium' in a leading St Petersburg newspaper. In the article, ostensibly a celebration of the thousand years of the Russian state, he attacked those he called 'the fashionable progressives, humanists, and liberals' who blindly followed Western slogans, arguing that Russia was still very young and could learn much from the West. But he also pointed out that a thousand years made Russia hardly youthful and that Russia had worthy traditions of its own to turn to in its hour of need. Russia should not look forward to ethereal ideals but backward towards practical goals. 'Instead of repeating the hackneyed, fashionable phrase "forward," is it not appropriate to say "back"! Even back to the middle of the ninth century, back a thousand years,' he wrote.

Kostomarov went on to outline the goals he espoused from the past. They were the ancient balance, as he believed it to be, between ruler and ruled, between the prince and the popular assembly, and between the centre and the various lands. This happy system, which, according to Kostomarov, had assured a maximum of personal freedom and regional independence, had been destroyed by foreigners, principally the Mongols, but was worthy of being resurrected. He concluded somewhat enigmatically:

In spite of the fact that our civilization differs greatly from the civilization of our ancestors of the ninth century, there is much in our present situation which links us to that epoch so far removed. If our present state structure has nothing in common with the way of life of the Krivichi and the Ilmen Slavs, the world of our moral powers, our ideas and ideals can still accommodate such chaos. The field of our spiritual and social activity is just as great and wide as was the land of our ancestors, and we lack *order* just as they did in that land. Just as our ancestors in the ninth century found it necessary to call in a princely clan, so too must we turn to the primary goals around which we must gather, and subordinate all our multifarious contemporary questions to them.[6]

This combined invocation of order and freedom seemed to appeal to many influential figures in Russian society and clearly marked the historian off from the most enthusiastic oppositionists.

Nevertheless, Kostomarov remained one of the most popular and active of the St Petersburg professors. He had a prominent role in a series of public lectures delivered at the City Hall in lieu of the closed university. This so-called Free University, for which Kostomarov had helped prepare the ground by publishing a series of articles in the St Petersburg press advocating freedom of speech and a university open to all, women as well as men, managed to get a stamp of approval from the Ministry of Education, and the funds raised therein were to be applied to the benefit of poor students. But the lectures were given in an atmosphere of tense excitement, and it was clear that the students had not yet given up their fight.[7]

Kostomarov's talks were very popular. On one occasion, over two thousand packed into the assembly hall, apparently the largest crowd of the kind ever seen there. The professor continued his course on Russian history by turning to the Muscovite era, which period he now habitually called that of *edinoderzhavie*. He was highly critical, of course, of the Muscovite state and its autocrats, and his attitude was noted both by the students, who responded to him warmly, and by police agents interspersed among the crowd. But while the latter reported to their superiors that Kostomarov's criticism of Ivan the Terrible might be a disguise for criticism of the monarchy and tsardom in general, they had to admit that he levelled no open attack on the government.[8]

Things reached a crisis in March, when P.V. Pavlov, one of Kostomarov's colleagues, delivered an address entitled 'The Millennium' which, though mild in content, was fiery in tone and ended by more or less openly challenging the authorities. The students went wild with delight, but Pavlov was immediately arrested and sentenced to administrative exile in Kostroma. Thereupon the student organizers of the lecture series decided to close down the Free University in protest and prevailed on almost all the professors to cooperate with them. Kostomarov alone refused to go along with this tactic and insisted on carrying on as usual. 'One should say,' he later wrote, 'that I, who had once enjoyed a great deal of affection among the students, began to lose much in their eyes.'[9]

The pressure on Kostomarov quickly mounted. A group of 'freethinking' and secular-minded students who accidentally had seen him at church for the Orthodox Easter service privately reproached him for lecturing in a free spirit and simultaneously submitting to traditional religious practice, a charge which offended his religious sensibilities and utterly infuriated him. Then the students asked Chernyshevsky, the historian's old acquaintance from Saratov, to intercede with him on their behalf. Chernyshevsky told Kostomarov that if he insisted on lecturing, there would be a tumult and many of the students would certainly be arrested. He, the professor, would be fully responsible; he would, in fact, be a kind of agent provocateur. Kostomarov replied firmly that he would not submit to 'despotism' either from above or from below. The two men parted in disagreement, their friendship ended.[10]

On 8 March, Kostomarov arrived at a crowded City Hall council chamber to face his critics and his supporters. He was to lecture on the Moscow *Stoglav*, or church council, of 1551. A student approached him as he went to the podium and told him that all the professors had stopped their teaching as part of the protest and that he should do so too. Kostomarov was already aware that his opponents planned to disrupt his talk. Nevertheless, he mounted the podium and announced the subject of his lecture to the audience. A great tumult immediately broke out, with whistles and jeering. When the crowd had quieted down a little, Kostomarov, whose face had paled to white, put it to them whether he should continue and stated that he valued free speech and served only science. Some people cried out for him to continue, but others jeered and whistled him down. In the end, he felt forced to retire, with some people shouting, 'Bravo, Kostomarov!' and others still jeering at him.[11]

Shortly afterwards, the government ordered the Free University closed. A petition signed by a number of prominent professors led by Kostomarov did not save Pavlov, who was sent into exile. The historian also requested that the authorities ignore the antics of the student demonstrators at his lecture, and in that the government acquiesced: no police investigation took place. Kostomarov, however, began to receive nasty unsigned notes, and criticism of him appeared in the liberal press. He replied by saying that whistling and mockery were a strange way of promoting 'liberal' and 'humanitarian' ideas, that the Western European revolutionary slogan Liberty, Equality, and Fraternity had been accompanied by the guillotine, and that even the Russian rebel Stenka Razin had mixed fine phrases with slaughter. What kind of 'liberalism' was this?[12]

Kostomarov, whose nerves were never very strong, seems to have been deeply disturbed by the controversy into which university politics had plunged him. He decided to resign his position as professor if he could obtain an alternate means of subsistence. He therefore approached Golovnin, the minister of education, and asked to be allowed to resign, but also to be allowed to continue his work on the Archeographic Commission and to travel for three years to Russia, Poland, and Austrian Galicia. Golovnin, who seems to have been personally sympathetic to the historian, endorsed the request and sent it on to the tsar with a suggestion that Kostomarov be retired with a small salary. The tsar approved the request.[13] 'That affair of the City Hall lectures,' the historian later reflected, 'made a deep impression on me and changed my convictions considerably. I had come to see that most of the Russian youth, in whose scholarly powers I had naïvely believed, could be easily carried away by noise and empty phrases, and put little stock in scholarship.'[14]

Having been freed from his university obligations in St Petersburg, Kostomarov immediately set out to fulfil his travel plans. On 31 May 1862, he left the capital for Vilnius, a historic and prosperous old city in Lithuania and at that time one of the principal centres of Polish culture in the Russian Empire. Vilnius had a rich intellectual tradition and many old monuments and buildings. But upon arrival Kostomarov quickly discovered that revolutionary feelings had not erupted in St Petersburg alone. In the streets of Vilnius, he was struck by the feverish temper of the population. Preparations were well under way for a Polish national uprising, and the Russian authorities seemed already to have lost control of the situation: rebel proclamations and leaflets bearing the words of revolutionary songs were being openly distributed in the streets.

Nevertheless, Kostomarov proceeded directly to his destination and soon made the acquaintance of a learned circle of Polish antiquarians, historians, and poets. He met the antiquary Mikolaj Malinowski, who regarded the excitement with caution; the elderly poet Antoni Odyniec, who recounted his memories of the great Mickiewicz, whom he had known personally; the younger poet Ludwik Kondratowicz, who was deeply devoted to democracy and the emancipation of the peasants, both Polish and Russian; Adam Kirkor, an ethnographer who was the publisher of the local Polish newspaper and was firmly committed to the cause of the common people; and Count Eustachy Tyszkiewicz, a leading figure in the cultural life of Vilnius. Tyszkiewicz was president of the Vilnius Archeographic Commission and warmly welcomed Kostomarov to one of its general meetings, where he introduced him in Polish as a man who was interested in and had made a positive contribution to Polish history. Noting that Polish was the working language of the session, Kostomarov politely replied in that language. That gracious response from an important Russian intellectual made a deep impression on the audience, but later it caused the historian much embarrassment, since it resulted in his being accused by some Russian patriots of softness towards the Poles in the heat of a dangerous situation. He defended himself by saying that he had been merely civil and would have been equally pleased to reply in French or German had he been welcomed as warmly in either of those foreign languages.[15]

From Vilnius, Kostomarov went on to Pskov and its environs, where he visited many old churches and monasteries. He was particularly impressed by Pskov's antique secular architecture, which had survived in relative abundance. From Pskov, he travelled back to St Petersburg, where after a few weeks' rest he again set off on a historical tour, this time of the Novgorod area. During these travels, Kostomarov paid close attention to the dialects spoken in the more remote villages of the Novgorod region and became more than ever convinced of their proximity to Ukrainian.[16] Upon his return to St Petersburg, he put the final touches to his history of Novgorod and Pskov, which was a summary of his work over the previous several years, and saw the manuscript to press. It appeared early the next year under the title *North Russian Popular Rule during the Feudal Veche Period: Novgorod, Pskov, Viatka*. The publication of the book, which was openly sympathetic to the free republican institutions of those old Russian commercial cities, served somewhat to rehabilitate Kostomarov in the eyes of the radical Russian intelligentsia.[17]

Another book appeared at roughly the same time which quite clearly re-established Kostomarov's oppositional credentials. In 1862, Kostomarov finally published his Russian-language drama on the life of Cremutius Aulus Cordus, which he had written in exile many years before. It was published by Kozhanchikov in St Petersburg and was, of course, a not so veiled protest against autocracy and despotism.[18]

In a certain way, however, Kostomarov remained on a very different course from the secularist and left-leaning radical Russian intelligentsia. For example, he continued to express an interest in all the Slavs and to mix that interest with his commitment to the Ukrainian awakening, a subject in which few Russian radicals were interested. Thus, at the beginning of May 1863 he joined his friend Father Stefan Opatovych and a number of other Ukrainians and sympathizers in a church service and memorial gathering in honour of Saints Cyril and Methodius, the apostles to the Slavs. Bilozersky, M.I. Sukhomlinov, D.H. Lebedyntsev, S.S. Artemovsky, N.I. Petrov, Z. Nedoborovsky, and a few others attended. Nedoborovsky's children were dressed in full Ukrainian costume, and Bilozersky sent a telegram of sympathy to Moravia, where, it seems, other commemorative gatherings were taking place. Afterwards, however, someone spread a rumour that Opatovych had held a memorial service for Polish insurgents killed during the uprising, and church officials accompanied by policemen arrived at his door to make inquiries. All the participants were thereafter interrogated by the police, and the matter went all the way to the metropolitan before it was resolved.[19] Kostomarov's Slavic and Ukrainian sentiments were not precisely leftist or oppositional, but they put him in an awkward position with regard to the Russian authorities.

Throughout 1863, however, Kostomarov continued to give considerable attention to Ukrainian affairs and worked hard at getting his project for the publication of Ukrainian books for the people accepted both in official government spheres and by the educated Ukrainian public. His strategy was to stress the usefulness of popular education and the continuing loyalty of the 'South Russian' people to the Russian state.

In early 1863, for example, Kostomarov deliberately published in a particularly conservative Russian journal an article on Russian-Ukrainian relations in which he stressed the friendly relations which, he claimed, had always existed between the Great and the Little Russian peoples. The article, entitled 'Prince Vladimir Monomakh and the Cossack Bohdan Khmelnytsky,' was ostensibly a survey of 'South Russian' history emphasizing Monomakh's commitment to both popular rule and the unity of all Rus', and Khmelnytsky's turn to Moscow and simultaneously held desire to retain old Cossack liberties and the independence of his country. Kostomarov maintained, further, that other Ukrainian Cossack leaders who wished to reunite with Poland had been continually overruled by 'the people,' who saw through false Polish promises of liberty and were intent on uniting with Muscovy. The Russian state had imposed serfdom on Ukraine only as a result of foreign influences, and even that illness recently had been cured. At present, concluded Kostomarov in making the main point of the essay, the demands of the 'Ukrainian' people were very modest:

We want to travel along the same road as the Great Russian people, as we have up to now. Let our pride and joy be a common one. We will march together towards victories in our internal life; together will we preserve our national unity from external enemies. We ask one thing of the Great Russian people and Great Russian society: respect for our language and an acknowledgment of our inalienable natural right to develop this language, and for our people to use its own language on the path of universal human development.

Kostomarov went on to flatter his Russian readers with an appreciative assessment of their supposedly positive attitude towards the Ukrainian awakening:

Up to now the greater part of thinking Great Russian society not only has refrained from any moral attack on the renaissance of our language, but has been sympathetic to us. We have faith in the entire Great Russian people; there is a noble absence of desire forcefully to assimilate the peoples who are united with it. The Great Russian people can be proud of this quality. If there is something contrary to this in our fatherland, then it does not arise from national feeling but from the influence of foreign ideas.

Kostomarov then turned to the accusations being made by the more extreme Russian nationalists, who were already shouting that Russia was being divided and who had adopted the American label 'separatists' and applied it to South Russian writers. 'These voices,' he continued, 'have been heard even in literature but, to the honour of the Great Russian reading public, have not been met with much sympathy.'

Every thinking Great Russian, who rejoices, as we do, in the wholeness of our common nation, understands that there can be no state disintegration where the subject is the affirmation of love and union between peoples. Can there be a danger for the Russian state when the two Russian peoples, South Russian and Great Russian, are bound by mutual respect for each other's nationality, when the South Russian considers it necessary to spread the Great Russian language and literature in his land and the Great Russian participates in the development and flowering of the South Russian language? ... Let the development and flowering of the South Russian national language be the cause of the entire Russian land and not just Southern Rus'! ... Let our national union show the world a high example of how related peoples can live in harmony ... Let it serve as a good example for all the Slavic peoples, who sooner or later must recognize that the separate efforts of each at the expense of the other lead only to enmity, weakness, and slavery, and that the one true way to salvation is to live, think, and act together in a spirit of mutual love and unity.[20]

In such a way did Kostomarov address the most conservative elements of official Russian society, whose overwhelming concern was the power and prestige of the Russian state. Those circles were important, of course, because they had the power to permit or to prohibit the production of Ukrainian books within the empire.

Kostomarov's strongly loyalist stance did not entirely escape the notice of those in power. Through his friend Countess Antonina Bludova, Kostomarov heard that official St Petersburg, including the tsar himself, was pleased with his article, which, of course, clearly distinguished the Ukrainians from the disloyal Poles. Bludova thereafter even seems to have arranged some meetings between the historian and the heir to the throne, Grand Duke Nikolai Aleksandrovich, in which various scholarly subjects are supposed to have been discussed.[21]

Successful as they at first seemed to be, such approaches to the most exalted St Petersburg circles were not Kostomarov's only tactic. In a parallel article published at about the same time in a much more liberal journal, Kostomarov with considerably greater bluntness argued for the publication and distribution of Ukrainian-language books for the Ukrainian-speaking people of the empire. In the article, he plainly stated the desirability of the progressive spread of education, which would raise the moral and material level of the masses. It could be achieved, he argued, only through the use of simple speech clearly intelligible to the common people, only through the use of the native tongue. The use of 'foreign' languages, he argued, including Great Russian (that is, so-called Common Russian), by contrast alienated most of the people from science, and the few who successfully took the path of higher education immediately scorned their origins and became cut off from their own people. That was one cause, Kostomarov continued, of the general prejudice against the South Russian language and people which was so common among the contemporary Russian public. The prejudice was shared even by such a famous liberal as the literary critic Belinsky, who cruelly mocked all efforts to develop a literature in Ukrainian. The fact of the matter was that, despite the claims of some that the Ukrainian language would disappear before the growing use of Russian or that the South Russian people themselves preferred Russian, Ukrainian had some thirteen million speakers and was not about to go away quietly; moreover, the historian continued, the language was greatly beloved by its speakers, who eagerly welcomed all publications in it. The South Russian language, Kostomarov emphatically concluded, was currently passing from the stage of poetry to that of science and scholarship, and what was most needed was a corpus of books on sacred and political history, geography, and the natural sciences.[22]

Kostomarov's campaign to begin the mass publication of Ukrainian books attracted many supporters who made significant financial contributions to the cause, but it soon ran into great difficulties as well. In particular, the editor of the influential *Moscow News* (*Moskovskie vedomosti*), Mikhail Katkov, fiercely attacked Kostomarov's proposals and accused him of dividing Russia and playing into the hands of the Polish insurgents. Katkov, urged on by letters from Yuzefovich in Kiev, even denied the existence of the 'two Russian nationalities' and claimed that Ukrainian was no more than a dialect of Russian and did not deserve to be raised to literary status any more than Provençal in France or Northumbrian in England. Katkov's attack was direct, crude, and vociferous. He raised accusations of 'separatism' and 'Ukrainophilism,' and soon other patriotic Russian editors also began to attack the effort to expand publication in the Ukrainian language.[23]

Kostomarov replied as best he could. He prepared a detailed and lengthy rejoinder to Katkov, but the censor would not allow it to be published. He did manage to publish a few shorter pieces, and in them he reiterated his loyalty to Russia and stated that the accusations of collaboration with the Poles were untrue. He noted that support for his proposals had come primarily from Left-Bank Ukraine, where the gentry was Ukrainian; practically nothing had come from Right-Bank Ukraine, where the gentry was Polish. Only a few Ukrainian priests and officials serving on the Right Bank had responded to his appeals. Moreover, he continued, the Ukrainian literary awakening had long been a thorn in the side of the Polish gentry of Ukraine because it proved that a separate Ukrainian language existed; that is, it proved that the common speech of the country was not simply a dialect of Polish, as the Polish patriots claimed, and that the land thus did not rightfully belong to Poland. Accusations of collaboration with the Poles against Russia were therefore pure nonsense.[24] Similarly, in other articles Kostomarov defended himself against the attacks of other Russian patriots who accused him of trying to divide Russia; and he reiterated the need for popular education in the native language and assured his readers that his 'federal' theories had to do only with history and not with current politics.[25]

Nevertheless, his limited and brief responses could not quell the torrent of criticism of the Ukrainian language that flowed from the Russian, especially the Moscow, press; Kostomarov, whose major rejoinder had been blocked by the censor, therefore resolved to take his case to the minister. He managed to obtain a personal interview with the minister of internal affairs, P.A. Valuev, who allowed the historian to visit him at his summer home. Valuev told Kostomarov that although his goal of spreading education through the publication of books in Ukrainian was praiseworthy, the government considered that current events were not conducive to the enterprise and that such a project might be used by persons of ill will to promote 'disorder and rebellion.' The government would no longer permit the publication of scientific or educational materials in the Ukrainian language.[26]

Greatly disappointed by Valuev's unsympathetic stand, Kostomarov approached Golovnin, the minister of education, who proved much more flexible. If the educational needs of the people demand it, the minister told the historian, then the publication of Ukrainian books was not only useful but unavoidable. Golovnin also suggested that Kostomarov might help to educate the Russian public concerning the status of the Ukrainian language by publishing an article on the subject in the official journal of the Ministry of Education. Kostomarov immediately did so, arguing in the strongest terms that the Ukrainian language was a truly independent Slavic tongue and not merely a local variant of either Russian or Polish.[27]

It did no good. Valuev had already issued his secret circular banning the printing of serious literature in Ukrainian. Kostomarov was compelled to shelve his project and deposit the money he had collected for it in a bank. It would be many years before books in Ukrainian were permitted in the Russian Empire.

The general reaction against things Ukrainian also touched Kostomarov personally. For example, at about the same time, the University of Kiev had elected him to fill its chair of Russian history. At first, Kostomarov was inclined to accept the position, but on discovering that the governor-general of Kiev, N.N. Annenkov, was strongly opposed to his candidacy on political grounds – he was once again accused of 'Ukrainophilism' – he declined. In compensation, however, the university awarded him an honorary doctoral degree for his research in 'Russian' history. Similarly, in 1864 the University of Kharkiv offered Kostomarov its chair of Russian history. This time, Golovnin himself intervened and advised the historian that, in view of the press campaign against him, it would be better if he declined the offer; Golovnin compensated Kostomarov by promising to support an application to the tsar for a full professorial pension for him for life. The combination of pressure and incentive worked; in compliance with Golovnin's advice, the historian refused the position in Kharkiv and received a university-level pension for the rest of his life. Privately, however, Kostomarov explained his situation in these terms, to Bilozersky's wife: 'The minister ... has told me that he will not confirm my appointment to any university, and that if I am walking the streets of St Petersburg whole and unharmed, I should thank the Lord God for it!'[28]

These years also saw a change in the direction of Kostomarov's historical interests. Before 1863, the scholar concentrated his attention on Ukraine, Kievan Rus', and early Novgorod – that is, Cossack Ukraine and the earlier periods of Russian history. However, as he moved forward in time, the role of Moscow became increasingly important, and Kostomarov was correspondingly drawn into the history of old Muscovy and to its role as a new centre for the gathering of the 'Russian' lands. Once again, however, it was 'the common people' who seemed to attract his special attention, and those periods in history in which the common people burst forth with greatest clarity were the ones on which he wrote with greatest sympathy. In the so-called Time of Troubles of the Muscovite state of the early seventeenth century, he once again saw the role of the common people as paramount, and that era was especially attractive to him. 'In all the history of the early Russian north,' he later reflected, 'there was no other period in which the people had so revealed themselves and by their own powers had been compelled to defend their political, social, and religious existence from external attacks and from internal disorders.' There was no other period, he continued in which the people

was involuntarily compelled to reveal the whole range of the spiritual qualities which were necessary for its salvation. This epoch, terrible and bloody, had the consolation that in living through it, the people came out as victors who had at least defended their independence and their social structure with those principles which had been earlier established. My earlier desire to work principally on the flow of life of the people had drawn me to this epoch ... I had worked on the epoch of Khmelnytsky and Vyhovsky, in which the activity of the popular mass had been very clearly expressed; I had been attracted to the history of Novgorod and Pskov, in which the popular mass had equally taken first place; I had been deeply attracted to the period of the wide independent action of the people which transpired during the stormy uprising of Stenka Razin. I also took up the Time of Troubles of the Muscovite state of the beginning of the seventeenth century with exactly this same interest in studying and revealing popular life in history.[29]

Kostomarov's unusual approach was to bear startling results.

They began to appear as early as 1862. In that year was published his 'Ivan Susanin,' a study of a quasi-official peasant hero of the Time of Troubles who had reputedly saved the life of newly elected Tsar Michael Romanov by leading a Polish raiding party into a great wood, in which they got lost; Susanin was killed by the Poles and thus seemed to have 'given his life for the tsar.' The story was a very popular one; the composer Glinka had made it the subject of his famous opera *Ivan Susanin*, named *A Life for the Tsar* in its early days. Kostomarov, however, informed a startled Russian public that there was absolutely no primary evidence in support of such a fairy tale. The leading astray of the Poles was pure fiction; there was no evidence that the party wished to kill the tsar; and the raiders were most probably not even Poles at all but 'Russians' – that is, Ukrainians or other East Slavs in the Lithuanian service, or even Russian 'bandits.' The entire Susanin episode, Kostomarov concluded, was a literary creation of early nineteenth-century Russian historians. It was a bookish invention with no basis in either contemporary documents or folk legend.[30] A Russian state hero had been demolished.

Reaction on the part of the defenders of such heroes was not long in coming. Kostomarov was accused of denigrating the nobility of Russian heroes and of promoting Little Russian figures over Great Russian ones. The historian does not seem to have been disturbed by such accusations, however, and probably even enjoyed the discomfort he had caused his state-oriented critics. He did not deign to reply to them. After all, the criticisms were, as he later recalled, little more than 'childish accusations' founded on 'false patriotism.' The sole duty of the historian was, as he put it, 'strict adherence to truth.'[31]

Kostomarov's preoccupation with Muscovite history soon led him to criticize other shibboleths of the Russian state. For example, in an article entitled 'Great Russian Freethinkers of the Sixteenth Century' he showed that many early Russian religious figures who had long been considered 'heretics' were actually pious Orthodox people who had simply come into conflict with the Muscovite state.[32] However, when Kostomarov dared to criticize Dmitri Donskoi, the hero of the Russian struggle against the Mongols, he stirred up a hornet's nest.

In 1864, in a lengthy article on the battle of Kulikovo Field, in which the Muscovite grand prince Dmitri Donskoi had defeated Mamai, the great khan of the Golden Horde, Kostomarov examined steppe politics of the fourteenth century and tried to show that Moscow was just one insurgent vassal among many and that Prince Dmitri, far from heroically leading his forces into battle, had delegated that task to others and later was found playing dead among the corpses until it was safe to come forward. Afterwards, he had even fled Moscow at the mere approach of Khan Toktamesh. The battle of Kulikovo Field, concluded the historian, was less important to contemporaries than it was later made out to be, and Prince Dmitri was anything but a great hero.[33]

Once again, Kostomarov's debunking caused a storm of controversy. Again, he was accused of depreciating Russian glory and denigrating its protagonists. The prominent defender of Russian historical traditions Mikhail Pogodin entered the fray, defended the valour of Prince Dmitri, and accused Kostomarov of simple prejudice against Moscow.

Kostomarov replied with a stern rejoinder about the importance of equanimity and objectivity for the historian. He assured Pogodin, in his own words, 'I love your Moscow and I grant her the honour of being *the gatherer of the Russian lands and founder of the state.*' He confessed only to an antipathy to that kind of patriotism which distorted history. He reiterated his position that Dmitri had shown little valour at Kulikovo Field and pointed out that he, Kostomarov, was merely paraphrasing the chronicles which were the primary sources for events in question.[34] Pogodin responded a second time, and others too sprang to the defence of Prince Dmitri, but Kostomarov stood his ground.[35] There is little doubt, however, that the historian's continued debunking of Great Russian heroes damaged his name in influential government circles and increased his reputation for having a 'Little Russian' bias in history. It helps to explain why, in spite of repeated offers from Ukrainian universities, he was prevented from accepting an appropriate appointment.[36]

In fact, Kostomarov's differences with the official Russian history written by Karamzin, Soloviev, and Pogodin went far deeper than any supposed Little Russian bias. Unlike that of those historians, Kostomarov's entire emphasis was on the people rather than the state, and he was never shy of saying so. Accordingly, in the theoretical article 'On the Relation of Russian History to Geography and Ethnography,' first published in 1863, he restated his fundamental ideas concerning the task of the historian and clearly postulated the primacy of 'the people.'

In Kostomarov's view, both ethnography and history had defined themselves too narrowly in the past. Historians had ignored the lower classes, and ethnographers had ignored the upper classes. In future, Kostomarov believed, historians should not restrict themselves to diplomatic issues, state structures, and laws, but address the real lives of the people, who exist apart from the state and, at times, in contradiction to the state. 'This is all the more so,' he wrote, 'since the people are not the mechanical power of the state, but rather its truly living force, its content, and the state, by contrast, is only the form, a dead mechanism which is brought to life only through popular impulses.' Ethnography too must expand its scope. It must examine law and administrative practices and the views of different strata of society. 'The ethnographer must be a historian of the present,' he concluded, 'just as the historian must ... present the ethnography of the past.'[37]

This was no idle theoretical construct. Throughout his long career, Kostomarov actively pursued the history of the people. Accordingly, in 1863, when he began to collect and reprint his works in *Historical Monographs and Researches*, the articles dearest to him, those which directly challenged official views of the state and of nationality, appeared in the first volume. Heading the list were 'Thoughts on the Federal Principle in Ancient Rus',' 'Two Russian Nationalities,' and 'The Characteristics of South Russian National History,' all from *The Foundation*. The same volume also contained his articles on the historical significance of Novgorod the Great and on Ivan Susanin.[38] There could be no question where his primary loyalties lay.

Nevertheless, the political reality of life in nineteenth-century autocratic Russia compelled Kostomarov to limit his radicalism to the realm of historical debate and to shun the pitfalls of contemporary politics. Thus, when conservative Russians among his readers, many of whom did not acknowledge the existence of a separate 'South Russian' or Ukrainian nationality, accused him of manufacturing artificial differences, of promoting the idea of 'Little Russian statehood,' or of preaching federalist solutions to Russia's contemporary problems, he was forced to deny the charges, limit his outline of Ukrainian aspirations to the linguistic sphere, and restate that his federalist interpretations of the past had nothing to do with the future.[39] Kostomarov remained an expert at clothing bold hypotheses in political innocence.

In the spring of 1864, the historian took a break from his vigorous writing and publishing activities and went on his third tour of Western Europe. He was accompanied by the young daughter of his friends Mordovets and Hanna Paskhalova, whom he had been helping to look after for some time. In Lviv, the capital of Austrian Galicia and the centre of a Ukrainian awakening somewhat parallel to the one taking place in the Russian Empire, the pair were warmly greeted by the local intelligentsia, and notices of their stay appeared in the press. They were similarly welcomed in Prague.[40] On this tour, Kostomarov spent three weeks in Vienna and made the boat trip down the Danube to Belgrade, the capital of Serbia. He was particularly fascinated by the Serbian attitude towards Orthodoxy, which he thought strongly mixed with local patriotism. He established contact with some Serbian scholars who had studied in the Russian Empire, including a certain priest who had studied at the Kiev Theological Seminary and who later disappointed Kostomarov by opposing the publication of the Bible and other religious books in the Ukrainian language. A single book language, Church Slavonic, this man seemed to believe, should hold all the Slavic peoples together.[41] Kostomarov also visited several Austrian and German cities and bathed in the sea at Ostend before returning to St Petersburg.

During the winter of 1864–5, Kostomarov buried himself in his study of the Time of Troubles. In spite of headaches, insomnia, and even the occasional hallucination in consequence, he was able to make steady progress. He also took time to engage in historical polemics in the press. When a certain M.I. Koialovich, a historian of the church union who approached Russian history from a conservative Slavophile perspective, published a series of lectures on what he called 'the history of Western Russia' in which he grouped the peoples of Lithuania, Western Belorussia, and Right-Bank Ukraine under the rubric 'the Western Russian people' and criticized 'theories about the unique nature of Little Russia' which he believed originated in a love of Cossackdom that had outlived its day, Kostomarov took him to task. Kostomarov pointed out that the Lithuanians were not even Slavs, let alone Russians, and that there were clear differences between Belorussians and 'Little Russians.' Koialovich's terminology, the historian maintained, arbitrarily lumped together diverse peoples with different histories and simultaneously cut off those peoples from their compatriots in Eastern Belorussia and Eastern 'Little Russia' who had been ruled for a longer period by the tsars of Moscow. Kostomarov further explained that the 'Russian people' definitely did not include the Lithuanians, but did include Great Russians and South Russians, who, of course, still had their differences. (The Belorussians he saw as comprising a subgroup of the Great Russian nationality.) Kostomarov further criticized Koialovich for anachronistically projecting the modern concept of the territorial state backward in Russian history and for his loose and uncritical use of the sources, and when the latter ventured to accuse him of a general prejudice against Great Russians, Kostomarov subjected his book to a devastating analysis and concluded that the reader would find a more reliable history of 'Western Russia' in Ustrialov's old general textbook – for which Kostomarov had little respect – than in the ostensibly specialized lectures of Koialovich.[42]

Kostomarov's polemic, of course, fell on deaf ears. In the years following, Koialovich, a native of Belorussia (Belarus') who, like Yuzefovich in Ukraine, largely rejected an independent or local identity for the sake of a wider 'all-Russian' one, continued to attack Kostomarov's historical and political ideas. He fiercely criticized any proposal for publications in Ukrainian, and in Aksakov's journal *The Day* (*Den*) he called Kostomarov and Mordovets 'stormy Cossacks,' 'wild horsemen,' and 'Turks,' to which Mordovets replied with sarcasm in the journal *The Voice* (*Golos*).[43]

These historical polemics took only a small part of Kostomarov's time. He still spent most of his hours working on the Time of Troubles and making historical and archaeological expeditions into the Russian countryside. In the summer of 1865, he visited a number of historical sites in the area just north of Moscow. He lingered for a while in the Cyril-Belozersky Monastery, where he made his way through a large collection of unpublished old manuscripts; then he went on to Kostroma, Yaroslavl, and Rostov before returning to St Petersburg.

Kostomarov remained in the capital only a short time, however, before setting off on another research trip, this time to Warsaw, to examine the Polish sources on the Time of Troubles. In Warsaw, he stayed at the home of Vasyl Bilozersky, who was now in government service and had been posted to the troubled Polish provinces. Kostomarov spent most of his time in the Krasinski Library, which he quickly discovered was a very rich source for both the Time of Troubles of Russian history and the Cossack era of Ukrainian history. In general, the historian's relations with the Poles with whom he had come into contact were good, and though it was often said that the Poles, whose insurrection had just been suppressed by Russian imperial troops, were usually very cold to Russians, Kostomarov found them hospitable. They obviously welcomed his interest in Polish history.

Kostomarov's interest in Polish history and culture was indeed real and growing. Not only did he visit Polish theatres and churches during his stay in Warsaw, but he also took an active interest in the excavations of old monasteries and churches then being carried out in the city by the Russian writer and archaeologist Vsevolod Krestovsky. Nevertheless, Kostomarov was struck by the way the Poles tended to idealize the old Commonwealth as a near paradise of individual liberty and happiness. The historian also noticed the many monuments to the heroes of the last years of independence and the adulation given the liberal Constitution of 3 May and the uprising of Tadeusz Kościuszko. He firmly believed that such affection was misplaced and that the freedoms of the Commonwealth, even in its dying days, were limited to the noble class, who cruelly oppressed the disenfranchised peasantry. It was here in Warsaw, he later recalled, 'that I conceived the idea of working on this era.'[44] He would write a history of the decline and fall of the Polish-Lithuanian Commonwealth.

Upon his return to St Petersburg, Kostomarov resumed his work on the Time of Troubles and became involved in some other projects. In 1865, his old master's dissertation on the church union, thoroughly revised and updated, appeared under a new and less controversial title. 'Fragments from the History of South Russian Cossackdom to Bohdan Khmelnytsky' this time passed the tsar's censor and escaped official condemnation. However, it retained Kostomarov's populist style and somewhat innovative explanations of the course of the church union, and it stood in clear contrast to Koialovich's more conventional and Muscocentric work on the same subject.[45]

At about the same time, Kostomarov's friend and publisher Mikhail Stasiulevich approached the historian with a view to publishing a new Russian journal to be devoted exclusively to history and culture. Remembering the literary accomplishments of Karamzin and Zhukovsky, Kostomarov suggested the name the *European Herald* (*Vestnik Evropy*) – which had earlier graced Karamzin's own journal – and agreed to contribute both articles and reviews. The new journal, originally envisioned as a kind of Russian *Historische Zeitschrift*, began to appear in March 1866, and in its first issue it carried this announcement: 'In so far as Russian history and the general history of the Slavs will be separated from general themes, this will be done only because of the necessity for a division of labour. Everything which relates to the history of Russia and the history of the Slavs in general will be looked after by our permanent collaborator and founder, N.I. Kostomarov, with whose support we today renew the *European Herald*.'[46] In fact, during the first several years of its existence Kostomarov remained a member of the editorial board, and his influence was so pervasive that the Russian writer I.S. Turgenev casually referred to the new periodical as 'Kostomarov's journal.'[47]

During its first two years, the *European Herald* printed the historian's lengthy study of the Time of Troubles in serialized form. It was also published later in book form in three large volumes.[48] Over the next several years, Kostomarov continued to write profusely for the *European Herald*, and though he eventually retired from the editorial board, he never stopped contributing. The journal itself quickly acquired a wide circle of liberal collaborators, and until the revolution of 1917 it occupied a prominent place in Russian life and letters.

Although primarily devoted to literary and intellectual pursuits, Kostomarov continued to have a private life. In the summer, he would get up early, go for a walk with a friend, and take a dip in the river before starting his day. In the evening, he would play host to a small circle of intimates such as Kozhanchikov, Mordovets, and A.A. Kraevsky, the editor of *The Voice*, the paper in which many of his shorter polemical articles appeared, or would visit Mordovets at his home. With Kraevsky and Mordovets, he would often joke about the rather shrill attacks in the Moscow papers on himself and on *The Voice*. Koialovich was the butt of more than one joke, and in the spring of 1866, when Katkov's *Moscow News* received a warning from the authorities to watch its language, Kostomarov proposed to Mordovets that they get together and drink champagne in honour of the joyous event.[49]

Kostomarov was now about fifty years old but was still not indifferent to feminine charms. At about this time, he took a fancy to the daughter of Mordovets's German landlord. She was a beautiful blond girl with fine features but was some thirty years the historian's junior. Still, he proposed to marry her, and he asked Mordovets to be his intermediary. The latter agreed somewhat reluctantly and seems to have been relieved when the girl told him that she respected Kostomarov as a writer but could not possibly marry such a peculiar person: 'He is so funny, he makes such faces,' she said.[50]

Public events also occasionally made themselves felt in Kostomarov's daily existence. In April 1866, a young Moscow student attempted to assassinate Tsar Alexander II in St Petersburg, and the historian, just emerging from the library, was caught up in the crowds. Those crowds, he noted, refused to believe that a real Russian would try to kill his own tsar, and at first laid the blame on the Poles; afterwards, when they had learned the assailant's Russian name, the people pretended that he was really of Armenian origin. Only very slowly did the truth sink in. A few months later, Kostomarov attended the execution of the young offender and was deeply impressed by the change in public mood and by the awe and respect for the life of the condemned student shown by the large crowds of people who were present. But that did not reduce the distress which the spectacle of public execution caused the psychologically delicate historian, and his sleep was disturbed for several weeks afterwards.

By 1867, Kostomarov was well into his work on the last years of the Polish-Lithuanian Commonwealth. Nevertheless, he still occasionally took time to do other things. That year the first posthumous edition of

Shevchenko's *The Minstrel*, or collected poems, was published by Ko-zhanchikov, with Kostomarov as co-editor. This carefully and lovingly edited volume contained several poems that had never before been published.[51] The historian also continued to address public issues in the press. The question of Panslavism, for example, still intrigued him, and it was being widely discussed in connection with a forthcoming con-gress of Slavic scholars from all over Europe to be held in St Petersburg and Moscow. When the Galician editors of a Panslavic Russian-language newspaper published in Vienna asked Kostomarov to contribute to their venture, he replied enthusiastically with an article favouring unity and mutual respect among the Slavs and supporting the idea of using the Russian language as the medium of communication among Slavs of different nationalities, but simultaneously cautioning that Russian should not replace local Slavic tongues in local development and main-taining that Russia should have no territorial ambitions at the expense of Austria, which contained so many well-developed Slavic peoples within its borders. [52] He also privately urged his friend Mordovets to send money to the Galician editors to aid them in the literary revival in their country.[53]

When the Slavic congress took place, however, Kostomarov took no part in it. Instead, he spent most of his time buried in his work on the fall of the Commonwealth. He limited his contact with the participants to a few informal meetings with Slavic friends from Bohemia and Gali-cia. Whether he did so out of simple enthusiasm for his work or out of fear of the aggressive Russian nationalism which at that time usually accompanied the expression and discussion of Russian Panslavic senti-ment remains an open question.[54]

What is clear, however, is that in the wake of the congress an anony-mous St Petersburg correspondent of Katkov's vociferous *Moscow News* fiercely attacked Kostomarov's cautious contribution to the Viennese Panslavic paper. The correspondent criticized the historian for recom-mending that Russian be restricted in favour of local Slavic languages, suggested that he should have advised the Austrian Slavs to put Slavic loyalties before state loyalties, insinuated that he was in league with the Poles against the Russians, and accused 'the Ukrainophiles' generally of wanting 'to plunder the Russian people.' Kostomarov immediately replied with his 'Clarification,' in which he stood his ground on all points and stressed that the Panslavism he supported was a cultural and intellectual, not a political, variety. Loyalty to one's own language and state must come first, Panslavism second. The accusations of collusion with the Poles, he maintained, were absurd; those concerning the Ukrainophiles' 'plundering' of the Russian people clearly ridiculous. He had met many Ukrainophiles, both Little Russian and Great Russian, who loved the Ukrainian language and people, but he had never met one 'who wished to plunder the Russian people.' They were a pure invention.[55]

Polemics with Russian nationalists did not remove Kostomarov for long from his more serious work on the last years of the Commonwealth, and his enthusiasm for the work remained high. Just as when studying early Russian history he had conversed with friends in Old Church Slavonic, so now did his work influence his ordinary speech, and he began to sport a Polish accent and write to friends in ostentatious Polish.[56] In general, he sympathized with the Polish peasantry against the Polish gentry, and, as he told one younger acquaintance, he distinguished clearly between the pious Catholic common folk and country priests, who, he thought, were generally broad-minded on religious issues and had little love for the old regime – many of the priests would have married had they been free to do so – and the 'fanatically' Catholic gentry and aristocracy, who seemed imbued with clericalism and a selfish love for the Commonwealth.[57] In June 1867, he went on a research trip to Vilnius and the Radziwiłł castle and archives at their family estate in Nesvizh (Nieświez), in what is today Belarus'.

In Vilnius, Kostomarov was shocked at the great changes that had taken place since the suppression of the insurrection of 1863. All the public institutions had been thoroughly Russified, his own former acquaintances had dispersed to other parts of the empire or abroad, and people were afraid to speak Polish in public. Moreover, a Russian bureaucrat in Vilnius had written a history of the insurrection in which he accused Kostomarov of sympathizing with the rebels and singing revolutionary songs. Many Poles believed the stories. Kostomarov hurried on to Nesvizh.

The historian was greatly impressed by the Radziwiłł family house, with its numerous paintings, artefacts, and manuscripts. He was disappointed, however, to learn that most of the family archives had recently been sent to Berlin at the request of the owners. But he did see many interesting things, including a full-length portrait of Bohdan Khmelnytsky, an unpublished letter of his son, Yury, explaining his relationship with the Poles, and the graves of many influential members of the Radziwiłł family.

Upon his return to St Petersburg, Kostomarov continued his work on the Commonwealth, made a side trip to Moscow to work in the archives of the Ministry of Foreign Affairs, and penned brief articles on Yury Khmelnytsky and on Muscovite church politics for the *European Herald*. By 1869, *The Last Years of the Commonwealth* was ready for press, and Kostomarov began printing it in the *European Herald*. It was afterwards reprinted in book form and filled two stout volumes of the historian's *Historical Monographs and Researches.*[58]

The subject of the book was Polish history, but the approach was classic Kostomarov. He began by stating that Poland and Rus' had a historical rivalry which went back to the time of Prince Vladimir and had continued more or less uninterrupted until the nineteenth century. Notwithstanding that rivalry, the fall of the Polish state had been caused not by unusually evil behaviour on the part of its neighbours but by the Polish state's own institutions and by underlying defects in the Polish national character. Like all Slavs, Kostomarov claimed, the Poles were given more to emotion than to intellect; they were brave but inconstant, subject to spurts of extraordinary activity followed by lethargy. The nobility spared no expense in its entertainments, but cruelly oppressed the peasantry; it was jealous of its prerogatives, but selfish when it came to public life. Polish history accordingly was filled with oppressive kings who went unchecked, 'confederations' of noble rebels who failed, extreme inequalities among the social classes, and constant disorder in public affairs. Even the loudly touted Constitution of 3 May could not correct those faults, and Poland was doomed to perish. 'That constitution,' wrote Kostomarov, 'left the peasants under the yoke of their owners and limited itself to a few fine phrases in their favour. It did not prepare for their peaceful future liberation, but rather for a bloody massacre. The resurrectors of Poland, to speak the truth, did almost nothing for her rebirth ...'[59] In his concluding statement, Kostomarov once again raised the spectre of the Ukrainian and Belorussian country folk. In spite of the fall of Poland, they continued to live under oppressive Polish landlords now protected by the conquering Russian state. The hard life continued for those people: 'For millions of Russian peasants, for those Russian masses for whom Russia and Poland have fought their centuries-old battle, and for whom rivers of blood have flown, for them the Commonwealth continues to exist.'[60] It was a severe judgment on the Polish gentry, who loudly proclaimed their liberal principles; but it was also a severe judgment on the Russian state.

During the period from 1861, when Kostomarov was busy teaching, contributing to *The Foundation*, writing polemics for the Russian press, and generally occupying himself with the intellectual and cultural life of the Russian capital, to 1869, when he put the finishing touches to *The Last Years of the Commonwealth*, the historian had a high profile in Russian society. He was a stimulating and popular university professor, a controversial historian, and a talented publicist. His historical tracts continued to breathe sympathy for the common people and firmly to remind his readers of the existence and rich heritage of what he called 'the South Russian people.' He was, in fact, an intellectual radical whose scathing criticism of the Russian autocratic state and its dark Muscovite past could be inferred on almost every page of his voluminous works. But in public life he remained moderate, even conservative, at times lashing out at those he considered 'intolerant' oppositionists and 'fashionable' liberals. These seemingly contradictory positions confused police spies and reactionary supporters of the autocracy, who would have loved to silence all criticism of their monarchy's shady past and stop every assertion of independent Ukrainian identity. But they also frustrated his admirers among the radical students and Westernizing liberals, who dearly wished that he would stand up and openly confront the tyrannical state, which, they believed, mercilessly stifled all attempts at significant change. However, Kostomarov never forgot the hard lesson he had learned during the reign of Nicholas I. He was careful never to overstep the established bounds of the censor or to involve himself in fruitless political gestures. He had found a way of continuing to fight for the causes in which he believed without being arrested or publicly reprimanded, and during the early 1860s he enjoyed some stunning if short-lived victories.

During the 1860s, Kostomarov published three important books, in which he set forth his thoughts on the hard life of the common folk and the advantages of popular rule. In numerous articles, he continued to assert the idea of an independent Ukrainian national identity and a partly independent Ukrainian historical process. Every book and almost every article was a masterpiece of artful craftsmanship, and his readership continued to grow. When he was still far from the end of his brilliant career, the booksellers undertook to reprint and distribute his collected works. 'At that time,' recalled D.A. Korsakov, a fellow historian and younger contemporary, 'Kostomarov's name thundered forth everywhere.'

The popular professor of St Petersburg University, who had only recently retired from his chair and was publishing volume after volume of his *Historical Monographs and Researches*, which simply delighted the young students by their lively depiction of events and the novelty of their point of view, was, according to the general consensus of the intelligentsia of that day, the very embodiment of Russian historical science. It is necessary to be well acquainted with the intellectual flowering of society in the 1860s in order to conceive fully of the fascination to which Kostomarov's name and writings gave rise. Each of his new articles in the journals was gobbled up by others and stimulated prolonged discussion and debate.[61]

Kostomarov was most certainly in his prime.

Yet these years were marked by significant set-backs and conspicuous failures. First, of course, Kostomarov's professional career was cut short, and he was deprived of the adulation of the masses of eager students who once had flocked to his lectures. Second, he was blocked from accepting positions in Kiev and Kharkiv, where he was especially beloved as a native son who had done well without ever forgetting whence he came. And third, and perhaps most important, his grand project for the mass production of popular literature in the Ukrainian vernacular was stopped almost before it started. These were hard blows, which changed the general course of his career; they were blows from which he never fully recovered.

But they did not defeat him. Deprived of the professor's lectern, he took up the author's pen with a flourish. He immediately composed brilliant short pieces on Ukrainian subjects, on Novgorod the Great, which he loved, and on Muscovite history and its icons, which he felt had been treated with too much respect. His articles on Susanin and Dmitri Donskoi were nothing short of sensational. They restored his reputation among the radicals but immediately alienated him from official circles and patriotic Russian acquaintances. In 1866, a former student, P.N. Polevoi, who had earlier honoured Kostomarov by inviting him to be his son's godfather, cut off all relations with him, and later he complained that Kostomarov had 'shown himself a partisan of some sort of ideal truth while denying everything in our historical past that was bright, great, and worthy.'[62]

Others, of course, saw his quest for truth in very different terms. Katerina Yunge, who knew Kostomarov well during this period, linked it to the historian's exceptional personality. 'He was characterized,' she wrote, 'by a complete lack of arrogance, rhetoric, and conceit, and displayed an unfailing courtesy towards people.'

I never saw any hostility or bitterness in Mykola Ivanovych. There was something clear and quiet about him, as there is with all those who look upon worldly affairs from some sort of distance. Misunderstandings and injustice stung him to the heart, but he would always try to forgive and explain the conduct of the perpetrators. He bore attacks [on him] in the press with equanimity, defending the right of everyone to have his own opinion. Sometimes it was even irritating how calmly he bore various insinuations. With regard to the frequent accusations concerning the destruction of ideals and the debunking of national heroes, he would say with a smile: 'What am I guilty of if I do not see or find these things in the sources? I know what is in the sources; what is not I do not know, and so I say: "I do not know this" or "This is not in the sources." What else can I do?' He knew that he sought only truth, implacable truth, and fearlessly went down the path indicated to him by his conscience. Truthfulness to an extreme was a characteristic of his personal life.[63]

Nevertheless, the support of a close circle of personal friends and supporters in St Petersburg was very important to Kostomarov. Just how important became clear in 1866, when Mordovets was compelled by family affairs to retreat from St Petersburg to Saratov. Kostomarov, greatly upset at the loss of another close friend, exclaimed to him, 'Without you, who will defend Little Russia from Koialovich and his type?' And when Mordovets replied, 'You,' Kostomarov remained unconvinced.[64] Right through to the early 1870s, he continued to suffer from bouts of depression and often would threaten to retire to an isolated monastery in the depths of the forest.[65]

But he struggled on and remained enormously productive. For a few years, he even tried his hand at Polish history, with spectacular results. 'The Last Years of the Commonwealth,' wrote his younger contemporary V.I. Semevsky, 'was one of Mykola Ivanovych's better compositions ... If we compare it to Soloviev's Fall of Poland, in which the author limits himself to the external depiction of events based primarily on Russian diplomatic reports, then we can see vividly the superiority of Kostomarov's talent.'[66]

While The Last Years of the Commonwealth was still being printed, Kostomarov was well into his next project and giving a series of public lectures on Russian history to the Artists' Club in St Petersburg. At the

same time, Kiev University again invited him to occupy its chair of
Russian history. Once again, however, the minister, this time Count
Dmitri Tolstoi, intervened, and he was prevented from accepting the
invitation. Once again, his pension was increased and he retreated to
pure scholarship. He would continue along that path for some time.
Kostomarov was not yet past his prime.

8

The Accomplished Historian

In the summer of 1870, Kostomarov went on a prolonged holiday to the Crimea. He visited resort towns, the sites of old Greek and Byzantine cities, and the great naval base at Sevastopol. He swam in the sea, viewed the ruins of Byzantine churches, and even found a monastery to visit. In Bakhchisarai, he saw the palace of the khans for the third time and noted that it had been kept in bad repair since the Crimean War, during which it had briefly housed a military hospital. From the Crimea, Kostomarov went to Odessa, where he had last been some twenty-four years before and had chanced upon his beloved Alina in the opera house. After a relaxing week in Odessa, he went on to Kiev, which he found greatly changed since his departure so many years before. He took time to look around his dear old city, the place where he had held so many youthful ideals, before returning to St Petersburg. He felt greatly refreshed upon his arrival home and shortly afterwards wrote to Mordovets, 'I feel so good that I look ten years younger.'[1]

Soon after his arrival in St Petersburg, Kostomarov published a précis of his lecture series to the Artists' Club in the *European Herald*. Entitled 'The Beginning of Central Rule in Ancient Rus',' the précis, which was the length of a short book, continued the discussion of the nature of Russian government and statehood that Kostomarov had begun in the 1860s in his *Foundation* article 'On the Federal Principle in Ancient Rus'.' In 'The Beginning of Central Rule in Ancient Rus',' the historian repeated his argument that early Rus' had known no central rule and even no clearly defined territorial statehood. The *veche* was powerful and the princes were not. That was true, he maintained, even in the northeast, in the principalities of Vladimir and Suzdal. Without actually naming them, he criticized other historians such as Sergei Soloviev for tracing autocracy and central rule back to those pre-Tatar times and claimed that only foreign conquest, that is, the Mongol invasion, finally united the lands of ancient Rus'. That unifying function, which was the result of force, he believed, was thereafter carried over to the Tatar khan's chief agent, the grand prince of Muscovy, who became the focal point of central rule in Rus'. Thus, just as many nineteenth-century Western European historians believed that most contemporary Western European states had their origins in foreign conquest, so too did Kostomarov believe that the modern Russian state, the Russian autocratic regime, traced its origins to foreign conquest and not to native developments. The foundation laid by the Tatars, Kostomarov concluded, was further strengthened by Byzantine monarchical principles and the violent changes wrought by Ivan the Terrible. His point, however, remained perfectly clear: the Russian monarchy was a foreign, not a native, creation.[2]

Because it was first published as a series of articles rather than in book form, Kostomarov's 'The Beginning of Central Rule in Ancient Rus'' received no notable reviews in the learned periodicals. But there is little doubt that his romantic association of early Rus' with Slavic liberty and his clever connection of centralized autocracy with foreign rule greatly irritated his scholarly opponents, both the official state historians like Soloviev, who traced that institution back as far as possible, and idealistic Slavophile historians like the Aksakovs and their friends, who claimed that autocracy was a deeply native Russian principle which had always been dear to the Russian people. The leading lights of the two schools, both of them centred in Moscow, were unquestionably offended by Kostomarov's attitude towards their favoured city.

In the following year, Kostomarov played the role of the iconoclast again and in three lengthy essays published in the *European Herald* attacked fashionable ideas about Russian history. In an article on the history of the *Raskol* and the *Raskolniky*, that is, of the schism of the so-called Old Believers, he set forth his view of the inflexible and 'formal' nature of Russian Orthodoxy. In 'On the Personality of Ivan the Terrible,' he fiercely criticized the work of the St Petersburg professor K.N. Bestuzhev-Riumin, who had tried to rehabilitate Ivan and credit him with the strengthening of the Russian monarchy. Kostomarov maintained that Karamzin's original estimation had been correct: Ivan was a cruel ogre whose disastrous foreign and internal policies had led Muscovy to the brink of utter ruin. In the essay 'On the Personalities of the Time of Troubles,' Kostomarov once again debunked a series of Russian heroes: M. Skopin-Shuisky, a military hero, may have been poisoned by the jealous tsar whom he served; D.M. Pozharsky, the hero of the recapture of Moscow from the Poles, was not much of a military leader and even less of a civic figure; Kozma Minin, the lowly butcher of the Volga who had led the common people against the Poles, was nothing but a brutal and cunning trickster who claimed to have religious visions in order to dupe the ordinary folk; and Ivan Susanin, as the historian had earlier maintained, was more legend than history.[3]

Once again, these startling revelations touched the patriotic nerves of a number of prominent Russians and prompted several rejoinders in the press. The St Petersburg historian I.E. Zabelin, for example, defended Russian honour in the pages of the conservative Slavophile *Russian Archive* (*Russkii arkhiv*), and the Moscow historian Mikhail Pogodin once again criticized Kostomarov in the Moscow newspapers. Kostomarov replied to the criticism graciously but essentially stood his ground on all points. His general thesis, the paucity of primary sources in support of the official historical icons, he maintained to the last.[4]

There can be no doubt that Kostomarov thoroughly enjoyed engaging in such polemics. The historical essays themselves were not lacking in humour, and Kostomarov, Mordovets, and their friends must have approached the task with their usual good cheer. In his reminiscences of those days, Mordovets wrote, 'The honourable historian was at heart a Ukrainian for whom life without laughter was the same as bread without butter or soup without salt.'[5] The polemics, however, were not without negative consequences.

Literary circles in Moscow seemed to come down hardest on Kostomarov. He had three great enemies in Moscow: Pogodin, Soloviev, and a conservative Slavophile historian named I.D. Beliaev. 'You see,' explained the historian to a younger friend, 'in general they do not like me in Moscow. They consider me an extreme Ukrainophile, a separatist, and a hater of Moscow. But ... history is not a panegyric. I have never denied the historical significance of either Moscow or the Great Russian people, but I just cannot be enthusiastic about Muscovite "orders" and Great Russian culture!' The historian then explained that Prince M.A. Obolensky, the director of the archives of the Ministry of Foreign Affairs who was deeply indignant about his work, had closed that institution to him, but that Nikolai Kalachev, an old friend, had welcomed him to the archives of the Ministry of Justice. The situation was difficult, but so far not all was lost.[6]

Still another figure arose to attack Kostomarov – Gennadi Karpov, a younger follower of Soloviev and a doctoral candidate in history at the University of Moscow. Karpov's doctoral dissertation was entitled 'A Critical Survey of the Treatment of the Main Russian Sources for the History of Little Russia,' and an entire chapter was a direct attack on the work of Kostomarov. So fierce was Karpov that the university faculty ordered him to rewrite and tone down several passages before the book could be printed.[7] Karpov criticized Kostomarov – especially his book on Khmelnytsky – for his treatment of 'Little Russian' history and, in general, accused him of extreme selectivity in his use of the sources. He questioned Kostomarov's trust in certain Ukrainian sources such as the chronicle of Velychko – which clearly explained Ukrainian Cossack concerns for their traditional rights and liberties – and criticized him for not making better use of various Moscow archives – indeed, of deliberately neglecting certain documents – and of Soloviev's *History of Russia*. Karpov, in essence, seemed to accuse Kostomarov of inventing history himself.[8]

The attack by Karpov, which was largely an attack on his personal integrity, greatly irritated Kostomarov. Nevertheless, he replied with a dispassionate – remarkably so, for Kostomarov – rejoinder. He explained that he had used Velychko with great care and in the knowledge that he was much more trustworthy than other sources such as the famous *History of the Ruthenians*. As for his alleged neglect of the Moscow sources and Soloviev, Kostomarov replied that those sources were excellent for the history of the Russian state during the seventeenth century but that was not his primary subject. He was writing about the Ukrainian struggle for independence from the Poles, and neither Soloviev nor many of the Moscow archival sources were useful for that subject. Essentially, Kostomarov defended the Ukrainians' right to have a history of their own and accused Karpov of pettiness in his critique.[9]

Several months later, however, Karpov attacked again, this time even more sharply, in a special pamphlet entitled *Kostomarov as a Historian of Little Russia*. He repeated his earlier criticisms, further stressed what he saw as Kostomarov's overreliance on the Cossack chronicles and exaggeration of Ukraine's traditional rights and privileges, and claimed that the Ukrainian revolt against Poland was primarily a religious conflict.[10] This time Kostomarov penned a very brief reply outlining his general approach to history and criticizing Karpov for placing too much emphasis on the religious struggle of the Orthodox Cossacks against the Poles – an emphasis common among most conservative Russian historians –

at the expense of social and other factors. Kostomarov also criticized Karpov for seeing the Cossacks, in Great Russian fashion, as a force separate from the common people; for the Ukrainian Kostomarov, the Ukrainian Cossacks *were* the Ukrainian common people. The historian ended this second rejoinder by stating his general theory that just as the Poles had their aristocracy and the Russians their patronizing attitudes, so too did the Ukrainians have their sense of brotherhood, as expressed in the popular Ukrainian saying *U liakhiv, pany, u Moskaliv, reb'iate, a u nas, braty*; and each of these expressions indicated something about the national character of the people concerned. The unstated implication, however, was that the Ukrainians did form a separate nationality and that their history should be seen in terms thereof.[11]

Kostomarov's discussion with Karpov seems to mark a turning-point in the story of his historical studies. Previously, he had spent a great deal of time in researching the history of Muscovy and its Time of Troubles – and before that, the history of Novgorod – but afterwards he devoted himself more and more exclusively to Ukrainian history of the Cossack period. He was returning to his earlier and most beloved interests; he was concentrating once again on what he considered his 'native land.'

Kostomarov began with ethnography. In 1871, he conceived the idea of writing a major work on the historical significance of Russian, particularly Ukrainian, folk-songs. It was intended to be an expansion of his second master's dissertation, written so many years before at the University of Kharkiv. At first, his work on the subject progressed very quickly, and by 1872 he was able to complete an introductory section on the pre-Cossack historical heritage of Southern Rus' as reflected in folk-song and to publish it in the Moscow journal *Conversation (Beseda)*.[12] However, that periodical soon thereafter ran into difficulties with the authorities and was forced to close down. Kostomarov was compelled to break off publication of the work and concentrate on other things.

One of them was the publication of a substantial work entitled 'The Legends of the Russian Primary Chronicle in Comparison with the Russian Folklore of Song, Tale, and Custom.'[13] The study analysed the *Chronicle of Nestor*, its authorship, and its accounts of the origin and dispersion of the Slavs, of the foundation of Kiev, and of the career of Prince Vladimir. Kostomarov treated the stories with considerable scepticism and compared them with folk legends touching upon the same themes. He tried thereby to show, as he later put it, that the earliest 'events of Russian history, which had thus far been considered as factually reliable, must be viewed more as an expression of folk fantasy which has been dressed up and presented as fact.'[14] His sceptical approach, which relied heavily on detailed content analysis and comparison with other sources, resulted in a significant revision of the older works of Tatishchev, Miller, and Karamzin and was an early precursor of the much later work of A.A. Shakhmatov (1864–1920), which finally clarified the provenance and character of the Nestor chronicle. It was a contribution to the textual analysis of a most important ancient historical source.

As usual, Kostomarov did not limit himself to office and library work, but continued to visit in person the places about which he was writing. In the summer of 1872, he made a major tour of the Ukrainian countryside in the company of the distinguished Ukrainian ethnographer P.P. Chubynsky. Chubynsky was in the process of compiling a major collection of Ukrainian folk material for the Russian Geographical Society, and Kostomarov took a keen interest in his work. The two scholars toured the Province of Kiev, where they visited sites of historical interest. They went to Korsun, to Kruty Yar, where Khmelnytsky had fought a great battle against the Poles, and to the Lebedinsky Monastery, which had a connection with the 1768 Cossack revolt against the Poles, the so-called *Koliivshchyna*, and the slaughter of Uman. From there, they went on to the Matroninsky Monastery, connected with the same events, and then to the town of Subotiv, where Khmelnytsky had been buried and where they discovered a wonderful portrait of this famous Cossack hetman, who had occupied so much of Kostomarov's life. In Chyhyryn, they heard folk-tales about Khmelnytsky and his son, Yury, from the mouths of the common folk. From Chyhyryn, Kostomarov returned to St Petersburg.

The results of Chubynsky's research came out in several bulky volumes in the years following. His was the greatest collection of Ukrainian folk material ever published and immediately won wide acclaim. Kostomarov participated in the project and was listed as co-editor of three large volumes,[15] though the extent of his contribution remains unclear.

During these same years, Ukrainian literature also attracted Kostomarov's attention, and in 1871 he published a critical survey of the extant corpus to date. He gave special credit to Kotliarevsky and Shevchenko and again acknowledged the latter not only as a national leader but as a 'prophet' of universal significance. Kostomarov compared Shevchenko with Pushkin and Mickiewicz and expressed the belief that although

Shevchenko yielded to them in education and artistry, he surpassed them in the liveliness of his ideas, in nobility of feeling, and in naturalness and simplicity. Of the writers who succeeded Shevchenko, Kostomarov gave a special place to Kulish for his novel *The Black Council* and to Marko Vovchok for her *Popular Tales*. He discussed the appearance and significance of *The Foundation* and suggested that its ultimate failure was a reflection of the undeveloped nature of Ukrainian society. At present, he concluded, it was impossible to turn the Ukrainian language into a vehicle for the expression of all contemporary branches of learning. It would be necessary first to expand the circle of the Ukrainian reading public by educating the common folk in their native idiom – a useful and essential enterprise which would not threaten the Russian imperial order – and only later to proceed to other things. But education in the Ukrainian language was just as necessary for the Ukrainian people as education in the Russian language was for the Great Russian people.[16]

That reflection upon the current state of Ukrainian literature and Kostomarov's concurrent study of the early history of Kievan Rus' and of Ukrainian folk-song were also accompanied by steady work on Ukrainian Cossack history. Kostomarov had already made serious contributions to the early history of the Cossacks and of their rise to power under Bohdan Khmelnytsky. He now turned to the following era, the period of the 1670s and 1680s, in which Petro Doroshenko was the dominant figure. 'In that way,' he later recalled, 'I hoped to write, little by little, the entire history of Little Russia, working it out period by period.'[17] He visited the Moscow archives in the pursuit of his goal and sent a great deal of material back to St Petersburg to be published later in the great collection entitled *Documents Relating to the History of Southern and Western Russia*.[18] He was further encouraged in his labours by a prize from the St Petersburg Academy of Sciences for *The Last Years of the Commonwealth*, although the award was not the first prize he and one of the referees had hoped for.[19]

Kostomarov's scholarly career underwent yet another change at this time. His eyes had bothered him for several years, and his vision had deteriorated. He had had trouble reading manuscripts and documents in the archives, and now he found it difficult even to work from published sources except for very short periods of time. Doctors had repeatedly advised him to control his close eye work and he had ignored their advice, but it could be ignored no longer. It was now clear to everyone, including Kostomarov himself, that he was in danger of going completely blind in the near future.

His friends, in particular Mordovets and Kozhanchikov, came to the rescue. They had long been urging Kostomarov to put aside his archival work and undertake something less strenuous. They suggested a series of reflective essays on Russian history as it was reflected in the lives of its principal figures. The reluctant historian finally agreed to their proposal and, thinking to imitate the parallel compositions of François Guizot and Joachim Lelewel, began to work. It was arranged that he would do no eye work but simply dictate his narrative to Bilozersky's wife, who would act as his personal secretary. The arrangement proved entirely satisfactory, and by 1873 the first sections of *Russian History in the Lives of Its Principal Figures*, those dealing with Prince Vladimir and his house, were ready for the publisher.[20] Simultaneously, Kostomarov, again apparently at the urging of his close friends, undertook to write a short autobiography. It too was dictated to Bilozerska, and later it was corrected and annotated by Kostomarov himself.[21] Both works revealed the historian's lively interest in 'personality' in history and were a testament to his prodigious memory.

On Kostomarov's name-day, 9 May, in 1873, a small group of his close friends and admirers gathered in his apartment to celebrate the thirty-fifth year of his literary activity. Among those present were Bilozerska, Nikolai Ge, I.F. Gorbunov, N.I. Katenin, Kozhanchikov, S.B. Maksimov, I.P. Minaev, F.K. Neslukhovsky and his family, Mordovets, and the priest Stefan Opatovych. Kostomarov and others delivered good-humoured recitations, and it was decided that a memorial album should be presented to the historian later in the year. This album had an illustrated cover executed by the painter Ge; it showed, in the centre, a Ukrainian *kobzar* with his instrument; behind him were Cossack burial mounds, the figures of Bohdan Khmelnytsky, Vyhovsky, Razin, Ivan the Terrible, and, further back, Prince Vladimir and Princess Olga; beyond them, in the far distance, were Riurik and other legendary figures. The album was formally presented to Kostomarov in December 1873.[22]

In the summer of 1873, Kostomarov made a second grand tour of Ukraine. He spent a week with friends in Ekaterinoslav (Dniprope-trovske) in the heart of the old Zaporozhian country. Then he toured the river rapids, which had once protected the Cossack settlements, and examined the remains of the old Cossack *Sich*, or fortress, on the island of Khortytsia. He visited the grave of the famous Otaman Sirko at the village of Kapulivtsi as well as other sites along the way. He was ever on the lookout for elderly Cossack minstrels or bandurists who could entertain him with historical songs and provide him with new ethnographic material. Leaving the country of the Zaporozhian Cossacks, he turned north to Kiev, where he remained for several days. There he visited his old apartments, which were at that time unoccupied. Chubynsky, who accompanied him, could see plainly that the recollections of the early years deeply moved the historian. Kostomarov, it seems, told him the story of his unhappy betrothal and his unfulfilled love. Chubynsky immediately made some inquiries among Kostomarov's old friends and acquaintances and discovered that Alina Leontievna had married a man named Kysil long before, had borne three children, had been widowed recently, and was living in the village of Didivtsi, near the town of Pryluky, in central Ukraine. Moreover, she was at that time visiting Kiev for medical reasons.

Kostomarov was greatly excited by the news. He conceived a passionate desire to see Alina once again and immediately wrote her the following note:

I heard about you by accident. At one time we were very close to each other. That was twenty-six years ago now. Bitter fate separated us. You are guilty of nothing against me, nor I against you. We can still meet in this world, although in old age. We can meet without the slightest reproach to each other on account of the past and with full respect for each other. I will be leaving Kiev, where I have been for a short time. If you have nothing against seeing me, then I say to you it would give me the greatest pleasure to see you, and in that case write me a few words and address the letter to Kiev, corner of Zhyliansky and Kuznechny Streets, care of Professor Volodymyr Bonifatiiovych Antonovych, for Mykola Ivanovych Kostomarov.[23]

Alina immediately replied that she sincerely wished to see Kostomarov once again, and the very same evening he went to visit her. It was a pleasant but sad meeting. Kostomarov had last seen her as a beautiful young girl, and now there stood before him a middle-aged woman who was unwell and was the mother of three growing children. Alina could barely rise to greet Kostomarov because of an illness which had affected her legs. She clasped his hand, and he fell to his knees before her as tears rolled down his cheeks. Her children, deeply moved by the scene, quietly went into an adjoining room. Alina sat the historian in an armchair and said: 'What is there to be done! Life has passed us by! No tears can bring back the past!' Kostomarov asked that the children be brought in so that he could get to know them. They spent the whole evening together. As Kostomarov rose to leave, he said to Alina, 'Let us go and get married tomorrow!' Alina replied jokingly that the next day was a day of abstinence and a wedding could not be celebrated. But Kostomarov returned the next day to see her again. Shortly afterwards, he returned to St Petersburg, where he wrote her a warm letter in which he called her his 'eternally dear and unchangeable Alina.'[24] They were to meet again.

After his return to St Petersburg, Kostomarov once again took up his work on Russian history in the lives of various figures and on other related subjects. He was also delving into Ukrainian ethnography and, in addition to his work on the history of Cossackdom as reflected in folk-songs, wrote a book-length review of the *Historical Songs of the Little Russian People* by V.B. Antonovych and M.P. Drahomanov. The publication of this collection was a significant event in Ukrainian cultural history, and Kostomarov recognized Antonovych and Drahomanov's achievement in the realm of historical commentary and scientific apparatus – they provided a full account of the geographical and linguistic provenance of each song – but he disagreed with their periodization and discovered a few pseudo–folk-songs in the collection.[25] In general, the historian recognized the progress in Ukrainian ethnography that had been made since his youth and revealed a more critically refined attitude than he had shown in his earlier studies in the field.

In the spring of 1874, Kostomarov visited Ukraine again. This time, he went directly to Didivtsi to see Alina and her family. He spent three relaxing weeks in the Ukrainian countryside enjoying the beauties of nature and attending a traditional peasant wedding ceremony. In spite of years of ethnographic studies of Ukraine, it was the first time in his life that he had witnessed such a ceremony, and it made a pleasant impression on him. In about the middle of May, however, he received a letter from his mother in St Petersburg asking him to return to the capital to look after his apartment while the landlord did some necessary renovations. He ended up spending most of the following months at a dacha, or country house, overlooking the Neva River just outside the city. In that refreshing environment, he amused himself by writing a historical novel about the times of Ivan the Terrible. The novel, entitled *Kudeiar* after a legendary Russian bandit who is one of the leading characters, was not without Ukrainian content, and when it was published the following year, it elicited some severe criticism from certain Russian reviewers, who accused the author of painting Russians such as Ivan himself in dark colours while painting Ukrainians such as the Cossack leader Dmytro Vyshnevetsky more favourably. In other words, Kostomarov once again was accused of a general prejudice against Great Russians. He replied to the criticisms by explaining that it was his goal to write what was as close as possible to historical truth and that the historical sources showed Ivan to be an evil character whereas they revealed nothing negative and a great deal positive about Dmytro Vyshnevetsky. Besides, he had painted many of Ivan's Russian advisers in a positive light, and there was no logical reason why readers should take Ivan alone as representative of the entire Russian people. Many years before, in his essay 'Two Russian Nationalities,' Kostomarov concluded, he had shown that the Russian and Ukrainian peoples complemented each other and that their continued cooperation was most desirable. He had not changed his position.[26]

Kostomarov wrote a second historical piece while staying at his dacha. This piece was requested by S.M. Shubinsky, the editor of a new illustrated journal entitled *Ancient and Modern Russia (Drevniaia i novaia Rossiia)*. Shubinsky wanted to launch his journal with an engraving of Nikolai Ge's dramatic painting depicting Tsar Peter the Great meeting with his son Alexei after enticing the rebel son home from exile abroad by false promises of paternal forgiveness. Kostomarov was asked to provide a historical commentary to accompany the engraving. In his study, which he entitled 'The Crown Prince Alexei Petrovich,' the historian painted a savage portrait of the great Westernizing Tsar and a pathetic one of his unrepentant son, who would have liked to undo many of his father's innovations. Bearing no love towards each other, they were both caught up in the cruel realities of the struggle for absolute power. The story ends with Peter breaking his pledge and ordering the torture and execution of his only male heir. Kostomarov, of course, is disgusted by the whole process. He concludes by rejecting both those historians like Pogodin who saw something noble in Peter's sacrifice of his only son for the sake of the welfare of the state and those who were especially critical of Peter. In Kostomarov's view, the entire history of the state was filled with injustice and falsehood, of which the story of Peter and Alexei was but one example.[27]

Kostomarov's stay at the dacha on the Neva proved most productive. In a very short period, he had composed two highly original literary pieces in entirely different genres. His stay was also enjoyable. His old friends Danylo Mordovets and Dmitri Kozhanchikov visited him at his retreat, and the time passed quickly. At the end of July, he left to attend an archaeological congress being held in Kiev.

The Third Archaeological Congress, as it was officially called, was an important event in Ukrainian cultural history. Numerous guests from France, Serbia, Bohemia, and all parts of the Russian Empire arrived in Kiev to take part in the discussions, to view the large archaeological exhibition that had been arranged by Professor Antonovych and his colleagues, and to visit local monuments of old Slavic culture, of which there was an abundance in the vicinity. Participants were taken down the Dnieper River in a steamboat to see the terrain and witness the progress of excavations at certain kurgans, or burial mounds, which contained rich treasures from as far back as Scythian times. They were also entertained by the famous blind Cossack bandurist Ostap Veresai, who enchanted the foreign guests with songs and dumas about old Ukraine. The local scholars treated Veresai with great respect, asking him to sing one or another historical song, and Kostomarov was deeply moved by the experience. Oral traditions also played an important role in the congress lectures: the three most notable papers – by Yakiv Holovatsky, Mykhailo Drahomanov, and Kostomarov himself – all dealt with or touched upon the subject. Before delivering his lecture, which was on Kievan Rus' and was never published, Kostomarov displayed his usual nervousness by walking tensely back and forth and smoking one cigarette after another. He was consoled, however, by the presence of Alina and her daughters and by the positive response of the assembled scholars, who greeted his lecture with prolonged applause. For the older Ukrainians present, Kostomarov was still the leading 'Ukrainophile,' a man to be respected and emulated; for the younger Ukrainians, he was a pioneer, a grandfather who had blazed the way for them during more difficult times.[28]

He had one unpleasant experience, however. One evening in the garden outside the lecture hall, he was approached by a man of similar age, who said to him: 'Oh, Nikolai Ivanovich, how glad I am to see you! It is so long since we last met!' Kostomarov merely glared at the old man and said: 'Yes, it is long. But all the same, I will not shake hands with you!' And he immediately got up and left. The old man, it seems, was Yuzefovich, the friend who had betrayed him to the tsar's police so many years before.[29]

But all in all there can be no doubt that Kostomarov greatly enjoyed the Third Archaeological Congress. Not only was his own paper very well received, but he was able to re-establish contact with many old acquaintances and take pleasure in the achievements of a younger generation of scholars led by Antonovych, Drahomanov, and Pavlo

Zhytetsky. He was also comforted by the friendship of Alina and her family. He left Kiev a happy man.

After spending a short time with Alina at her pleasant home in Didivtsi, Kostomarov returned once more to misty St Petersburg. He was accompained this time by Alina's twelve-year-old daughter, Sophia, whom he enrolled at the Smolny Institute for young women in the capital. Thereafter, he resumed his work on Russian history in life stories.

The year 1874 proved an interesting one for the Ukrainian circle in St Petersburg. Panteleimon Kulish, after an absence of over ten years, returned to the capital and once again tried his hand at historical writing; his appearance was like that of a bright meteor in the night. Other newcomers included the composer Mykola Lysenko, the singer Oleksander Rusov, and the blind bandurist Veresai, all of whom thrilled the Ukrainian circle; and finally, in the words of Mordevets, the 'sympathetic and gifted Goldshtein, who later died a heroic death in Serbia.'[30]

Kostomarov continued with his work, but he had not progressed far before tragedy struck again. In January 1875, he was afflicted by a severe case of what seems to have been typhoid fever. Moreover, while he lay delirious on his sickbed, his mother took sick and died. Kostomarov himself was very close to death, and only the diligent care of his physician and the constant support of a number of his close friends kept him alive. During that time, a letter arrived from Alina asking Kostomarov about his health. Mordovets wrote a reply in which he informed her of the historian's very serious but not entirely hopeless state; she immediately rushed to the capital. For a long time, Kostomarov remained very weak, and only when he had recovered somewhat was he told of his mother's death and allowed to see Alina. The unexpected news of his loss deeply disturbed the exhausted historian, who had quarrelled with his mother shortly before becoming ill. He thought that his complaints and demands had driven her to her death, and severely blamed himself, and only the repeated assurances of his friends could soothe him a little. Kostomarov spent the rest of the winter recuperating but by the spring was well enough to accompany Alina to Didivtsi. There, on 9 May 1875, they were married in the village church by the local priest. Kostomarov was finally reunited with his beloved.[31]

Alina's love and care were to prove a source of great consolation to the historian during the last years of his life. He had lost his mother, who had for many years looked after his daily needs, but he had gained a wife and family who surrounded him with warmth and support.

Although there was much sadness in the reunion, at the many years he and Alina had been forced by circumstances to spend apart, there was also much joy. The joy was of great importance to Kostomarov since his physical health never completely recovered from the blow it had been dealt during the previous winter. He had already looked much older than he really was, and now he aged even further. Moreover, he remained weak, and his eyes continued to deteriorate. Very seldom now could he work without the assistance of a secretary. As a result, he was compelled to spend less time labouring in library and archive and visiting historical sites and more time working and relaxing in his St Petersburg or his Ukrainian home.

These changes in his style of life had a direct effect on the kind of work Kostomarov produced. In the years after 1875, he did less writing of original historical monographs based on archival research and more writing of popular history, syntheses, historical novels, and polemical articles crystallizing his views. But the quantity of the work he produced remained formidable; there seemed to be no end to his creative energy.

Moreover, in spite of his physical handicaps, Kostomarov still ventured occasionally into the countryside. In 1876, he visited the Lake Ladoga region, where he frequented local churches and monasteries. Thereafter, he tended to spend his summers in Ukraine, and from his base in Didivtsi he made various expeditions into the countryside to visit the sites of famous events. With Teofan Lebedyntsev, who was soon to found a journal specializing in Ukrainian history and ethnography, he visited the town of Bila Tserkva, and with the young literary and art critic Vasyl Horlenko he visited the sites of the battles between the Cossack hetman Severyn Nalyvaiko (d. 1627) and the Poles. He also began serious work on the reign of the controversial hetman Ivan Mazepa (d. 1709), who had led a major revolt against Tsar Peter the Great and had joined the forces of the Swedish king Charles XII at the battle of Poltava. He visited the ruins of Mazepa's capital at Baturyn, wrote articles on the reign of Peter the Great and the activities of Mazepa, and toured other spots connected with the age of Mazepa. His work on Mazepa's era and Peter the Great was, of course, a natural continuation of his previous work on the various Cossack hetmans before Mazepa.

The quiet progress that Kostomarov and his colleagues had made in the field of Ukrainian studies during the early 1870s and, in particular, the very successful Third Archaeological Congress of 1874 alarmed conservative Russians in Ukraine, who saw a 'separatist' threat to the Russian state in every manifestation of what they termed 'Ukrainophilism.' In May 1875, Kostomarov's old foe Yuzefovich loudly complained to the central government about the 'Ukrainophiles' and warned the authorities that they had on their hands what he called 'a revolutionary phenomenon dangerous to Russia's interests.' Yuzefovich specifically attacked Kulish, Shevchenko, Drahomanov, and Kostomarov. In particular, he accused Kostomarov of trying to alienate Little Russians from the Russian state by vilifying its history. 'The historian Kostomarov,' he wrote, 'is a man of undoubted talent, but is weak-hearted and without character.'

He is extremely sensitive and terribly carried away with himself. And that leaves him susceptible to being pushed or led in any direction. Kostomarov, who is gifed with – in addition to talent – a good heart and all the traits of an honourable man, has never taken a firm stand in his entire life and has always been guided by outside influences because of his lack of character. He began by being a keen Panslavist, the founder of the Cyril-Methodian Society, which supported the unification of all the Slavs under the Russian state. Later on, he gave himself over entirely to the Polish-Ukrainophile trend under the influence of Bilozersky and Kulish. He published his 'Two Russian Nationalities' in *The Foundation* and invented Russian historical federalism in order to show the essential lack of ethnic and state unity in Russian life. On the eve of the Polish uprising ... he went to Lithuania, where he fraternized with the Poles, and then later he wrote against Poland. More and more aroused by his instigators, he finally struck out with the spitefulness of a chained dog at all that is holy and venerable in Russian history. The fruits of Kostomarov's activities form a whole historical literature comprising a particular school and, of course, for a long time have been tearing the patriotic feelings out of our alienated youth.

Yuzefovich concluded his attack by pointing to places in Kostomarov's novel *Kudeiar* where he believed the historian was denigrating the Russian state and simultaneously praising 'traitors and rebels.'[32]

Largely as a result of Yuzefovich's denunciations, Alexander II appointed an imperial commission of high government officials to investigate the Ukrainian movement. Yuzefovich himself was appointed to the commission, the conclusions of which were never really in doubt. The commission recommended that the government adopt firm measures against the 'Ukrainophiles,' including a prohibition of all publications

in the Ukrainian language, of all stage performances and printed lyrics
to songs in Ukrainian, and of all public lectures in that language. The
long series of measures recommended by the commission also included
a ban on the import of Ukrainian-language books and the exile of
Drahomanov and Chubynsky from 'Little Russia.' However, no specific
action was to be taken against Kostomarov. On 18 May 1876, Alexander
II approved the measures at Ems, Germany, where he was taking the
cure, and they became law.[33]

The Ems *Ukaz*, or Ems Decree, as it came to be known, struck a
terrible blow at the Ukrainian movement in the Russian Empire. The
previous restrictions on the public use of the Ukrainian language were
greatly strengthened, and once again Ukrainian activities temporarily
ground to a halt. The Ukrainian circles in Kiev were devastated, their
organizations dissolved. Antonovych was compelled to keep a low
profile, and Drahomanov was dismissed from the university. Drahomanov, however, immediately went abroad with the support of his colleagues, the circle generally known as the Kiev *Hromada*. He was to
continue the publication of Ukrainian books abroad and to publicize the
persecution of the Ukrainian language in Russia.

Drahomanov took into account Kostomarov's previous efforts at
publishing in his plans for the publication of Ukrainian books in Western Europe. It was well known, of course, that Kostomarov had collected a great deal of money for the purpose, and Drahomanov hoped
to obtain access to it. Perhaps, he ventured, the cautious Kostomarov
would help fund a Ukrainian translation of the Bible?

But Drahomanov was to be bitterly disappointed. Kostomarov, in
spite of his outrage at the repressive actions of the Russian government,
refused to release the funds to Drahomanov and refused to have anything to do with the publication of political pamphlets or any other
unauthorized literature in Western Europe. He expected that sooner or
later government policy would change and another opportunity would
arise for the publication of Ukrainian books within Russia itself. 'With
every new reign,' he replied to Drahomanov on 8 January 1877, 'there
is a new policy and new conditions ... I do not share your plans for
publishing abroad with the goal of serving Little Russia. There is no
Little Russian public but only the [common] people, who need elementary books and not journalism. This kind of literature is necessary, and
it is possible only with the full agreement of the authorities, not with
any kind of opposition.'[34]

In fact, during the next few years, Kostomarov went quite far in his policy of trying to accommodate the Russian government. In 1877–8, when war broke out between Russia and the Ottoman Empire and patriotic Slavophiles began rallying to the colours for the sake of Russian prestige and the 'liberation' of the Balkan Slavs from Turkish rule, Kostomarov swallowed his distaste for his reactionary allies and supported the war effort. He thought it Russia's 'historical mission' to liberate the South Slavs, and he refused to share the doubts of certain liberal war critics.[35] His position was roundly criticized by Drahomanov, who thought that 'the Turks back home' were more dangerous than the Turks abroad and that 'clean deeds demand clean hands.'[36]

When the war with Turkey ended, Kostomarov once again took up the cause of reform. His approach remained cautious, and eventually his tactics began to pay off. During the 1870s, repressive measures had brought the government of Alexander II no relief, since Russian terrorists continued to disrupt Russian public life and to make attempts on the life of the tsar. In 1880, therefore, under the influence of his moderate adviser General M.T. Loris-Melikov, Alexander II initiated a series of liberalizing reforms and moved towards granting Russia a constitution. At that time, Kostomarov and his Ukrainian allies pushed especially hard to get the ban on Ukrainian activities and publications lifted, and they enjoyed some modest success. In December 1880, the tsar approved the Kostomarov Award, to be granted by the Academy of Sciences to a scholar who would prepare a Ukrainian-Russian dictionary. Kostomarov had initiated the idea by transferring the funds he had earlier collected for the publication of Ukrainian books to the Academy for that purpose. There were severe restrictions on the project – the government insisted that the dictionary use Maksymovych's etymological orthography, which looked very much like Russian, rather than Kulish's phonetic orthography, which looked quite different from Russian – but at least the project had been approved.[37] Thereafter, the governors-general of Kiev and Kharkiv provinces submitted memoranda to the central authorities for further amelioration of the laws restricting the use of Ukrainian, and Kostomarov spoke out in a series of toughly worded articles in favour of books for the common people in the Ukrainian language. He maintained that it was difficult for many people in Little Russia to write in Great Russian rather than their native language, and that the laws impeded the progress of science, especially the history, ethnography, geography, archaeology and philology of the 'Little Russian people.' He argued that negative laws even alienated Russian speakers in Ukraine who had come to sympathize with the situation of the Little Russian nationality and that the restrictions on the publication of music and song in Ukrainian were undesirable in the eyes of locals, of all Russia, and of 'the entire Slavic world.' He concluded by saying that Ukrainian should be permitted in Russia just as Breton was permitted in France, Walloon in Belgium, and Scottish in Britain. Russian would continue as the language of administration, and tolerance of Ukrainian would not place a brake upon the use of Russian.[38] Such arguments made some impression on the authorities, and the laws restricting the printing and the public use of Ukrainian were slightly ameliorated.[39]

But then disaster struck. On 1 March 1881, Alexander II was assassinated by terrorists in the streets of St Petersburg. All Russia went into shock, and Kostomarov, sick with a cold at the time, was no exception. On 11 March, he wrote to his old Saratov friend I.U. Palimpsestov concerning the 'tragic events which are transpiring before our eyes' and quoted Pushkin on the terror and 'the horror of our days.' He told Palimpsestov that he admired Alexander II not only as his monarch but also as a good man, 'whom, in truth, history would judge to be the best ruler of the dynasty.' He thought it sad and shameful that men like the assassins, 'wild and unthinking animals' as he called them, were walking on city streets rather than lurking in deep forests. But in response to an inquiry by Palimpsestov about their former common friend Chernyshevsky, who some years before had been imprisoned and then exiled to Siberia for life merely for expressing socialist ideas in some of his writings, Kostomarov said that he found such a sentence utterly unacceptable and affirmed that he stood by the idea of complete freedom of speech.[40]

For some time after the death of Alexander II, Kostomarov and his colleagues continued to press the authorities to loosen the bonds restraining the public use of the Ukrainian language. In general, the historian made only very modest demands which in no way threatened the established powers. His recommendations to 'the Ukrainian intelligentsia,' a small but ever widening circle of writers, intellectuals, and social activists, considerably narrowed the scope of Ukrainian activity from what he and his friends of the 1840s had once privately dreamed. The situation was difficult, and Kostomarov advised caution.

For example, in an article entitled 'The Goals of Ukrainophilism,' published in the *European Herald* in 1882, Kostomarov took an indisputably moderate position. Although he firmly restated the existence of a Little Russian language and nationality – something still being denied by many Russian journalists and public figures – Kostomarov explained that the Little Russian people had repeatedly lost its ruling or intellectual class to the Poles and to the Great Russians. By the beginning of the nineteenth century, the upper class, who were enamoured of French and German, had become completely cut off from the common people among whom they lived. As a result, the Little Russian or Ukrainian people was now exclusively restricted to the country folk, who alone preserved the ancestral tongue. But with the passage of time interests changed. Now it was admitted that the common man was the spiritual equal of his social superiors. Certain individuals had expressed an interest in the common people and had begun writing in their language. At first, the literature written in that language had been scorned by many, but it was a real language with rights equal to those of any other language. Only works in that language could describe the land and people of Little Russia, 'that cradle of the Russian nation,' as they really were. Writers like the novelist Nechui-Levytsky, who wrote in the simple, unaffected language of the country folk, could do it best. What was now necessary was further work acquainting educated society with the ways of the common people and further work widening the intellectual horizon of the people itself. Accordingly, dictionaries, practical texts, and simple works for the common people were more important than exalted literary or poetic masterpieces. Kostomarov concluded that he shared the general goal of full development for the Ukrainian language but advised that it be undertaken slowly, methodically, and from the bottom up.[41]

Kostomarov's moderate proposals had no effect on the government of the new tsar, Alexander III. The laws restricting the use of the Ukrainian language, though they had been modified in the last days of the previous tsar, remained in place. Moreover, Kostomarov's caution aroused the criticism of many 'Ukrainophiles,' who were now more and more openly identifying themselves as 'Ukrainians' (*Ukraintsi*). From his safe haven in Switzerland, for example, Drahomanov scorned Kostomarov's proposals and engaged in an open campaign against the repression of the Ukrainian language in Russia.[42] Similarly, in Austrian Galicia, a leading Ukrainian activist, Volodymyr Barvinsky, rejected Kostomarov's program for the Ukrainian intelligentsia and in the leading Galician Ukrainian newspaper *Action* (*Dilo*) urged the Ukrainian intelligentsia to become active in all spheres of public life and to develop their language as quickly as possible at all levels including that of high literature. After all, he argued, that was what the Germans, the Czechs, and many other peoples had done, and they had all been successful.[43]

Barvinsky's comments did not go unnoticed by Kostomarov. He immediately replied with two personal lettters to the Galician activist explaining that his recommendations concerned only the Ukrainian lands inside the Russian Empire and that in Galicia, which enjoyed the advantage of being governed by a constitutional regime, he favoured the immediate and full development of Ukrainian language and culture.[44] In fact, immediately after Kostomarov's death, Barvinsky's brother, Oleksander, was busily engaged in the vast project of translating into Ukrainian and publishing in Galicia all Kostomarov's major historical works dealing with 'Southern Rus'.' Together with a Ukrainian translation of his most famous historical novel, *Kudeiar*, they formed a substantial contribution to the corpus of Ukrainian-language literature published in Galicia during the 1890s.[45]

During the 1870s and 1880s, all the 'Ukrainophiles' had united solidly around the cause of free development for the Ukrainian language in the Russian Empire. There were other questions, however, on which agreement was more difficult to obtain. One, for example, was the general attitude towards the role of the Cossacks in Ukrainian history. It was an especially important question because pride in the independence, liberties, and physical prowess of the Cossacks was playing a significant role in the building of the new sense of Ukrainian national identity.

For many years, Kostomarov and his old colleague Panteleimon Kulish had been quietly drifting apart on the Cossack question. Kostomarov, on the one hand, essentially remained an admirer of the Cossack phenomenon and a critic of the Polish and Russian states against which the Cossacks had repeatedly rebelled. Kulish, on the other hand, had increasingly come under the influence of Polish historiography and during the 1860s and 1870s had come to regard Polish activity in Ukraine as having exerted a 'civilizing' influence; he had also come to be very critical of the violence and anarchy arising from the Cossack resistance to the Poles. Kulish and Kostomarov thus drifted apart in their thinking and consequently in their personal relations. After Kulish returned to St Petersburg from his stay in the Polish provinces as a government administrator, the two men met infrequently, and Kostomarov never once visited Kulish at his home. The historian, it seems, was further irritated by Kulish's repeated reference to him as a 'foreigner,' which he saw as a denial of his Ukrainian background. Matters came to a head when Kulish published a critical three-volume history of the Cossack era entitled *The History of the Reunification of Rus'* (*Istoriia vossedineniia Rusi*) containing personal attacks on Kostomarov and Shevchenko – he labelled the latter a 'drunk' – and followed it with a series of articles characterizing the Cossacks as little more than 'plundering bandits' who were just as harmful to society as modern 'socialists, communists, and nihilists.'[46]

At that point, Kostomarov, who as recently as 1873 had used his influence to get Kulish appointed to the Archeographic Commission, turned sharply against his former friend and authored a piece, 'On the Cossacks,' in which he called Kulish a 'fanatical' opponent of Cossackdom. Kostomarov admitted that there was both good and bad in Cossack history but denied that Kulish had uncovered any new information about the Cossack revolts of old.

Kostomarov said that Kulish should judge the Cossacks by standards contemporary to them rather than by modern standards, and he defended the Cossacks' respect for family, their honour as rebels – the Serbs and Bulgarians were similarly rebelling against the oppressive Turks – and their civic creations, including the Hetman state and the renewed Orthodox church. He further argued that the unbiased Arab traveller Paul of Aleppo had greatly admired the orderliness of the Hetman state under Bohdan Khmelnytsky and that that state was recognized and respected by Moscow for two centuries. Would Moscow have approved of 'bandit' institutions? Kostomarov thought not. Moreover, Kulish's personal attack on Shevchenko reminded the historian of the Christian fanatics of the Middle Ages who persecuted all artists and scholars who happened to disagree with them. One would expect better from the 'former patriarch of the Ukrainophiles,' who had at one time truly respected and loved Shevchenko.[47]

Kulish did not deign to reply directly to Kostomarov's criticisms but continued his drift away from traditional Ukrainian Cossackophilism. Within a few years, he had published an amazing little booklet examining the whole question of Polish-Ukrainian relations. In the booklet, entitled *An Easter Egg for the Ruthenians and Poles for Easter, 1882* and published in Ukrainian in Galicia, Kulish offered his hand in friendship to the Poles with the understanding that both peoples had made serious mistakes in the past. He particularly blamed religious leaders, both Polish Catholic and Ukrainian Orthodox, for preaching hatred and intolerance of their rivals. Moreover, he scolded Ukrainian historians – without actually mentioning Kostomarov by name – for idealizing the Cossacks, for relying too heavily on biased clerical sources and slanted and untrustworthy folk material, and for generally denigrating the Polish role in Ukrainian history.[48]

Kostomarov replied immediately. In a long letter to the editor of the *European Herald*, he described Kulish's unexpected conversion to Polonophilism and stated that his honoured opponent had completely misunderstood the essence of Polish-Ukrainian relations. Kulish had a bookish concern with reconciling the intelligentsias of the two peoples, which was well enough, but the real problem was an economic one. Ukrainians did not hate the Poles or Catholics as Poles or Catholics, but they did feel a deep antagonism to being economically subjected to Polish landlords. The landlord-slave relationship had been the crux of the problem throughout history. Kulish was wrong, stated Kostomarov, when he said that landlord rule was the only option for the Ukrainian nation. The Cossacks had proved otherwise by setting up their own social and economic order. As for the historical sources, most of the Ukrainian chronicles had been written by Cossack laymen and not by priests or monks, and historical songs and other folk material remained a true reflection of the common people's view of itself. Kostomarov concluded that all religious denominations contain truly spiritual people on whom no blame can be laid, but that the same denominations were also subject to unhealthy political and economic influences. The true Christian should rise above those influences and stand always on the side of the oppressed.[49]

The admonitions had absolutely no effect on Kulish. In 1882, he published a booklet in Galicia entitled *Homestead Poetry* (*Khutorna poeziia*) which contained twenty-five poems and two essays. These creations once again proclaimed his love of high culture – especially Shakespeare, whom he intended to translate into Ukrainian – and the Ukrainian language, his disdain for Cossack violence, and his admiration for the state builders Peter the Great and Catherine the Great. At the same time, in a section devoted to his memories of the Kiev awakening of the 1840s, he distanced himself from Kostomarov and the illegal organization of the Cyril-Methodian Brotherhood, though he openly espoused some of its Panslavic and Christian principles. In general, Kulish was more and more taking on the garb of a cultivated conservative, retaining from his earlier beliefs only his love for the Ukrainian language and a belief in its full development as a vehicle of higher culture.[50]

Kostomarov could not remain silent at these grandiose assertions. He immediately penned a commentary on Kulish's work in which he attacked the project for the translation of Shakespeare into Ukrainian. First, he claimed, Ukrainian literature needed original creations, not translations; the common people – the only ones who still spoke Ukrainian – had no use at all for Shakespeare but only for simpler, more practical works. In Russia, the Ukrainian intelligentsia could already read Shakespeare in Russian; only in Galicia, therefore, would Kulish's Shakespeare be of any use. Second, while something might be said for Peter the Great, Catherine, who had suppressed both the Zaporozhian Cossacks and the Ukrainian Hetmanate, was indefensible; all she had done was replace those institutions with serfdom, social inequality, and the slavery of the common people. Kostomarov went on to attack Kulish's effort to distance himself from the Cyril-Methodian Brotherhood. He claimed that there was nothing illegal in the behaviour or intentions of the brethren and that in fact no actual organization had existed from which Kulish had to distance himself. Kostomarov concluded by noting that Kulish greatly admired the work of Kotliarevsky, who had begun the rebirth of Ukrainian literature in the early nineteenth century. But Kotliarevsky, argued Kostomarov, was very 'democratic' and used the language of the simple folk to create high literature. Instead of translating Shakespeare for the sake of the Galicians, said Kostomarov, Kulish would be better off imitating the methods of Kotliarevsky.[51]

These discussions with Kulish were not the only journalistic articles produced by Kostomarov during his last years. He continued to write both polemical articles on various historical questions and lengthy reviews of recent literature. Most of the material dealt with issues of Ukrainian culture. Such were his reviews of Antonovych's history of the Grand Duchy of Lithuania, Drahomanov's work on Ukrainian folk-song, and the first volumes of the new journal of Ukrainian studies *Kievan Antiquity* (*Kievskaia starina*), a publication of the kind Kostomarov had waited all his adult life to see. When a new issue of *Kievan Antiquity* arrived at his home, the elderly historian would immediately put aside all other work and go through it eagerly.[52] Moreover, he contributed to it as often as he could, and he corresponded with the editor, Teofan Lebedyntsev, whom he encouraged to try the censors by publishing as much material as possible in the Ukrainian language.[53]

Kostomarov also continued to write lengthy reviews of books on Russian history and to engage in polemics with figures such as his old foe the historian Koialovich. In particular, Kostomarov critiqued the last of Koialovich's major works, a history of Russian historiography, which he had written from an ultra-conservative Slavophile point of view. Kostomarov noted that Koialovich was still criticizing his writings on Russian federalism some twenty years after they had been written and was still unable to distinguish between the federal principle (which Kostomarov claimed existed in old Rus') and federal institutions (which Kostomarov made no claims for). Moreover, the Ukrainian historian continued, Koialovich was still accusing him of valuing Ukrainians above Russians when in fact in his essay 'Two Russian Nationalities' he had clearly stated that while Ukrainians were more friendly and poetic than Russians, the latter were more practical. Thus, each people had its own qualities. Finally, Kostomarov mocked the blind Slavophile hostility to both German and Pole and the Slavophile rejection of everything foreign. The Slavophiles even attacked the Western European enlightenment and tried to depict the liberation of the serfs as a return to old Russian principles, when it was clear that the Russian Orthodox church, fearing for its property, had rejected the reform at first and that Western European, especially French, ideas of personal freedom were the motivating force behind the emancipation.[54]

Indeed, Kostomarov's historical and literary interests remained quite broad. Viliam Berenshtam, who knew him well during these years, later recalled that Kostomarov could still recite entire verses of Mickiewicz by heart some forty years after he had first studied them and also had a good knowledge of Shakespeare, Byron, Schiller, and Goethe. He also followed developments in Russian literature, his favourites being Turgenev and Leo Tolstoy. He was especially drawn to Tolstoy's religious works, though he seemingly never shared the tendency of Tolstoy and Dostoevsky to reduce the future happiness of mankind solely to moral reform.[55]

Although during his last years Kostomarov spent more and more time writing historical polemics such as the critique of Koialovich and the commentaries on Kulish, he did not entirely abandon scholarly research and writing. In 1879, he began publishing the results of his research of the past several years on the successors of Hetman Yury Khmelnytsky. The work, on the stormiest and most confused period of Cossack Ukraine, he entitled *The Ruin* (*Ruina*) in imitation of popular lore about the era. Like his earlier works on Ukrainian history, *The Ruin* contained much action and plenty of stimulating dialogue. But Kostomarov was dealing with a confused period, and he was unable to maintain a clear story-line. Thus, while there are plenty of negative characters in *The Ruin*, including several Cossack leaders, there are no real heroes and few historical judgments, especially about Ukrainian independence. For example, on the one hand Kostomarov points to the 'tragic fate' of Ivan Vyhovsky, the hetman who tried in vain to gain 'federative liberty' (*federativnaia svoboda*) for Ukraine in union with Poland, only to be murdered by his Cossack rivals, and he clearly describes Hetman Petro Doroshenko's plan 'to make Ukraine an independent state' (*sdelat Ukrainu samobytnoi derzhavoi*) under the distant protection of the Ottoman sultan. On the other hand, he states that Vyhovsky never realized that there was no salvation 'for his beloved homeland' other than through firm loyalty to the Russian tsar, and he makes no final judgment on either Doroshenko's policy or his character. *The Ruin* is a complex but equivocal and highly restrained book about a chaotic but important period of Ukrainian history, a period in which several Cossack hetmans directly opposed Russian imperial interests.[56]

In 1882, having completed his work on *The Ruin*, Kostomorov published his last major historical work. This study was on the era of Hetman Ivan Mazepa, who had ended his long reign by allying himself with Charles XII and the Swedes during their invasion of the Russian Empire. Mazepa was traditionally a negative figure in Russian eyes, far more so than either Vyhovsky or Doroshenko, and Kostomarov dealt with the subject of his 'treason' with great delicacy. The historian managed to weave into his narrative a great deal of material about the oppression of Ukraine under the Muscovite yoke, about the heavy exactions of Muscovite governors and emissaries, about the burdens imposed by the presence of Peter the Great's army, which was billeted in Ukraine, about the unpopular, forced, and illegal service of the Ukrainian Cossacks outside their own country, and about what he called the Muscovites' 'most barbaric destruction' of Mazepa's capital at Baturyn along with all its inhabitants. Kostomarov also quoted Mazepa's own words to his followers upon their going over to the Swedes, his words to the Zaporozhian army, which later joined him, and his words to the Ukrainian population as a whole in his 'universals,' or proclamations. In all these documents, Mazepa referred to 'the rights and privileges of Ukraine' and of the Cossack Host, and in his speech to the army he declared, 'The time has come to throw off the hated yoke and make our Ukraine a free country and one that is completely independent (*ni ot kogo nezavisimoiu*).'

But Kostomarov's judgments are uniformly against Mazepa and the Ukrainian rebels. They are, in fact, suspiciously shrill. The Zaporozhians are not defenders of Ukrainian liberty but lovers of anarchy and 'haters of Moscow'; Mazepa is not a Ukrainian patriot but a vain aristocrat and a traitor to the tsar. 'As a historical personality,' wrote Kostomarov in his brief conclusion, 'Hetman Mazepa was not representative of any national ideal.'

He was an egoist in the full sense of the word. A Pole by education and habit, he went over to Little Russia and made himself a career there. He submitted to the Moscow authorities and, as we have seen, did not shrink from any kind of immorality. The truest description of his personality would be to say that it was a complete lie. He lied to everyone and deceived every-one: the Poles, the Little Russians, the tsar, and Charles. He was ready to do evil to anyone if it was to his profit or if it saved him from danger. He used the Little Russians' desire to preserve the autonomy of their land and their nationality and tricked the officers into believing that he had a plan for the independence of Ukraine. But at the same time ... he thought to put Ukraine under Poland ... In folk-songs and legends he was some kind of evil and inimical being; he was not even a man but an evil accursed power: 'Cursed Mazepa!'

Kostomarov ended with a surprising, indeed startling, change of subject. He concluded by stating that Mazepa should not be confused with the Ukrainian people, who did not like him and did not support him, and that it was incorrect to see 'the *Khokhol*-Mazepa' behind every manifesta-tion of modern Ukrainian feeling. Contemporary Ukrainophiles, in particular, should not be accused of disloyalty to the Russian state merely because they strove to protect Ukrainian individuality and the Ukrainian language. Ukrainians, he assured his readers, had 'an instinc-tive feeling of loyalty to that state.'[57]

Kostomarov's work on Mazepa and his followers was to be his final major contribution to Russian and Ukrainian historiography. It was the last work for which he did intensive research in the archives. He still had the strength, however, to compose a number of lesser pieces for which intensive eye work was not necessary. He particularly wanted to write a popular outline of Ukrainian history in the Ukrainian language, but he was never able to begin that task. He did start to write a histori-cal novel in Ukrainian about the times of Hetman Doroshenko and the ruin, entitled *The Chernihiv Girl* (*Chernigovka*); he completed the novel in Russian but kept the dialogues of the characters in the original Ukraini-an. Shortly afterwards, he completed and published a second novel in the same genre, entitled *Forty Years* (*Sorok let*).[58]

Throughout his later writings, Kostomarov remained true to the ideal and to the method he had espoused as a youth. His ideal was to write the history of the common man; his method was to investigate the ethnographic sources. In his final contribution to Ukrainian ethnography, entitled *The History of Cossackdom in the Monuments of South Russian Folk-song Creation*, he returned to the themes he had originally dealt with in the 1840s in his dissertation on the historical significance of Russian popular songs. This enormous work, which Kostomarov began by publishing in the journal *Russian Thought* (*Russkaia mysl*), was later to fill several hundred pages of closely packed Cyrillic type in his collected works. It treated Ukrainian folk-song in historical sequence but narrowed its historical significance somewhat from that which Kostomarov had allowed it in the 1840s. In the 1880s, Kostomarov thought historical songs useful primarily as offering a picture of the people's view of itself.[59] Kostomarov was also considerably more critical now in his approach to folk-song and was constantly on the lookout for fakes. In an 1880 letter to his old Kharkiv friend Oleksander Korsun, he referred to 'the pseudo-folk creations' and 'false chronicle tales' with which Sreznevsky had embellished his *Zaporozhian Antiquity*.[60]

Although his physical condition prevented Kostomarov from doing as much scholarly work as he wished to do – his great project of writing the history of the Ukrainian people through folk-song remained incomplete – he retained his enthusiasm for the revival of Ukrainian culture and kept his lively and humorous disposition. He would still often joke with Mordovets about public affairs and write him elaborate letters in Church Slavonic on various historical and literary subjects. On their walks together through the Russian capial, Kostomarov would still get carried away in learned discussion and, shedding his usual hypochondria – which worsened during his later years – would pay absolutely no attention to the weather but plunge on enthusiastically through rain and wind.[61]

His absent-mindedness eventually was to have serious consequences. In the fall of 1881, crossing a street in St Petersburg, he was hit by a wagon. His head was slightly injured and he was badly scratched, but he recovered quickly. Shortly afterwards, he was well enough to attend an archaeological congress in Tbilisi. The elderly historian was greatly honoured at the congress, where he happened upon many an old friend, such as the Georgian writer Akaki Tsereteli, who had frequented the evening parties of the St Petersburg *Hromada* during the 1860s.[62] The most emotional reunion, however, was with Mykola Hulak, his old friend and colleague from the Cyril-Methodian Brotherhood. The two men were greatly moved at meeting after so many long years and embraced and kissed oblivious of the crowds of people milling about them. The historian, it seems, never forgot Hulak's selfless attempt to take all responsibility for the brotherhood's illegal writings onto himself, and Hulak had apparently forgotten and forgiven all Kostomarov's weakness under arrest, and took pride in his friend's great success as a Russian historian and leader of the Ukrainian national movement.[63] At the same congress, a distinguished German scholar made a complimentary speech in Kostomarov's honour, and the Ukrainian received a warm ovation.

At the beginning of 1884, Kostomarov was involved in another traffic accident, again being hit by a wagon while crossing a St Petersburg street. This time, however, the consequences were much more serious. He was badly injured and was carried home unconscious. Shortly afterwards, he caught a heavy cold and began to have stomach trouble. His memory, which had always been superb, began to fade. He was able to spend the spring and summer at Alina's house in Didivtsi, but he never recovered his health. He returned to St Petersburg in the fall still suffering from chest and stomach problems. He was under constant medical attention and was forced to spend a great deal of time in bed. By the spring of 1885, he had still not recovered. After Easter, he could no longer get up from bed, and those around him knew he was dying. His family and friends took turns sitting by his bedside. On the evening of 4 April 1885, he took the last sacraments. On the morning of 7 April, he died, not having lost consciousness until the very end.

The distinguished Ukrainian historian was buried in St Petersburg, where he had lived and worked for most of his adult life. The entire Ukrainian community in the capital and Kostomarov's many Russian friends and colleagues attended his funeral. A long funeral procession made its way through the streets of the city to the Volkovsky Cemetery, where he was buried. Delegations came from Kiev, Kharkiv, Odessa, Poltava, and Kazan, and wreaths were received from the youth and villagers of Ukraine, from groups of female students, from the 'Siberians' (perhaps Ukrainians and others who had been exiled to Siberia), and from newspapers and journals and other institutions. A contingent of students carried the casket, and three generations of Ukrainians spoke over Kostomarov's grave. His dear old friend Danylo Mordovets gave the principal oration in Ukrainian, in which he declared that the historian's glory would last as long as there was a Ukraine.[64]

Kostomarov reached the pinnacle of his success during the last fifteen years of his life and then began his professional decline. In the early 1870s, he was still in his prime, writing innovative new works on the older period in the history of Southern Rus' and engaging in sharp polemics with Russian historians about the principal icons of Russian history. The polemics reached a high point when the Moscow historian Gennadi Karpov published a brochure attacking Kostomarov's ideas with unusual directness. Thereafter, the Ukrainian historian devoted himself more and more exclusively to specifically Ukrainian history and composed only the occasional essay on one or another aspect of north Russian or Muscovite history.

Changes in Kostomarov's daily way of life accompanied the shift in his professional interests. His eyes had been giving him more and more trouble with the passing of the years, and he grew less able to undertake serious archival work. Accordingly, he turned to writing reflective essays and polemical articles which would not require serious eye work. The first major fruit of that effort, a project which was to engage his attention repeatedly until the end of his life, was his history of Russia in life stories, which he dictated to Bilozersky's wife. (The final sections of this voluminous work were published only after the historian's death.) Second, Kostomarov wrote a number of important reviews and polemical articles examining recent historical literature, including various works by Antonovych, Drahomanov, Kulish, and Koialovich. Third, he produced three major works on Ukraine, two of them full histories – *The Ruin* and the work on Mazepa – and the third on ethnography – his unfinished book on historical songs about the Cossacks. Fourth, he continued to raise his pen in defence of the Ukrainian language, and he defended the 'Ukrainophile' cause. His position, he argued, was a normal and healthy one in view of the real needs of the people of Southern Rus', and it created no political danger to the unity of the Russian state.

In defending the Ukrainian position from the attacks of its reactionary opponents, Kostomarov was compelled to give a high profile to his loyalty to the Russian state and to take a blamelessly moderate position. He was, after all, writing in the very capital of the empire during a time of general political reaction. But not all Ukrainians agreed with his strategy. During Kostomarov's lifetime, the émigré Mykhailo Drahomanov and the Galician Volodymyr Barvinsky were critical of his moderation. Moreover, a few years later an openly political generation of Ukrainians within the empire itself accused Kostomarov of restricting the functioning of the Ukrainian language by means of what they called a 'theory of home use.' Such, for example, was the accusation of the Ukrainian literary critic Serhii Yefremov at the turn of the century.[65] Kostomarov's polemics in defence of the Ukrainian language, however, were written for publication in the Russian Empire in the nineteenth century and had to pass the test of the official censors of their day. There can be no doubt that the historian would have taken a very different position if he had been free to do so and if the political realities of his day had allowed. As it was, he favoured the full development of the Ukrainian language in Galicia, where such an undertaking was possible, and he suggested 'priorities' only with regard to the tasks of the Ukrainian intelligentsia in Russia. Thus, while Kostomarov might criticize Kulish's project for the translation of Shakespeare into Ukrainian in the 1880s, that did not mean he considered such a project undesirable in an ideal sense. It merely had to be put off into the future.

Similarly, the goals and methods of Kostomarov's historical work did not change significantly during his final years: he still aimed at writing the history of 'the common man,' and he still sought to find the necessary source material in the realm of ethnography. It was only his critical sense that had sharpened with the years. That, in part, explains his great admiration for the work of his younger contemporary Volodymyr Antonovych, whose goals and ideas did not substantially differ from his own.[66] Similarly, in 1881, when a young student of the Zaporozhian Cossacks named Dmytro Yavornytsky approached the elderly Kostomarov about the writing of a general history of the Zaporozhians, the latter advised him in the following words:

Before you write a history of the Zaporozhian Cossacks, travel about the whole Zaporozhian land. Then gather together the archival material about the Zaporozhians which is preserved in various places. Look at all the Zaporozhian artefacts collected in various museums, and furthermore, do not forget the Cossack dumas and historical songs, which live on in the memory of our elderly folk, and most of all [are kept alive] by the blind bandurists and kobzars.

The young historian took the advice to heart and during the next decade produced a major synthesis of Zaporozhian history which clearly derived much of its inspiration from the words of the author's venerable mentor.[67] It is quite clear, then, that Kostomarov's general approach to Ukrainian history did not falter with his death in 1885, but was taken up by a younger generation of Ukrainian historians, who were to develop it further.

The last years brought changes that nevertheless provided a consistency in Kostomarov's personal life. In 1875, he lost his beloved mother, but at the same time he gained a wife and children who would accompany him on the final stages of his life's journey and console and strengthen him in their own way. Before 1875, Kostomarov had spent many summers travelling abroad and in northern Russia; after that date, he retreated almost every summer to his wife's cottage at Didivtsi, whence he spent many happy hours exploring the Ukrainian countryside with learned friends and fellow cultural enthusiasts. During his early years he had written humorous letters in Church Slavonic to his friend Kulish; in the 1880s, he parted company with Kulish, but he continued to write fanciful letters in Church Slavonic, now to Danylo Mordovets.

In religion and morality too, Kostomarov remained fairly consistent. He never lost a certain humility and simplicity. 'There was absolutely no envy in Mykola Ivanovych,' wrote Bilozerska, who knew him through many long years, 'neither towards younger scholars nor towards those who had already succeeded in winning an honourable name for themselves in science. He could be just even with fierce enemies.' Bilozerska went on to say that he had two main character traits: 'abhorrence of all violence whatever the source, and a deep spirituality ... The Orthodox rites were full of poetry for him.'[68] None of those personal strengths diminished during his last years.

The biggest change in Kostomarov's personal life during his later years was in the state of his health. The historian had always been something of a hypochondriac and had constantly worried about his headaches, his nerves, and his general disposition. The worries had given rise to his particular affection for hydrotherapy, his swims in the Volga and the Neva, his visits to spas and bathing resorts in Western Europe, and so on. The weakness of his eyes had also long worried him.

In the 1870s, however, the health problems became very real. First, his eyes grew steadily worse, to the point where it became impossible for him to carry on with his usual reading and archival work. Accordingly, he turned to polemics, reflective essays, and historical novels. Second, he was struck down with typhoid, from which he never fully recovered. His terrible experience with the fever recalled to him his own mortality and left him infirm and unable to work normally or undertake any difficult travelling. But he struggled on and remained in good humour to the very end.

In general, Kostomarov's last years were moderately happy and fairly productive. His health had been badly broken, and he was unable to write the intensively researched histories to which he was accustomed, but he persevered, and with the support of his wife, her children, and his friends he managed to write and to publish until the end. In spite of numerous peronal tragedies and frequent political defeats, Kostomarov had lived a life of great faith and had achieved much. He died as he would have wished, surrounded by family and friends and still at work. He was indeed a lucky man.

9

Conclusions

From the time of his intellectual formation in the 1830s and 1840s to that of his death during the last quarter of the nineteenth century, Mykola Kostomarov held to certain ideals and values. Though the reigning tsar or the political climate changed several times during his life, and though Kostomarov did not hesitate to mould the form of his message to suit the times, he never altered his general course, and he remained true to most of the ideas he had espoused during his youth.

Kostomarov was raised by his father to respect the ideals of the rationalist enlightenment of the eighteenth century. But from the beginning those ideals were moderated and balanced by a warm feeling for religion which in all probability had been acquired from his mother. In university, Kostomarov wholeheartedly adopted the principles of the romantic movement led by the German philosopher Herder, which saw poetry as the fruit of the genius of the common people and the vernacular language as the vehicle and repository of the national spirit. Under the influence of Gogol's historical novel *Taras Bulba*, Maksymovych's collection of folk-songs, and Sreznevsky's tales of old Zaporozhia, Kostomarov absorbed the idea of nationality as defined by language and ethnicity and began to take an interest in the common Ukrainian people, among whom he had always lived but to whom he had hitherto given no thought. Kostomarov too began to collect folk-songs and, as soon as his Ukrainian was good enough, to write poetry and drama in that language. It was not long before he had embraced the idea of full literary development for the Ukrainian language and a corresponding development in Ukrainian political affairs. His first dissertation for the master's degree at the University of Kharkiv revealed not only a feeling for religion but also an intense interest in Ukrainian history and the fate of the common people; his second dissertation unequivocally posited the existence of the 'Little Russian' people as a 'nationality' separate from and equal to the 'Great Russian.' This represented a new emphasis, an innovative use of the word 'nationality' (*narodnost*), and a clear break with the unilinear, state-oriented, and monarchical scheme of his renowned predecessor Nikolai Karamzin.

Although Karamzin's patriotic Russian historical scheme was dominant during Kostomarov's youth, it was not without rivals. Competing ideas were privately expressed in certain circles among the 'Little Russian' nobility of Left-Bank Ukraine, who were for the most part descendants of the Cossack officer class of earlier days. These circles were made up of local patriots, Little Russian particularists, country gentlemen who cultivated the memory of their Cossack ancestors and were jealous of their traditional rights and privileges. Their heroes were the great Cossack hetmans, Bohdan Khmelnytsky and others, their historiography was best represented by the anonymous *History of the Ruthenians*, which for many years circulated in manuscript, and by the history of Mykola Markovych, which had been an instant success in Little Russia.

Kostomarov became aware of this Little Russian historical tradition during his early days in Kharkiv, but he formed his own ideas on entirely new principles. Those principles were ethnolinguistic and democratic. Thus, while he respected them, he did not rely primarily on the historic-rights claims of his Little Russian predecessors, played down the roles of their hetman heroes, and claimed to dismiss their historiographical legacy, which he believed to be somewhat fanciful.

Nevertheless, Kostomarov retained a great deal from his aristocratic forerunners. He too was a local patriot and he too was interested in Cossack history. Although he often denigrated them, he often cited as authorities the old Cossack chronicles and the history of Markovych. It might even be argued that Kostomarov merely changed the emphasis within a well-established historiographical tradition. Thus, the young Kostomarov spoke somewhat less about the legal-historical concept of 'Little Russia' (*Malorossiia*) and correspondingly more about the vaguer but more flexible ethnolinguistic concept of 'Southern Rus'' (*Iuzhnaia Rus'*).

Kostomarov's ideas about the nationality of what he called 'Southern Rus',' about its history and its political predicament under the Russian tsars, were further elaborated and defined during the period he spent in reading, researching, and teaching in Volhynia and Kiev. During the

Kiev period, he met and befriended Taras Shevchenko and Panteleimon Kulish, who each in his own way exercised a powerful influence on him. Both Shevchenko and Kulish were of purely Ukrainian ethnic background and had a more intimate knowledge of the Ukrainian language and culture than did Kostomarov. There can be no doubt that Shevchenko's stunning poetical compositions deepened Kostomarov's already considerable sympathy for the enserfed Ukrainian peasantry and that discussions with Kulish sharpened his appreciation of the intricacy and unique character of the history of Southern Rus'.

But the influence flowed in the opposite direction as well. By the time he was teaching at Saint Vladimir's University in Kiev, Kostomarov had studied Czech, Polish, and Serbian and was thoroughly acquainted with the national awakenings taking place among the various Slavic peoples of Eastern Europe. He was aware of the belief in language, folk poetry, and nationality shared by his fellow 'awakeners,' and, like many of them, he united his commitment to the Ukrainian revival to a general faith in the resurrection of all the Slavic peoples. When this disposition was linked with a commitment to the replacement of monarchy by nationality and to democracy and the cause of the common people, the result was the new Panslavic federalism expressed in the program of the Brotherhood of Saints Cyril and Methodius. Kostomarov's personal religious beliefs, moreover, coloured his ideas about Panslavic federalism in a way that heightened the idealism and sense of moral justification of the Cyril-Methodian circle. In his exalted view, republicanism created the high culture of ancient Greece and the achievements of ancient Israel, Christianity saved Rome from its emperors, and the Cossacks held high the torch of freedom before Polish kings and Muscovite tsars. The idea that 'Ukraine' – and in this case he used the name 'Ukraine' (*Ukraina*) rather than 'Little Russia' (*Malorossiia*) or 'Southern Rus'' (*Iuzhnaia Rus'*) – had preserved its ancient Slavic virtues and maintained its abhorrence of royal idolatry and would one day become 'an independent republic in a Slavic union' thus emerged. It was, as Mykhailo Hrushevsky, writing in Soviet Ukraine during the 1920s, was to stress, a 'revolutionary' message in religious clothing, and Kostomarov was nothing less than 'the precursor of a modern Ukraine.'[1]

However, these idealistic and far-reaching plans did not escape the notice of the authorities. Kostomarov and his comrades were betrayed and arrested. They were locked up in the Peter and Paul fortress in St Petersburg and subsequently sent into exile. Shevchenko, who received the stiffest sentence, was to have his health irreparably broken by his hard experiences in Central Asia. But Kostomarov suffered too. The shock of his betrayal by a man he had thought a trusted friend and of his sudden arrest on the eve of his wedding day was too great for his delicate and nervous personality, and psychologically he was completely crushed. He collapsed in confusion before his interrogators. For a time, he was forced to voice support for the tsar's rule and gratitude for the tsar's personal magnanimity, and in the psychological confusion of the moment he may even have been sincere. But the bout of obsequiousness did not last. The mild climate and leisurely way of life of his Saratov exile restored his health and once again strengthened his resolve.

In Saratov, Kostomarov was soon privately comparing Tsar Nicholas with the Roman tyrant Tiberius, completing his study of Bohdan Khmelnytsky and the Ukrainian struggle for independence, and beginning another on the revolt of Stenka Razin. In his study of Khmelnytsky, it was not the Cossack leader himself who emerged as hero but the Cossacks and common Ukrainian people. Kostomarov in fact was quite critical of Khmelnytsky when he saw him as failing to support the interests of the common people.

Bohdan Khmelnytsky was Kostomarov's masterpiece. It immediately established him as a major Russian historian and the foremost expert on Ukrainian history. He was to return to the book again and again during the course of his life, and he continually revised and improved it. Originally a highly colourful work written for the general public, it took on a more serious and scholarly character better appreciated by the specialists. Some later historians have judged that during his last years Kostomarov presented a more positive picture of Khmelnytsky's role in Ukrainian history and that in Kostomarov's later view the great Cossack hetman gained a fuller appreciation of Ukrainian 'statehood' and independence over the course of his struggle – an appreciation the historian shared.[2] But the general character of Kostomarov's thought remained unchanged: to the end of his career, he showed an abiding loyalty to the cause of the common people, continued to criticize the state structures which held the people in check, and viewed 'the state' itself in a largely negative light.

Similarly, in his book on Stenka Razin Kostomarov maintained that responsibility for the revolt clearly lay at the door of the state, which had treated its subjects so badly they were forced to rise in revolt. With a view to the tsar's censors, however, Kostomarov concealed that message behind vivid presentations of the cruelty, brutality, and senselessness of the revolt. After all, the tsar himself was to read the book before the historian could receive an academic position. Indeed, it is one of the ironies of history that Tsar Alexander II and the professional revolutionary Karl Marx both studied Kostomarov's book and critically evaluated his attitude towards popular revolt from their own viewpoints. To have satisfied both those very divergent points of view was no mean achievement indeed.[3]

Kostomarov's release from penal exile and his triumphant appointment to the University of St Petersburg opened a new chapter in his life and gave him an opportunity further to elaborate his views on Russian history. He did so in a whole series of important books and articles published in the 1860s and 1870s. His fundamental ideas on Russian history were formulated in detail in his volumes on Novgorod and the *veche* system and on Muscovy and the beginnings of central government, and in a series of essays in the Ukrainian journal *The Foundation*.

Several important themes emerged from all these writings. First, there was a clear division between older Russian history and recent Russian history – that is, between the period of Kievan Rus' and the subsequent *udel*, or feudal, period and the period which began with the Tatar conquest and the rise of Muscovy. The older period Kostomarov drew in bright colours as one of individual freedom, religious tolerance, and national concord. There were no firmly centralized state structures – there was, in fact, no real 'state' – but rather decentralized forms. The 'federal principle' was ascendant. The powers of the princes were limited, and the *veche*, or popular assembly, reigned supreme. That was true in 'Southern Rus'' and also in 'Northern Rus'.'

The Tatar conquest shattered this idyll of early Slavic happiness. As in Western Europe, so in Rus' did foreign conquest bring statehood, centralized government, and oppressive rulers. First, the Mongol khans and after them the Muscovite tsars established central rule in northeastern Rus'. The *veche* system and popular rule – Kostomarov did not dare to call it 'republicanism' out of fear of the government censors – lived on in Novgorod, which had always been especially close to Southern Rus' by virtue of certain old ethnic ties, but Muscovite aggression eventually put an end to the *veche* system of Novgorod, and the victory of statehood, central rule, and monarchy was assured. The new principles of autocratic rule, religious conformity, and national exclusiveness came to the fore. The old principles of individual liberty and religious and national tolerance disappeared from Muscovy and the lands it conquered.

But the old principles did not disappear elsewhere. They lived on in

Southern Rus', most notably among the Zaporozhian Cossack brotherhood and among the Don Cossacks, who lived in the borderlands of the Muscovite state. Razin's revolt was a flashback to the golden liberties of earlier times. The principal facts of Ukrainian history also gestured back to those times. Kostomarov's perception of the continuity between the history of ancient Southern Rus' and Cossack history was so strong that it became the basis of the second great pillar of his historical thought, the existence of 'two Russian nationalities.'

Kostomarov gave the essence of his interpretation of Russian history in his path-breaking essay 'Two Russian Nationalities' and in a series of related books and articles. According to that interpretation, the ancient Rus' polity (*russkii materik*) and the modern Russian people (*russkii narod*) had never been an undivided, organic whole, but had always been composed of more than one nationality (*narodnost*). Ancient tribal differences had taken hold in various principalities, and by the fifteenth century the Slavic tribes of the territory that later became Russia had been grouped into four: Novgorod, Muscovy, Lithuania (that is, Belorussia), and Rus' (that is, the later Little Russia or Ukraine). These four nationalities were later reduced to two: Northern Rus' and Southern Rus'. This clear distinction, which Kostomarov traced back to the most ancient times, was formed by geography and historical circumstances and was revealed in the different characters of the two nationalities in question. Thus, the Great Russians of the northeast were practical and materialistic with little poetry or love for nature, and the Little Russians of the south were impractical and poetic with a great love for nature. The Great Russians were stiff, formal, and intolerant, and that disposition gave rise to schisms and heretical sects of various sorts; by contrast, the 'South Russians' were flexible and tolerant, and sectarianism did not appear in their land. The Muscovites were suspicious of foreigners and sealed them off; but Southern Rus' was filled with Poles, Jews, and Tatars and for centuries tolerated them well. The Great Russian had autocracy, the village commune, and the ability to found a state; the Southerner had personal freedom and individual ownership but was weak in the management of a state. The Northerners were autocratic, the Southerners democratic. But both these peoples shared a common religion, a common book language, and, in the early days, a common ruling house, the house of Riurik. They needed each other and had qualities that complemented each other's. Together the two separate nationalities formed the Russian people, the Russian nation, and had made Russia what is was.

Kostomarov's interpretation of Russian history and understanding of Russian nationality was obviously different from the unilinear, official, state-centred, and monarchical scheme of his predecessor Karamzin and his contemporary Sergei Soloviev, both of whom concentrated on dynastic history and thought of nationality in terms of politics and religion rather than language and ethnicity. Nor are Kostomarov's ideas those of the twentieth century, which generally accepts the existence of three East Slavic nationalities which long lived within the boundaries of a single Russian, and for many years Soviet, state. Kostomarov concentrated entirely on what he and his contemporaries called 'Great Russian' and 'Little Russian' and largely ignored the 'Belorussian' people, whom he considered a subgroup of the 'Great Russian.' Moreover, Kostomarov's vocabulary, 'North Russian,' 'South Russian,' and so on, is somewhat foreign to the twentieth century, which generally has replaced those terms with the clear-cut 'Russian' and 'Ukrainian.' It seems clear, therefore, that Kostomarov's thought stands half-way between the unified monarchical-dynastic interpretations of Russian history and nationality postulated by Karamzin and his successors and the trifold ethnolinguistic interpretation of the history of the East Slavic peoples accepted by most twentieth-century historians. This trifold ethnolinguistic interpretation received its first clear formulation in a famous essay by Mykhailo Hrushevsky published in 1904.[4]

Furthermore, once Kostomarov had first opened the door to new thinking about the importance of nationality and ethnicity, his ideas were taken up by others, who developed them further. Accordingly, while the Ukrainian circles of his day accepted Kostomarov's ideological postulations as a positive statement of the real existence of a separate South Russian nationality, in the 1890s a younger generation of Ukrainian activists questioned the historian's apparently moderate political stance and his placing equal emphasis on the unity in Russian history and the complementarity of the two Russian nationalities on the one hand, and the divergence in history and the distinctiveness of the nationalities on the other. For example, when the Galician Ukrainian activist Oleksander Barvinsky questioned Kostomarov's friend and younger contemporary Volodymyr Antonovych about this equal emphasis, Antonovych replied that, given the political restraints on publishing in mid-nineteenth century Russia, Kostomarov had to include such passages simply to satisfy the censor. Antonovych told Barvinsky that had Kostomarov been free to do so, he most certainly would have written something quite different.[5] Similarly, later generations of Ukrainian historians, eager to stress the existence and separateness of the Ukrainian nationality throughout the ages, often reprinted Hrushevsky's essay of 1904 but almost completely ignored Kostomarov's innovative but less far-reaching statement of some forty years earlier.[6]

The reason for the neglect of Kostomarov's historiographical legacy is obvious: he did not develop the principle of nationality to its 'logical conclusion' but went only half-way down the road on which he had set out. In other words, Kostomarov did not completely abandon the old unilinear, state-centred, monarchical system elaborated by Karamzin and his successors. His conservatism was apparent, of course, in his constant emphasis on the unity as well as the divergence in Russian history, but also in his belief that 'South Russians' were incapable of carrying on an active political life and had to give in to the practical, state-oriented 'North Russians'; it was especially apparent in his last works, on the history of the Cossacks after 1654, in which he displayed no faith in the political potential of the Ukrainian nationality and severely criticized all the Ukrainian leaders who had dared to challenge the Russian state. Thus, wrote Hrushevsky of his illustrious predecessor, 'the political struggle in Ukraine at the end of the seventeenth and in the eighteenth century lost all rationale, all significance, and all content in the way he presented it.'[7]

Kostomarov's reluctance to break completely with the old state-oriented, dynastic view of Russian history shows most clearly in his last work, on Russian history in life stories. In this synthesis of Russian history to the time of Catherine the Great, Kostomarov seems to have abandoned almost completely the theoretical position he had taken in his dissertation on Russian popular poetry and in his essay on the two Russian nationalities. He does not divide Russian history into two parallel streams with two parallel sets of life stories, one for the north, beginning, perhaps, with the Tatar conquest and ending with the Russian emperors of the eighteenth century, and one for the south, beginning with Grand Prince Vladimir and ending with the political absorption of Ukraine into the Muscovite state at the time of Mazepa. Instead, he freely mixes northern and southern figures and arranges them chronologically; his only clear periodization is dynastic, a division into the house of Prince Vladimir and the house of Romanov. Moreover, the sharp criticism of official Russian heroes which had characterized his earlier work is somewhat muted, and the work as a whole lacks the oppositional edge of some of the earlier essays. Most of the biographies, of course, are of princes and rulers. Thus, in spite of his double commitment to the cause of the common people and the cause of the Ukrainian national awakening, Kostomarov largely abandoned his general theoretical position of the 1840s and 1860s and retreated to the comfort and security of the official scheme of Russian history, which was generally accepted in his day and in no way directly challenged the legitimacy of the Russian state or the authority of its conservative protagonists.

But the conservative streak in Kostomarov's historiographical legacy was not unequivocal. He remained critical of the general direction of Russian political development and suspicious of Westernizing historical concepts introduced by official historians like N.G. Ustrialov, Mikhail Pogodin, and Sergei Soloviev. His partial rejection of the values of the Westernized governing class was accompanied by an emphasis on Russia's early Slavic heritage. That would have allied him with the conservative Moscow Slavophiles, especially Konstantin Aksakov, whom he somewhat admired, had it not been for his shift in emphasis from the old Muscovy, which they idealized and he disliked, to Kievan Rus', which they ignored and he promoted. It was freedom-loving, tolerant, and cosmopolitan Kievan Rus' which Kostomarov upheld as the ideal, and his position marked him off clearly both from liberal Westernizers who rejected Russia's past for the sake of 'progress' and from the Moscow Slavophiles, who fully accepted that part of Russia's past which Kostomarov considered dark and oppressive. He published in 'liberal' journals and applauded the emancipatory reforms of Alexander II but remained critical of fashionable liberalism and Westernizers; he espoused Panslavism and welcomed the Slavophile replacement of state history and diplomatics with a new focus on the history of the Russian people but sharply criticized the early Moscow Slavophiles and their even more reactionary successors in the Slavic Benevolent Societies. He was neither Westernizer nor Slavophile but shared some ideas with the first camp and other ideas with the second. He was most certainly his own man.

Kostomarov's unique position in Russian intellectual history is manifest in his original contribution to Russian and Ukrainian historiography. Not only was his emphasis on the history of the common people alien to the state school and more serious than that of the Slavophile school, but he also opened up entirely new areas to historical inquiry. He was the first to write specialist monographs on the *veche* in Russian history, on the life of Bohdan Khmelnytsky, and on Stenka Razin and popular revolts in general. Having postulated the novel idea that there existed two separate Russian 'nationalities,' he was the first to formulate clearly the contemporary problem of Russian-Ukrainian relations; that is, he boldly stepped beyond the traditional demand of the Ukrainian landed nobility for restoration of their rights and liberties under the Treaty of Pereiaslav (1654), by which the Hetmanate was joined to Muscovy, and entered the modern world of linguistic and ethnic distinctions and claims. Moreover, as his Ukrainian successor Antonovych was later to explain, he was the first systematically to gather archival sources for the history of Ukraine and on the basis of primary material write a scholarly history of the Cossack era. With regard to Ukrainian history, at least, before him was chaos, after him came order.[8]

But it was not mainly Kostomarov's innovative archival work that made him famous. Rather it was his brilliant narrative style, his exciting presentation, and his use of local colour and anecdote based on a close reading of chronicle and contemporary source to produce vivid and believable images of historical personalities and events. Simply put, it was his artistry as a writer that made him a household name. By reason of his artistry, Antonovych likened him to the famous French romantic historian Augustin Thierry, and the comparison was not inappropriate.[9] Kostomarov had, in the words of his younger contemporary D.A. Korsakov, 'an unusually lively relationship with Russian history. It was not for him some sort of abstract philosophical ideal to be resolved, nor was it simply the gathering of chronicle or archival materials.' Korsakov went on to say: 'Russian history was for him a contemporary reality emerging from the depth of the centuries. He lived through the events which he had gotten from the sources in the very same way that he lived through contemporary political, social, and intellectual life.'[10] V.O. Kliuchevsky, a student of Soloviev and the last great pre-revolutionary synthesizer of the state school, wrote of Kostomarov, 'For him, Russian history was a museum, an ample collection of rare and commonplace objects.'

He passed by the latter with indifference and lingered by the former long and attentively. A short time later, the reading public would receive an excellent monograph in one or two volumes and would read it through with delight and take the first opportunity to marvel how and of what materials such an attractive story was composed. In that way, a series of historical images taken from the historical past and unbreakably bound with it by the author was created. We say, this is a Kostomarov Ivan the Terrible, a Kostomarov Bohdan Khmelnytsky, a Kostomarov Stefan Razin, just as they said, this is Antokolsky's Ivan the Terrible, this is Ge's Peter the Great, and so on. ... We need living portraits and Kostomarov gives us such portraits. Kostomarov has related all this, all that was dramatic in our history, especially in the history of our south-western borderlands. He has related it as a real master storyteller who experiences a deep satisfaction from his own tale.[11]

Kostomarov was indeed a historian-artist and a master painter of icons. Moreover, in painting his colourful icons, icons of evil Muscovite tsars, of hesitant Ukrainian hetmans, and of popular heroes both Russian and Ukrainian, Kostomarov deliberately destroyed the official icons that had preceded his, shifted the focus of Russian history from the rulers to the ruled, and in the process created a new field, 'South Russian' or Ukrainian history, as a legitimate specialty in and of itself.

There remained, of course, several problems with Kostomarov's methodology. First, his search for the 'popular spirit' and the personification of this supposed spirit in certain figures had an element of the unreal, the metaphysical, the mystical. Second, ethnography and folklore were useful but inadequate tools for the tasks he had set himself; that is, he lacked a firm sociological base and was not methodical in his reconstruction of events over long periods of time. In other words, his histories remained unconnected, at least in part, and consequently lacked overall movement and direction. His were isolated portraits, without a past and without a future. 'We do not find in him,' concluded Hrushevsky, 'a clear construction of the social-historical process ... We need historians, not icon painters.'[12]

If Kostomarov's skill as a painter of historical portraits was both a gift and a drawback, so were other of his qualities. For example, he worked always from primary sources, both chronicles and archival documents. On the one hand, this practice represented a tremendous advance over his predecessors, especially his Little Russian predecessors – Dmytro Bantysh-Kamensky, whose archival base was quite limited, and Mykola Markovych, who relied heavily on the fanciful *History of the Ruthenians*. Kostomarov's archival work threw new light on many areas of Russian and Ukrainian history and greatly increased the factual base for further studies in those fields. On the other hand, by burying himself in the primary sources, Kostomarov was apt to lose a wider perspective, and in some areas he fell behind current research. That was particularly true in his ethnographic studies, which ignored the significant theoretical advances of his time, especially Grimm's comparative approach, and remained wedded to the conceptions of the 1830s.[13]

Similarly, while Kostomarov's quest for fresh primary sources, which took him to renewed searches of the Moscow archives and to the investigation and study of previously unexamined Polish material, represented a step forward, it was a somewhat faltering step. For his use of Polish sources was confined largely to published chronicles, memoirs, and histories, which left him only with the old Muscovite archives for a more thorough investigation of the contemporary documents. Thus, in many ways, concluded Hrushevsky, in spite of marked ideological differences with his conservative, Karamzinite predecessor Bantysh-Kamensky, Kostomarov looked at the same papers in Moscow as he, and arrived at the same conclusions in his work on Ukrainian Cossack history; both of them viewed unsympathetically the struggle for autonomy by the Ukrainian political and military leadership and uncritically accepted the claim of the Moscow scribes that the common people did not support that struggle.[14] Kostomarov's rejection of the supposedly class-bound 'estate' or local patriotism of the Ukrainian hetmans of the eighteenth century and their historiographical spokesmen of the very early nineteenth century – the anonymous author of the *History of the Ruthenians*, Markovych, and others – has been seen as a step backward by some intellectual supporters of full Ukrainian independence during the twentieth century.[15]

But the entire question of Kostomarov's severe treatment of Russian and Ukrainian political leaders remains unresolved. Was his unsympathetic treatment merely the reflection, even the logical conclusion, of his primary commitment to the cause of the common people, whom he invariably saw as severely oppressed by the state and its ruling classes? In other words, was it an extrapolation of a basically anarchistic attitude towards state and society? That is, in fact, the simplest and most universally applicable answer. But several caveats must be mentioned.

First, there remains the real possibility that Kostomarov amended the content of his historical portraits in order to get his writings passed by the tsarist censors. Thus, for example, his severe treatment of Ukrainian leaders such as Khmelnytsky and Mazepa may have been a tactic, the object of which was to get controversial Ukrainian subject matter legally published; he almost admitted as much in his letter to Ivan Aksakov published in 1906. If so, then Kostomarov may not have had as negative a view of Ukrainian statehood as is sometimes suggested, and the model of Kostomarov as fundamentally an 'anarchist' breaks down. Second, Kostomarov may have drawn his harsh portraits of Ivan the Terrible and other Muscovite leaders partly out of an ethnic bias against his 'Great Russian' compatriots. (That was, in fact, the accusation lodged against him in his own lifetime by a great number of his more unscrupulous Russian critics.) If there is any merit at all in this argument, then the model of Kostomarov as anarchist once again begins to break down. Moreover, when put to the test of real action in the political arena, Kostomarov's social thought turns out to be very moderate indeed.

Kostomarov, in truth, was not easily roused to participation in the confusing turmoil of active political debate. Although it is clear from his historical polemics that he was an opponent of autocracy, of a privileged nobility, and of a disenfranchised and enserfed peasantry, he never directly entered the political arena to condemn those long-standing Russian institutions. Having learned the consequences of illicit political/cultural activity in an authoritarian state during the 1840s, he thereafter carefully limited himself to historical controversies which could be discussed more or less freely under the conservative regimes of Nicholas I and his successors. Of course, an attentive reading of his major works clearly reveals his unbending commitment to the welfare of the common people and his admiration for the liberty and equality which he believed were represented in the *veche* system of old Rus' and the Zaporozhian Cossack brotherhood of old Ukraine. But even those positive values had to be hidden to a degree behind a veneer of Aesopian language meant to mislead and placate the authorities.

It was, in fact, only the fate of Kostomarov's beloved 'Southern Rus'' that roused him from his extreme caution and drew him into the dangerous waters of active political debate. But even the political debate was carried on largely within the narrow parameters of legal public discourse in the pages of officially sanctioned journals and newspapers published in St Petersburg, Moscow, and Kiev. Thus, the mature Kostomarov refrained from openly proposing any form of federal or republican reorganization of the Russian Empire – ideas that were basic to the Cyril-Methodian program – and limited himself to polemics affirming the existence of the 'Little Russian' nationality, the dignity and independence of the Ukrainian language, and the need for Ukrainian-language schools. His habit of caution in political debate became so ingrained, moreover, that even in his widely read letter to Alexander Herzen, which was not subject to the emasculating red slashes of the censor, Kostomarov's demands remained extremely modest. Certainly, he welcomed, was even overjoyed at, Herzen's admission of the possibility of Ukrainian independence and his proposals concerning a democratic Slavic federation, but in spite of his obvious solidarity with these far-off theoretical goals he limited his practical demands to the abolition of special privileges for the nobility and the establishment of government-supported Ukrainian-language schools. Thus, if the Russian tsar were willing to transform himself into a ruler of free people and cease being, in the historian's own words, 'the voracious lord of a Tatar-German Muscovy,' Kostomarov was willing to continue to live under his sceptre. In that way, the historian's theoretical radicalism, as expressed in his *Books of the Genesis of the Ukrainian People* and in his fiery polemics on various historical questions, was transformed into a modest political program which he believed was not beyond the realm of practical implementation by the conservative bureaucrats of nineteenth-century Russia. During the 1860s and most of the 1870s, his moderate approach to practical politics gained the wholehearted support of the historian's fellow 'Ukrainophiles,' and to the beginning of the 1880s Kostomarov remained the unrivalled ideological leader of what later came to be called 'the Ukrainian national movement.'

During the very early phase of the movement, the national awakening of the 1840s, there seems to have been a general consensus among the Cyril-Methodians on certain basic points. All the members, including Shevchenko and Kulish, seem to have shared to some extent the national and the libertarian, egalitarian, Panslavic, and religious ideals expressed in *Books of the Genesis of the Ukrainian People*; all of them looked for inspiration to the stormy events of seventeenth-century Ukraine. However, as the years rolled by and the contributors to the national awakening slowly grew in number, minor differences of emphasis among the original Cyril-Methodians took on a more serious character. Shevchenko, one critic has argued, unlike Kostomarov abandoned the ideals of seventeenth-century Ukraine in favour of universal principles. And by the late 1870s, furthermore, Kostomarov and Kulish were openly quarrelling over the Polish role in Ukrainian history.[16]

Whereas Kulish now defended the Polish gentry and their emulators, the Cossack officer class which held power during the period of the Hetmanate – even accusing Kostomarov of a general prejudice against the Poles – Kostomarov remained true to his earlier ideals and continued to defend the anti-Polish Cossack rebels and the common people he believed they represented. His historical judgements of the Poles were severe, his polemics against them sharp. The tone of his anti-Polish rhetoric was so acrimonious, in fact, that during the period before 1863 it shocked and alienated several of his more liberal Russian colleagues.

But that did not mean Kostomarov's seeming antagonism towards the Poles was rooted in simple ethnic or religious prejudice. His major disagreements with the Poles were political, economic, and historical: he was fundamentally opposed to the landlord-serf relationship which characterized Polish-Ukrainian relations in his time and which had its origins in the social structure of the old Polish-Lithuanian Commonwealth. He saw in the Polish national movement and the insurrection of 1863 an attempt to resurrect that state and include in it the Ukrainian lands west of the Dnieper. That he would never accept.

He did, however, recognize the achievements of Polish writers and cultural figures in his time and indeed was profoundly influenced by them. Thus, while still a very young man, Kostomarov studied the Polish language assiduously, read Polish literature, fell in love with Mickiewicz, and adopted and moulded many of the poet's religious and political ideas to fit the Ukrainian context. (It might even be argued that Kostomarov's own life work and some of his historical ideas – such as his positive notion of Slavic antiquity – paralleled those of the radical Polish historian Joachim Lelewel, although there is little evidence of a direct influence in Kostomarov's autobiographical writings.) In later life, Kostomarov cultivated contacts with Polish colleagues, befriended Polish exiles, consorted with Polish figures in St Petersburg, spoke Polish in Vilnius on the eve of the insurrection, wrote Polish history, and looked kindly upon the hard life of the Polish country folk. He knew Polish culture far more intimately than did his liberal Russian critics, and he did not share the blind hostility to Catholicism and to everything Polish that was propagated by reactionary Russian Slavophiles like his long-standing antagonist M.I. Koialovich. His beloved Alina had strong Polish roots.

Kostomarov's relations with the Jews were somewhat less complex. He saw the Jews as the willing collaborators of the Poles in the oppression of the Ukrainian people during the period of the Commonwealth and, when he visited Right-Bank Ukraine in the 1840s, formed the impression that their role had hardly changed over the years. He had little or no interest in Jewish cultural and religious life, believed that certain Jewish sects may have used Christian blood in their religious rites, mocked Jewish objections to the use of the term *Zhyd* in Ukrainian, and seems to have had no sustained personal contact with Jews. His letters to Kharkiv from Volhynia, which, it is true, were written in a very black mood, abound in simple prejudice.

Nevertheless, Kostomarov's antagonism towards the Jews, like his antagonism towards the Poles, had its limits. Once again, his disagreement with the group in question was not so much ethnic or religious as it was economic and historical. He believed that if the Jews would give up what he called their economic monopoly within the Pale of Settlement, they should be given full civil rights. In 1858, he even signed a protest against the anti-Jewish attacks of one of the more reactionary Russian periodicals. Moreover, he objected in principle to all theories of racial superiority and firmly rejected the Eurocentric premises of his Polish-Ukrainian colleague Franciszek Duchiński. Kostomarov had faults, and prejudice against the Jews was one of them, but he was not anti-Semitic in the modern sense of the term.

Kostomarov's idiosyncratic attitudes towards Poles and Jews, though noteworthy, do not form the most enduring part of his historiographical legacy. Far more important and influential were his fundamental ideas about Russian and Ukrainian history. His critique of the unilinear, Karamzinite scheme of Russian history was later expanded and elaborated by others so that the idea of three distinct East Slavic nationalities could finally emerge; his stereotypes of Russian formalism and Ukrainian freedom had a power that even today has not been lost completely. Moreover, Kostomarov's novel interpretation of the unique character of Kievan Rus' was unhesitatingly accepted by Soloviev's pupil Kliuchevsky and through him came to exercise a determining influence on how almost all modern Russians view the early medieval Russian legacy. (The same ideas only reinforced Ukrainian notions about the uniqueness of their historical legacy.) Similarly, Kostomarov's ideas about the negative influence of the Tatar conquest were to a greater or lesser extent absorbed into the general historiographical tradition of modern Russia, and even casual observers do not hesitate to remark that Russia's 'backwardness' and its tradition of autocratic rule have something to do with its Tatar heritage. Kostomarov's 'ethnographic' explanations, if that is what they should be called, had limitations and in later years were increasingly replaced by more sophisticated social and economic explanations – Novgorod's commercial activity, for example, replaced the southern ethnic ties identified by Kostomarov as the accepted 'cause' of the city's democratic constitution – but many of his theories, especially the fundamental one, of the separate existence of an independent Ukrainian nationality, are alive today. His penchant for bold hypothesis was not without lasting fruit.

Kostomarov's work as a poet, a dramatist, and a writer of fiction shines less brightly than does his work as a historian. Not originating from central Ukraine and not having a native fluency in the Ukrainian language, he could never compete with a Shevchenko or a Kulish.

Nevertheless, his contribution to Ukrainian literature was real and important. His poetry, his two plays, and his several dramatic fragments published in 1838 and 1839 were original and pioneering and went well beyond the imitation of folk-song so common at that time by injecting a historian's conscience and a historian's sense of reality into the whole field of Ukrainian belles-lettres. Moreover, at this early date, enthralled by the renaissance of the Slavic peoples, Kostomarov could not help but touch upon general human themes, and he enriched Ukrainian literature with translations from Byron, Mickiewicz, and the Královédvorský manuscript. But reprimanded by the Russian authorities for his efforts and mocked by Kulish and others, he quickly gave up writing in Ukrainian, and those works remained, as it were, the 'sins of his youth.'

In the Saratov years and in later life, Kostomarov turned to writing fiction in Russian. His novel on the rebellion of Stenka Razin, *The Son*, was admired by the political left, and his story of the time of Ivan the Terrible, *Kudeiar*, was defended by patriotic Ukrainians, but the two books never won much praise from the critics. Literary historians like P.N. Polevoi and Alexander Brückner considered the first somewhat arid and the second much too fanciful.[17] Kostomarov would be a footnote in Russian literary history were it not for the fact of his enormous prestige as a historian, his pioneering position in Ukrainian letters, and his continuing popularity among the general reading public.

Finally, there is the drama of Kostomarov's personal life. He led a partly charmed, partly tortured youth that left him nervous and unstable but with a warm feeling for religion that strengthened him in times of difficulty and remained with him throughout his life. He sought a certain ideal of feminine beauty and thought that he had found it in his beloved Alina, only to lose it on the eve of his wedding night. The loss almost broke him, but he persevered and eventually recovered. Afterwards, he was attracted to various women from time to time and was able to find friendship and solace of other kinds, but it was to be many long years before he was reunited with his first and only true love.

A devoted mother, good friends, and intellectual endeavours took the place of his missing wife. Tatiana Petrivna brought stability and order to his home life, and he was dependent on her to the time of her death. But it was with his close circle of personal friends that he really shone. Whether with Shevchenko and Kulish in Kiev; Pypin, Chernyshevsky, and Mordovets and his wife in Saratov; or Bilozersky, Mordovets, Kozhanchikov, Ge, Kraevsky, and Father Opatovych in St Petersburg,

Kostomarov revealed himself an interesting, lively, good-humoured, enthusiastic friend who brought good cheer as well as lofty ideals into the lives of those around him. With such friends, he not only shared adventures of the mind but also indulged his great love for music and art. Kostomarov attended the opera frequently and enjoyed visiting art galleries and museums. In spite of his debunking of the hero Ivan Susanin, he heard Glinka's opera many times with great pleasure. He even loved animals and in later years took to visiting the St Petersburg Zoo. He had no personal enemies.

His close friends were a great solace to Kostomarov, who suffered enormously both from the loss of Alina and from repeated buffeting by unsympathetic government officials who would not allow him to teach where he wished, by unfeeling censors who mutilated some of his best work, and by cruel publicists who savagely attacked him in the press. He suffered from recurring bouts of depression, but with the help of Mordovets and others he came out of them unharmed. This pattern continued for many long years, until he was finally and completely reunited with the girl of his dreams, now become the middle-aged mother of three. At this point, rather late in life, the nervous, idiosyncratic bachelor finally began to disappear and the devoted father and family man emerged.

Throughout his life, Kostomarov was sustained by a deep Christian faith and a profound commitment to the cause of the common Ukrainian people, from whom, in part, he came. His Christian faith was a truly spiritual one, steeped in the oriental tradition but unsullied by excessive sectarianism or hostility to other traditions. His commitment to the common Ukrainian people was neither over-abstract nor over-intellectual but moderated by repeated personal contact with the people themselves. He had prejudices, and several of his bold hypotheses, both historical and ethnographic, were clearly wide of the mark, but much of his work has stood the test of time and has shaped our thinking and feeling about contemporary Russia and modern Ukraine. Mykola Kostomarov was born, educated, formed, and first arrested in Ukraine; was jailed, taught, wrote, and lived many long years in St Petersburg, Russia; and travelled across the Slavic world and throughout Western Europe. Today, however, he must be considered one of the creators of the modern world.

Notes

Introduction

1 There is an analysis of these materials in Iu.A. Pinchuk, 'Dozhovtneva i radianska istoriohrafiia pro M.I. Kostomarova iak istoryka,' *Istoriohrafichni doslidzhennia v Ukrainskii RSR*, no. 4 (Kiev, 1971), 124–50, especially 133. The more important essays sympathetic to Kostomarov were written by men like V.I. Semevsky, A. Markevich, V.B. Antonovych, A.N. Pypin, and others cited in the present work. Unfriendly treatments were by P.N. Polevoi and others. Of the numerous memoirists treating of Kostomarov, his close friend Danylo Mordovets (Mordovtsev) was both the most prolific and the most important.

2 The most important of these previously little known documents was the full text of *Books of the Genesis of the Ukrainian People* (*Knyhy buttia ukrainskoho narodu*), which was discovered by the Ukrainian literary historian Pavlo Zaitsev and immediately published in the short-lived Ukrainian journal *Nashe mynule*, no. 1 (1918), 7–35. This work is now a bibliographical rarity, but on its basis the text of the *Books* has been reprinted many times. I have used the editions cited in the bibliography. At this point, mention should also be made of a rather full collection of documents on the Cyril-Methodians which the Ukrainian historian Mykhailo Hrushevsky somehow managed to get published in Kiev in 1915, a year in which censorship restrictions were still rather tight. See his 'Materiialy do istorii Kyrylo-Metodiivskoho Bratstva,' in *Zbirnyk pamiaty Tarasa Shevchenka* (Kiev, 1915), pp. 1–157. These documents, together with the authentic texts of the *Books*, were reprinted much later in an extensive collection under the title *Kyrylo-Mefodiivske Tovarystvo*, 3 vols (Kiev: Naukova Dumka, 1990–1). The publication of the latter collection, of course, was made possible by the Gorbachev reforms.

3 M.A. Rubach, 'Federalisticheskie teorii v istorii Rossii,' in *Russkaia istori-cheskaia literatura v klassovom osveshchenii*, ed. M.N. Pokrovsky, vol. II (Moscow: Izdatelstvo Kommunisticheskoi Akademii, 1930), pp. 3–120.

4 N.L. Rubinshtein, *Russkaia istoriografiia* (Moscow: Gospolizdat, 1941), pp. 423–40.

5 *Ocherki istorii istoricheskoi nauki v SSSR*, ed. M.V. Nechkina et al., vol. II (Moscow: Akademiia Nauk SSSR, 1960), pp. 129–46.

6 Ivan M. Myhul, 'M.I. Kostomarov in Recent Soviet Ukrainian Historiography,' *Laurentian University Review*, X, 1 (1977), 85–95.

7 V.E. Illeritsky and I.A. Kudriavtsev, *Istoriografiia istorii SSSR* (Moscow: Vysshaia shkola, 1971), p. 244.

8 A.N. Tsamutali, *Borba techenii v russkoi istoriografii vo vtoroi polovine XIX veka* (Leningrad: Nauka, 1977), pp. 129–33. Tsamutali did note, however, that, in his work on Bohdan Khmelnytsky, unlike his conservative rival Sergei Soloviev (1820–79) Kostomarov examined social as well as religious factors, and that later on Kliuchevsky further developed some of Kostomarov's ideas.

9 Iu.A. Pinchuk, *Istoricheskie vzgliady N.I. Kostomarova: Kriticheskii ocherk* (Kiev: Naukova Dumka, 1984). Pinchuk's book gave rise to a fairly substantial review article by R.P. Ivanova, 'Knyha pro M.I. Kostomarova,' *Ukrainskyi istorychnyi zhurnal*, no. 1 (1985), 144–7.

10 Volodymyr Miiakovsky, 'Shevchenko i Kostomarov,' *Shevchenko*, no. 7 (New York: UVAN in the USA, 1958), 16–30; 'Knyha pro Kyrylo-Metodiivske Bratstvo,' *Suchasnist*, no. 3 (Munich, 1963), 85–96.

11 Dmytro Doroshenko, 'A Survey of Ukrainian Historiography,' *Annals of the Ukrainian Academy of Arts and Sciences in the U.S.*, V–VI, no. 4 (New York, 1957), 132–45. Doroshenko's treatment was considerably more serious and more extensive than the parallel article on Kostomarov in Anatole G. Mazour, *Modern Russian Historiography*, 2nd ed. (Princeton: Van Nostrand, 1958), pp. 152–7.

12 Dennis Papazian, 'Nicholas Ivanovich Kostomarov: Russian Historian, Ukrainian Nationalist, Slavic Federalist,' unpublished Ph.D. diss. (University of Michigan, 1966); 'N.I. Kostomarov and the Cyril-Methodian Ideology,' *Russian Review*, XXIX, 1 (1970), 59–73.

13 A.G. Bespalova, 'Kostomarov, Nikolai Ivanovich,' in *Modern Encyclopedia of Russian and Soviet History*, vol. XVII (Gulf Breeze, Fla. 1980), pp. 233–5.

14 G.S.N. Luckyj, *Between Gogol' and Ševčenko: Polarity in the Literary Ukraine, 1798–1847* (Munich: Wilhelm Fink, 1971); *Panteleimon Kulish: A Sketch of His Life and Times* (Boulder: East European Monographs, 1983); *Young Ukraine: The Brotherhood of Saints Cyril and Methodius, 1845–1847* (Ottawa–

Paris: University of Ottawa Press, 1991); ed. and trans., Pavlo Zaitsev, *Taras Shevchenko: A Life* (Toronto: University of Toronto Press, 1988).

15 N.I. Kostomarov, *Istoricheskie proizvedeniia. Avtobiografiia*, ed. V.A. Zamlinsky (Kiev: Izdatelstvo pri Kievskom Gosudarstvennom Universitete, 1989) contained several portraits of figures from Ukrainian history, while N.I. Kostomarov, *Russkaia istoriia v zhizneopisaniiakh ee glavneishikh deiatelei* (Moscow: Mysl, 1991) focused on Muscovite and Russian history. A photoreprint of the full work under the same title appeared in Moscow in 1990–1 and was published by 'Kniga.' For translations into Ukrainian, see Mykola Kostomarov, *Istoriia Ukrainy v zhytiepysiakh vyznachniishykh iei diiachiv*, trans. O. Barvinsky (Lviv: Naukove Tovarystvo im. Shevchenka, 1918; reprinted Kiev: Ukraina, 1991), and *Haleriia portretiv*, trans. Mykola Illiash (Kiev: Veselka, 1993).

16 V.A. Zamlinsky, 'Zhizn i tvorchestvo N.I. Kostomarova,' *Voprosy istorii*, no. 1 (Moscow, 1991), 234–40; Iu.A. Pinchuk, 'Do otsinky naukovoi i hromadskoi diialnosti M.I. Kostomarova,' *Ukrainskyi istorychnyi zhurnal*, no. 3 (Kiev, 1992), 3–11.

17 Iu.A. Pinchuk, *Mykola Ivanovych Kostomarov, 1817–1885* (Kiev: Naukova Dumka, 1992). 233 pp.

Chapter 1: Youth and Education

1 N.I. Kostomarov, 'Avtobiografiia,' in *Istoricheskie proizvedeniia. Avtobiografiia*, pp. 426–7. The ethnolinguistic border separating Ukrainian- from Russian-speaking lands seems to have run through the middle of Voronezh province, though the country folk on the Kostomarov estate were exclusively Ukrainian.

2 Ibid., p. 428.

3 Ibid., p. 431.

4 Alina L. Kostomarova [Kragielska], 'Nikolai Ivanovich Kostomarov,' in *Avtobiografiia N.I. Kostomarova*, ed. V. Kotelnikov (Moscow: Zadruga, 1922), pp. 94–5; Dennis Papazian, 'Nicholas Ivanovich Kostomarov,' p. 26, confirms this on the basis of materials from Kostomarov's personal archive (*lichnii fond*) in the Central State Historical Archive in St Petersburg, and adds that Tatiana Petrivna was left with only forty-seven serfs.

5 'Avtobiografiia,' p. 432.

6 Ibid., p. 439.

7 Ibid., p. 442. On Lunin, see Hans Hecker, *Russische Universalgeschichtsschreibung von den 'Vierziger Jahren' des 19 Jahrhunderts bis zur sowjetischen 'Weltgeschichte'* (Vienna: Oldenburg, 1983), pp. 89–92.

8 'Avtobiografiia,' p. 446. Kostomarov intended to write the history of the other regiments of the area as well and thus compose a general history of Sloboda Ukraine, but he never got around to it. In 1847, his history of the Ostrogozhk regiment was confiscated by the police, and it was never returned to him.

9 Ibid., pp. 446–7. In the earlier version of his 'Avtobiografiia,' dictated to N.O. Bilozerska ('Avtobiografiia N.I. Kostomarova, zapisannaia N.A. Belozerskoi,' *Russkaia mysl*, nos 5, 6 [Saint Petersburg, 1885], no. 5, p. 202; hereafter cited as 'Avtobiografiia–1885'), Kostomarov tells a parallel story, but one which mentions the influence of Nikolai Gogol: 'At that time [that is, the fall of 1837], having already read something by Gogol, I stumbled upon *Vechera na khutore bliz Dikanki* and *Taras Bulba*. That was the very first awakening of that feeling towards Little Russia which was to give a completely new direction to my activity. I read Gogol with enthusiasm, I reread him, and I could not read him enough. "How all of this surrounded me and I did not see it, I don't know!" I thought to myself; "It is necessary to study this very well (*khoroshenko*)!" I then obtained the little collection of Ukrainian songs of Maksymovych ...'

10 'Avtobiografiia,' p. 448. He also visited the nearby town of Dikanka since rumour had it that Gogol was visiting there, but the rumour turned out to be false. See 'Avtobiografiia–1885,' no. 5, p. 203.

11 'Avtobiografiia–1885,' no. 5, p. 203; V.I. Semevsky, 'Nikolai Ivanovich Kostomarov, 1817–1885,' *Russkaia starina*, no. 1 (Saint Petersburg, 1886), 182; A.N. Pypin, *Istoriia russkoi etnografii*, 4 vols (Saint Petersburg: Stasiulevich, 1890–2), III, 164; Papazian, 'Nicholas Ivanovich Kostomarov,' p. 51.

12 The central figures of the tragedy are Petro Chaly and his son Sava, who served under the Cossack hetman, or leader, Ostrianytsia. After Ostrianytsia's death, the Cossacks elect Petro as their new hetman, whereupon the brave and ambitious Sava is somewhat disgruntled and the Poles, who rule the country, make use of Sava's disaffection. They acknowledge him as the official or crown hetman. Sava, who now serves the Poles, steals the young Kateryna from her betrothed, the Cossack Hnat Holyi, and marries her. In revenge, Holyi sows mistrust of Sava both among the Polish rulers led by Stanisław Koniecpolski and among the Ukrainian Cossacks. Sava begins to feel the pressure: the Poles demand that he swear a new oath of loyalty to the king and promise that he will hold to the pro-Polish Uniate, or Eastern rite, Catholic church. Sava refuses, and the Poles confiscate his possessions. The Cossacks too take their revenge by killing both Sava and Kateryna. Only then is the duplicitous role of Holyi discovered, and he too is killed. Hetman Petro rushes to the scene

but arrives too late to prevent the bloodshed. See Iieremiia Halka, *Sava Chaly: Dramaticheskiia stseny na iuzhno-ruskom iazyke* (Kharkiv, 1838), reprinted in M.I. Kostomarov, *Tvory v dvokh tomakh*, 2 vols (Kiev: Dnipro, 1967), I, 145–202. There is a good summary and analysis in Mykola Zerov, *Lektsii z istorii ukrainskoi literatury* (Oakville, Ont.: Mosaic Press, 1977), p. 85.

13 It appeared in the collection *Zbirnyk tvoriv Iieremii Halky* (Odessa, 1875). It is unknown whether Kostomarov himself played a role in the preparation of this volume. For an exploration of folk motifs in *Sava Chaly*, see O.I. Honchar, *Ukrainska literatura pered-Shevchenkivskoho periodu i folklor* (Kiev: Naukova Dumka, 1982), pp. 254–7. On the review in *Otechestvennye zapiski*, see the discussion in Luckyj, *Between Gogol' and Ševčenko*, p. 70. Kostomarov erroneously believed that this review was authored by the progressive Russian literary critic Vissarion Belinsky. See 'Avtobiografiia–1885,' no. 5, pp. 204, 221n2. By contrast, *Moskvitianin*, no. 5 (Moscow, 1841), 446, was quite critical in directly attacking *Otechestvennye zapiski* for its favourable attitude towards Ukrainian literature.

14 The texts of both *Ukrainskii ballady* (1839) and *Vitka* (1840) are reprinted in *Tvory v dvokh tomakh*, I, 37–83.

15 'Avtobiografiia,' p. 450.

16 Semevsky, 'Kostomarov,' p. 183, writes that 'without a doubt this theme arose because of the reunification of the Uniates [with the Orthodox], which occurred at that time and attracted great interest.'

17 A. Korsunov [O. Korsun], 'N.I. Kostomarov,' *Russkii arkhiv*, no. 10 (Moscow, 1890), 199–200; summaries in Dmytro Doroshenko, *Mykola Ivanovych Kostomarov* (Kiev–Leipzig: Ukrainska nakladnia, 1920), pp. 14–15, and Papazian, 'Nicholas Ivanovich Kostomarov,' pp. 52–3. The material from Korsun's *Snip* (1841) is reprinted in *Tvory v dvokh tomakh*, vol. I; it includes the translations from Byron and 'Pereiaslavska nich.' Later on, Kostomarov criticized his early loose treatment of history – overreliance on Sreznevsky and other dubious sources – and what he called the 'conceited airs' composed in imitation of Schiller ('Avtobiografiia,' p. 454).

18 Korsunov, 'N.I. Kostomarov,' 207. See also the brief discussions in Luckyj, *Between Gogol' and Ševčenko*, p. 141, and Doroshenko, *Mykola Ivanovych Kostomarov*, p. 16.

19 On the *Istoriia Rusov*, see Doroshenko, 'A Survey of Ukrainian Historiography,' pp. 76–92, which gives further references.

20 Mykola Kostomarov, *Naukovo-publitsystychni i polemichni pysannia Kostomarova*, ed. M. Hrushevsky (Kiev: Derzhavne vydavnytstvo Ukrainy, 1928), pp. 1–40, reprints Kostomarov's 'O prichinakh i kharaktere Unii v zapad-

noi Rossii.' See especially p. 33 and Hrushevsky's introductory remarks, pp. vi–viii. Kostomarov's 'rationalist' approach was evident in the epigram with which he prefaced his study:

O Bozhe mii neskinchenyi	O my God eternal
Dyvytysia hore,	Look upon the grief,
Shcho teper na sim sviti	Faith fights faith
Vira viru bore.	And gives the world no relief.
O Bozhe mii neskinchenyi	Oh my God eternal
Shcho sia teper stalo?	What shall happen now?
Use vira, use vira,	It's all faith, all faith,
A mylosti malo.	And the kindness is hollow.

Ukrainian folk-song

21 See the article on Betsky by A. Isichenko in the *Ukrainska literaturna entsyklopediia*, vol. I (Kiev, 1988), p. 157, 'Do mari'i Pototskoi' is reprinted in *Tvory v dvokh tomakh*, I, 89, and 'Obzor sochinenii pisannykh na malorossiiskom iazyke' is reprinted in *Tvory*, II, 375–93.

22 'Obzor,' especially p. 378.

23 'Avtobiografiia,' p. 456.

24 An examination of the St Petersburg archives reveals that the assistant curator of the Kharkiv school District, N.A. Tsertelev, wrote to St Petersburg complaining about the dissertation, and that although Uvarov and his advisers found nothing in it against the government or the Orthodox church, the minister vetoed it because of its controversial subject matter – in Uvarov's own words, 'the contemporary nature of events relating to our destruction of the Uniates.' See James T. Flynn, 'The Affair of Kostomarov's Dissertation: A Case Study of Official Nationalism in Practice,' *Slavonic and East European Review*, LII (London, 1974), 188–96. In the 1920s, I. Aizenshtok, 'Persha dysertatsiia Kostomarova,' *Ukraina*, no. 3 (Kiev, 1925), 21–7, clearly demonstrated that Bishop Innokenty and local university officials – including Hulak-Artemovsky – initiated the destruction of Kostomarov's work on the union, which was, in Innokenty's own words, 'not only of historical, but also of state significance' and viewed things in what he called 'an un-Russian manner' (*neporusski*; p. 23, n4).

25 'Avtobiografiia–1885,' no. 5, p. 205.

26 'Avtobiografiia,' p. 457.

27 In I. Aizenshtok, 'Do etnohrafichnykh planiv 1840-kh rokiv,' *Za sto lit*, IV (Kiev, 1929), 13.

28 'Avtobiografiia–1885,' no. 5, p. 205.

29 N. Kostomarov, 'Perviia voiny malorossiiskikh Kozakov s Poliakami,' *Molodyk za 1844* (Kharkiv, 1843), 46–70, dealt with the revolt of the Cossack leader Severyn Nalyvaiko against the Poles (1595–6), and 'Russko-polskie velmozhi, Statia pervaia: Kniazia Ostrozhski,' ibid., 186–203, dealt with the Ukrainian magnate family which once owned most of the Province of Volhynia. See 'Avtobiografiia,' pp. 459–60.

30 Quoted in Pinchuk, *Mykola Ivanovych Kostomarov*, p. 52.

31 'Avtobiografiia,' p. 460.

32 N. Kostomarov, *Ob istoricheskom znachenii russkoi narodnoi poezii* (Kharkiv, 1843) is reprinted in full in *Etnohrafichni pysannia Kostomarova*, ed. M. Hrushevsky (Kiev: Derzhavne vydavnytstvo Ukrainy, 1930). There is a detailed analysis in P.M. Popov, *M. Kostomarov iak folkloryst i etnohraf* (Kiev: Naukova Dumka, 1968), pp. 16–28, and in my 'Mykola Kostomarov and East Slavic Ethnography in the Nineteenth Century,' *Russian History*, XVIII, 2 (1991), 166–71.

33 'Avtobiografiia,' pp. 460–61.

34 *Otechestvennye zapiski*, XXXIII, 3 (1844), ii, cited and reprinted in V.G. Belinsky, *Polnoe sobranie sochinenii*, vol. VIII (Moscow, 1955), pp. 152–3.

35 *Biblioteka dlia Chteniia*, LXVI, sec. 6 (1844), 12, cited and quoted in Popov, *Kostomarov iak folkloryst i etnohraf*, pp. 29–30.

36 *Moskvitianin*, no. 3, pt 2 (1844), 144–54, as analysed in Popov, *Kostomarov iak folkloryst i etnohraf*, pp. 30–2, who notes that later scholars such as O.O. Potebnia and A.N. Pypin, like Sreznevsky before them, saw much value in Kostomarov's pioneering work. Similarly, K.M. Sementovsky, who wrote under the pseudonym K. Kalaidensky, penned a highly favourable review in *Maiak*, XXX (1844), 81, cited in Pinchuk, *Mykola Ivanovych Kostomarov*, pp. 47, 211n33.

37 In fact, as early as 1843, while still working on his dissertation, Kostomarov published 'O tsikle vesennikh pesen v narodnoi iuzhnorusskoi poezii,' *Maiak*, XI, 21 (1843), 58–71, reprinted in *Etnohrafichni pysannia Kostomarova*, pp. 118–26, in which, discussing Ukrainian folk-songs of the springtime, feast of Saints Peter and Paul, and feast of Saint John the Baptist cycles, he touched upon epic/mythological themes and noted that the essence of the Saint John the Baptist feast (*Kupalo*) lay in the pre-Christian cult of fire and water. See the discussion in Popov, *Kostomarov iak folkloryst i etnohraf*, pp. 33–4.

38 Ivan Franko, *Narys istorii ukrainsko-ruskoi literatury do 1890*, in his *Zibrannia tvoriv u piatdesiaty tomakh*, vol. XLI (Kiev, 1984), p. 281.

39 These issues were first analysed in detail by Oleksander Hrushevsky [A.S. Grushevsky], 'Iz kharkovskikh let N.I. Kostomarova,' *Zhurnal Ministerstva*

Narodnogo Prosveshcheniia n.s. XIV, 4 (Saint Petersburg, 1908), 233–95, and 'Ranniia etnograficheskiia raboty N.I. Kostomarova,' *Izvestiia Otdeleniia Russkogo Iazyka i Slovestnosti*, XVI, 1 (St Petersburg, 1911), 77–120.

40 According to Kostomarov, Herder 'dealt a decisive blow to old ways of thinking and set the flag of nationality [*narodnost*] upon an unshakeable foundation.' In Popov, *Kostomarov iak folkloryst i etnohraf*, p. 21. For a spirited though highly contentious discussion of Herder's influence on the 'Kharkiv Romantics,' see L.K. Polukhin, *Formuvannia istorychnykh pohliadiv M.I. Kostomarova* (Kiev: Vydavnytstvo AN URSR, 1959), pp. 59–69, who points out that both Metlynsky and Lunin were strongly influenced by Herder, and that they passed this influence on to Kostomarov. More generally, see J.P. Sydoruk 'Herder and the Slavs,' *Ukrainian Quarterly*, XII, 1 (New York, 1956), 58–62.

41 'Zapiska N.I. Kostomarova ob ego uchenykh trudakh, sostavlennaia v 1870 g.,' *Russkaia mysl*, no. 6 (St Petersburg, 1885), 44.

Chapter 2: Schoolteacher and University Professor

1 'Avtobiografiia–1885,' no. 5, p. 206. See also A. Markevich's entry on Kostomarov in the *Russkii biograficheskii slovar*, vol. IX (St Petersburg, n.d.), pp. 305–19, especially p. 307.

2 'Avtobiografii,' p. 462; Volodymyr Miiakovsky, 'Kostomarov u Rivnomu,' *Ukraina*, no. 12 (Kiev, 1925), 29–30.

3 P. Kulish, 'Vospominaniia o Nikolae Ivanoviche Kostomarove,' *Nov*, IV, 13 (St Petersburg, 1885), 62, 64, quoted in Luckyj, *Panteleimon Kulish*, p. 23.

4 Kulish, 'Vospominaniia o Kostomarove' p. 72. See also Kostomarov, 'Avtobiografiia,' p. 462. Kostomarov's letter to Sreznevsky is in Aizenshtok, 'Do etnohrafichnykh planiv,' p. 15.

5 Miiakovsky, 'Kostomarov u Rivnomu,' p. 30.

6 M. Kostomarov, letter of 13 November 1844 to K.M. Sementovsky, in *Ukraina*, no. 12 (Kiev, 1925), 42–6.

7 For a description of the Rivne gymnasium at the time of Kostomarov's stay there, see A.I. Popov, 'N.I. Kostomarov: Prepodavatel rovenskoi gimnazii,' *Istoricheskii vestnik*, no. 3 (1917), 716–35.

8 Miiakovsky, 'Kostomarov u Rivnomu,' p. 36; Semevsky, 'Kostomarov,' p. 185.

9 In Miiakovsky, 'Kostomarov u Rivnomu,' p. 32.

10 Ibid., p. 33.

11 'Avtobiografiia,' pp. 464–8. See also S. Zhuk, 'Kostomarov i Shevchenko u Pochaevi,' *Tserkva i narid* (1938), 616–23, cited in Metropolit Ilarion

[I. Ohiienko], *Fortetsia pravoslaviia na Volyni: Sviata Pochaivska Lavra* (Winnipeg, 1961), pp. 368–9.

12 M. Kostomarov, letter to K.M. Sementovsky, in Miiakovsky, 'Kostomarov u Rivnomu,' pp. 54–66; 'Avtobiografiia,' pp. 468–70.

13 Kostomarov's map is reproduced in his letter to Sementovsky, which is the most detailed account of his Easter, 1845, expedition; see n12, above.

14 In Miiakovsky, 'Kostomarov u Rivnomu,' p. 35.

15 'Avtobiografiia–1885,' no. 5, p. 209.

16 Ibid.; 'Avtobiografiia,' p. 473.

17 Nikolai Ge, 'Kievskaia Pervaia Gimnaziia v sorokovykh godakh,' in *Sbornik v polzu nedostatochnykh studentov universiteta sv. Vladimira* (St Petersburg, 1895), pp. 59–60, quoted in Markevich, 'Kostomarov,' p. 308.

18 Kostomarova, 'Nikolai Ivanovich Kostomarov,' pp. 10–16.

19 'Avtobiografiia–1885,' no. 5, p. 210.

20 'Avtobiografiia,' p. 473; 'Avtobiografiia–1885,' no. 5, p. 210.

21 'Avtobiografiia,' pp. 474–5. There is some uncertainty concerning the origin of the name of the Cyril-Methodian Brotherhood. In his 'Avtobiografiia–1885,' no. 5, p. 210, Kostomarov writes: 'At that time [that is, in 1846], V.M. Bilozersky had the idea of ordering a ring in commemoration of the founding of the society with the inscription "Cyril and Methodius. January, 1846." That was the reason that later on the Third Department designated our society by the name of those two Slavic enlighteners.'

22 M.I. Kostomarov, 'Spohad pro dvokh maliariv,' in *Spohady pro Tarasa Shevchenka*, ed. I.O. Dzeverin (Kiev: Dnipro, 1982), p. 133, reprinted from *Osnova*, no. 4 (St Petersburg, 1861), 44–56.

23 See, in particular, M. Kostomarov, 'Lyst do vydavtsia-redaktora *Russkoi stariny* M.I. Semevskoho,' in *Spohady pro Tarasa Shevchenka*, ed. Dzeverin, pp. 138–44, which is reprinted from *Russkaia starina*, no. 3 (St Petersburg, 1880), 597–610, where Kostomarov writes: 'When I turned our conversation to this question [of Slavic reciprocity], I felt Shevchenko's most enthusiastic sympathy about it and this, in particular, brought me closer to him.' However, in his 'Avtobiografiia–1885,' no. 5, p. 211, Kostomarov writes: 'When I informed Shevchenko of the existence of the society, he immediately expressed his willingness to join, but he related to its ideas with [such a] great fervour and [such an] extreme impatience that it became the cause of many disputes between Shevchenko and myself.'

24 Kostomarov, 'Lyst do Semevskoho'; 'Avtobiografiia,' p. 476. According to Semevsky, 'Kostomarov,' pp. 185–6, the possibility of Kostomarov's teaching history at the University of Kiev had been raised at least a year

earlier, when he had first arrived in Rivne, but his first application was not successful and in fact *complicated* his second application.

25 Kulish, 'Vospominaniia o Kostomarove,' p. 65, quoted in Doroshenko, *Mykola Ivanovych Kostomarov*, pp. 21-2. Doroshenko has somewhat simplified the text. Kulish continued: 'In his memoirs about Shevchenko, [Kostomarov] speaks evasively, as if he did not know him well. [But] I have grounds for saying that in my absence they were as close to each other as one could expect from people who were so naturally gifted and were in their youth during the just but severe reign of Nikolai Pavlovich.'

26 Kostomarov wrote this recollection in the introduction to the Prague edition (1876) of Shevchenko's *Kobzar*. The passage is quoted in full in V.I. Semevsky, 'Kirillo-Mefodievskoe Obshchestvo 1846–47 g.,' *Russkoe bogatstvo*, 5, 6 (St Petersburg, 1911), no. 5, p. 105.

27 Kostomarova, 'Nikolai Ivanovich Kostomarov,' pp. 25–32; Doroshenko, *Mykola Ivanovych Kostomarov*, p. 23; Pinchuk, *Mykola Ivanovych Kostomarov*, p. 68.

28 Oleksander Hrushevsky, 'Malovidoma statia Kostomarova z 1846 r.,' *Zapysky Naukovoho Tovarystva im. Shevchenka*, LXXXIX (Lviv, 1907), 161–4. Hrushevsky suggests that Kostomarov's unsigned 'Mysli ob istorii Malorossii,' *Biblioteka dlia Chteniia*, IX (St Petersburg, 1846), 21–42, was published in that journal to counter disparaging remarks about Ukraine's 'Asian' character that had been published in it earlier.

29 'Avtobiografiia,' p. 477.

30 Ibid., pp. 477–9.

31 Panteleimon Kulish, letter of 11 September 1846 to M. Kostomarov, in *Za sto lit*, II (Kiev, 1928), 58, quoted in Luckyj, *Panteleimon Kulish*, pp. 34–5. Kulish continued: 'God's grace is given to us all, and in every nation a man of clear mind and goodwill may accomplish a great deal for its honour and its future power (moral or material). Up to now, few such have appeared in Little Russia. All our better minds turned inwards towards our families ... It was not until you opened your mouth to say *ex cathedra* "the soul of this people is insignificant" that the most passionate feelings of Little Russian activists became centred on the people. You may scold the baseness of the country's representatives, but do not call its soul insignificant. This is unforgivable blasphemy.' Unfortunately, Kostomarov's letters to Kulish of this period have not been preserved.

32 Nikolai Kostomarov, *Slavianskaia mifologiia* (Kiev: Bainer, 1847; photoreprinted London–The Hague: Mlyn, 1978). Kostomarov's 'Byzantinism,' which, of course, was not synonymous with loyalty to the official tenets

of the Russian Orthodox church, was clearly defined first by Mykhailo Hrushevsky, 'Z publitsystychnykh pysan Kostomarova,' in *Naukovo-publitsystychni i polemichni pysannia Kostomarova*, especially p. viii.

33 In general, Kostomarov was interested in only the 'high' mythology of the Slavs; 'low' mythology or demonology, as he called it, was in his opinion primarily the domain not of the historian but of the ethnographer. See the discussion in Popov, *Kostomarov iak folkloryst i etnohraf*, pp. 38–42. Popov also maintains that Kostomarov thought that mythology originated primarily among the educated classes, who passed it on to the popular masses. Thus, says Popov, though Kostomarov seems to have been aware of Jakob Grimm's theory of the folk origin of pagan mythology, he did not accept it in his own work.

34 'Avtobiografiia–1885,' no. 5, p. 212; 'Avtobiografiia,' pp. 478–80; Semevsky, 'Kostomarov,' p. 187, stresses that the absence of a legal department of Slavic studies forced the brethren underground. Of course, Semevsky himself was writing under the conditions of censorship prevalent in 1885.

35 Kostomarova, 'Nikolai Ivanovich Kostomarov,' pp. 35–7.

36 Kostomarov, 'Spohad pro dvokh maliariv,' p. 133, quoted in full in Pavlo Zaitsev, *Taras Shevchenko: A Life*, ed. and trans. George Luckyj (Toronto: University of Toronto Press, 1988), p. 122.

37 Panteleimon Kulish, letter of 2 May 1846 to M. Kostomarov, in Volodymyr Miiakovsky, 'Liudy sorokovykh rokiv: Kyrylo-Metodiivtsi v ikh lystuvanni,' *Za sto lit*, II (Kiev, 1928), 52–3. See also the discussion in Luckyj, *Panteleimon Kulish*, pp. 32–3.

Chapter 3: The Cyril-Methodian Brotherhood

1 'Avtobiografiia–1885,' no. 5, p. 211.

2 This possibility was first suggested by Volodymyr Miiakovsky, 'Shevchenko in the Brotherhood of Saint Cyril and Methodius,' in *Shevchenko and the Critics*, ed. George Luckyj (Toronto: University of Toronto Press, 1980), pp. 371–2.

3 Ibid.; 'Avtobiografiia–1885,' no. 5, p. 214.

4 Miiakovsky, 'Shevchenko in the Brotherhood of Saints Cyril and Methodius,' pp. 272–3.

5 Ibid., p. 371.

6 'Avtobiografiia,' p. 471.

7 Polish influences on the Cyril-Methodians are examined in great detail by Vasyl Shchurat, 'Osnovy Shevchenkovykh zv'iazkiv z poliakamy,' in his

Vybrani pratsi z istorii literatury (Kiev: AN RSR, 1963), pp. 242–353. Doroshenko, *Mykola Ivanovych Kostomarov*, p. 24, selected the two organizations mentioned above as being particularly influential.

8 'Avtobiografiia–1885,' no. 5, p. 211.

9 Iulian Belina-Kendzhytsky [Julian Bielina-Kedrzycki], 'U Shevchenka v Kyievi. 1846 r.,' in *Spohady pro Tarasa Shevchenka*, pp. 153–60.

10 Panteleimon Kulish, 'Istorychne opovidannia,' *Tvory*, vol. VI (Lviv, 1910), p. 381, quoted in Luckyj, *Panteleimon Kulish*, p. 27.

11 'Statut Kyrylo-Mefodiivskoho Tovarystva,' in *Kyrylo-Mefodiivske Tovarystvo*, I, 150–1. Text in Russian. There is a convenient Ukrainian version in *Knyhy buttia ukrainskoho narodu*, ed. K. Kostiv (Toronto: NTSh, 1980), p. 100. See also *Le livre de la genèse du peuple ukrainien*, ed. Georges Luciani (Paris: Institut d'études slaves de l'Université de Paris, 1956), p. 40.

12 Russian text in *Kyrylo-Mefodiivske Tovarystvo*, I, 151–2. There is a Ukrainian version in *Knyhy buttia*, ed. Kostiv, pp. 100–1. See also *Le livre de la genèse*, ed. Luciani, pp. 40–1.

13 Both Ukrainian and Russian texts in *Kyrylo-Mefodiivske Tovarystvo*, I, 170–2. See also *Le livre de la genèse*, ed. Luciani, pp. 41–2.

14 Ibid.

15 Russian text in *Kyrylo-Mefodiivske Tovarystvo*, I, 172; Ukrainian translation in *Knyhy buttia*, ed. Kostiv, p. 103; French translation and discussion in *Le livre de la genèse*, ed. Luciani, p. 42.

16 The texts of both *Panich Natalich* and Kostomarov's note on Panslavism are given in *Kyrylo-Mefodiivske Tovarystvo*, I, 262–4.

17 The texts of both letters are given in Mykhailo Vozniak, *Kyrylo-Metodiivske Bratstvo* (Lviv, 1921), pp. 95–7.

18 The 'Law of God' label has been accepted by the Russian historian P.A. Zaionchkovsky, *Kirilo-Mefodievskoe Obshchestvo (1846–1847)* (Moscow: Izdatelstvo Moskovskogo Universiteta, 1959) who, as is clear from the title of his book, also refers to the Cyril-Methodians as forming a 'society' rather than a 'brotherhood,' the latter being a less secular term. By contrast, most Ukrainian historians prefer the term 'brotherhood' (see Vozniak, n17, above) since it accords well with the religious tradition of the Ukrainian people, which, they think, the Cyril-Methodians were trying to invoke. Ukrainian historians also seem to prefer the title *Books of the Genesis of the Ukrainian People*, given the work's importance in the evolution of Ukrainian political thought. For a critique of Zaionchkovsky's position from the Ukrainian point of view, see Volodymyr Miiakovsky, 'Knyha pro Kyrylo-Metodiivske Bratstvo,' pp. 85–96.

19 Both the Russian and the Ukrainian texts of *Knyhy buttia ukrainskoho*

narodu under the title *Zakon Bozhyi* are given in *Kyrylo-Mefodiivske Tova-rystvo*, I, 156–9. There is an English translation in *Knyhy buttia*, ed. Kostiv, pp. 107–21, who also reprints Luciani's Ukrainian text (first published by Pavlo Zaitsev, 1918) and his annotated French translation.

20 From the 1930s through to the 1980s, it was incumbent upon Soviet historians to divide what they called the 'Cyril-Methodian Society' into a 'revolutionary-democratic' wing headed by Shevchenko and a 'liberal-bourgeois' wing headed by Kostomarov and Kulish. See, for example, H. Serhienko, *T.H. Shevchenko i Kyrylo-Mefodievske Tovarystvo* (Kiev, 1983). However, while it is clear that Shevchenko's social views were expressed more emotionally than those of Kostomarov and the others, there was no clear division among the brethren, and all members seem to have supported the ideology outlined by Kostomarov in the programmatic documents of the organization. With the advent of 'glasnost' in the Soviet Union, it became possible for Soviet Ukrainian authors to come closer to this point of view. See, for example, P.M. Fedchenko, 'Schevchenko, Kulish, i Kostomarov u Kyrylo-Mefodiivskomu Tovarystvi,' *Radianske literaturoznavstvo*, no. 7 (Kiev, 1989), 29–36.

21 See the line-by-line analysis of Mickiewicz and Kostomarov by Dmitry Čiževsky, 'Mickiewicz and Ukrainian Literature,' in *Adam Mickiewicz in World Literature*, ed. W. Lednicki (Berkeley and Los Angeles: University of California Press, 1956), pp. 409–36.

Chapter 4: Arrest, Imprisonment, and Exile

1 'Avtobiografiia–1885,' no. 5, pp. 212–13.

2 Ibid., p. 214.

3 Ibid., pp. 214–15.

4 Ibid., p. 215; Doroshenko, *Mykola Ivanovych Kostomarov*, pp. 33–4.

5 Ibid., pp. 34–5; Papazian, 'Nicholas Ivanovich Kostomarov,' pp. 188–9.

6 Doroshenko, *Mykola Ivanovych Kostomarov*, pp. 36–7, gives an outline of the process. The pertinent documents, including Petrov's original denunciation before Traskin, are given in *Kyrylo-Mefodiivske Tovarystvo*, I, especially 24–8.

7 The protocol of Kostomarov's 15 April interrogation is given in *Kyrylo-Mefodiivske Toyvarystvo*, I, 275–9.

8 The text of Kostomarov's testimony is given ibid., pp. 279–87.

9 Ibid., pp. 294–5; 'Avtobiografiia,' p. 483.

10 *Kyrylo-Mefodiivske Tovarystvo*, I, 295–304.

11 'Avtobiografiia,' p. 485.

12 Kostomarova, 'Nikolai Ivanovich Kostomarov,' p. 42; Doroshenko, *Mykola Ivanovych Kostomarov*, p. 39.

13 C.H. Andrusyshen and Watson Kirkconnell, trans., *The Poetical Works of Taras Shevchenko* (Toronto: University of Toronto Press, 1964), pp. 301–2. For the context of the writing of this poem, see Zaitsev, *Taras Shevchenko*, pp. 142–3.

14 'Avtobiografiia,' p. 485; Doroshenko, *Mykola Ivanovych Kostomarov*, p. 41.

15 See especially Luckyj, *Young Ukraine*, pp. 66–7.

16 See 'Arest gg. Kulisha i Kostomarova po razskazu nemetskikh gazet v 1847 g.,' *Russkaia starina*, no. 9 (1885), 123–5.

17 'Avtobiografiia,' pp. 468 ff.; 'Avtobiografiia–1885,' no. 5, pp. 219–20.

18 In his 'Avtobiografiia–1885,' no. 5, p. 220, Kostomarov reports that the tsar himself uttered these words. In 'Avtobiografiia,' p. 488, he says they were uttered by Orlov.

19 For the full text of the letter, see P.L. Iudin, 'K biografii N.I. Kostomarova (Pismo grafa Orlova M.L. Kozhevnikovu),' *Istoricheskii vestnik*, XCIV (1903), 562–4. See also 'Avtobiografiia,' p. 488, which quotes Dubelt.

20 'Avtobiografiia,' p. 489.

21 In P.L. Iudin, 'N.I. Kostomarov v ssylke,' *Istoricheskii vestnik*, C (1905), 136–53, especially 142.

22 Kostomarova, 'Nikolai Ivanovich Kostomarov,' pp. 55–76.

23 'Avtobiografiia–1885,' no. 6, p. 21.

24 Iudin, 'Kostomarov v ssylke,' p. 144, discusses Kostomarov's experiences at the *Saratovskie gubernskie vedomosti*.

25 Ibid., p. 147. See also 'Avtobiografiia–1885,' no. 6, p. 21.

26 For the text of the play, see 'Kremutsii Kord,' in *Tvory v dvokh tomakh*, I, 292–332. There is a brief summary in Ie. Shabliovsky, 'N.I. Kostomarov v gody revoliutsionnoi situatsii,' in *Revoliutsionnaia situatsiia v Rossii v 1859–61 gg.*, vol. V (Moscow, 1970), pp. 101–23, especially p. 107, who incorrectly states that Kostomarov composed this work in prison.

27 In Pinchuk, *Mykola Ivanovych Kostomarov*, p. 91.

28 'Avtobiografiia,' p. 491.

29 Ibid., p. 490.

30 I.U. Palimpsestov, 'Iz vospominanii o Nikolae Ivanoviche Kostomarove,' *Russkoe obozrenie*, no. 7 (1895), 155–80, especially 168.

31 Ibid., p. 162.

32 'Avtobiografiia–1885,' no. 6, p. 23; N.G. Chernyshevsky, 'Po povodu "Avtobiografiia" N.I. Kostomarova,' in his *Polnoe sobranie sochinenii*, vol. I (Moscow, 1939), pp. 757–77. As late as 19 January 1851, however, the historian had still not given up hope of marrying Alina. On that date, he

wrote to V. Bilozersky: 'I have made a request to get married, but they would not allow me to go to Kiev. Not for anything. Grief, grief! grief! Grief on all sides!' In Pinchuk, *Mykola Ivanovych Kostomarov*, p. 94, citing 'Pisma N.I. Kostomarova k V.M. i N.M. Belozerskim,' *Kievskaia starina*, 10 (1897), 136.

33 N.G. Chernyshevsky, letter of 15 November 1851 to I.I. Sreznevsky, in his *Polnoe sobranie sochinenii*, vol. XIV (Moscow, 1949), pp. 220–1.

34 'Avtobiografiia–1885,' no. 6, p. 25; 'Avtobiografiia,' p. 491; Chernyshevsky, 'Po povodu "Avtobiografiia" N.I. Kostomarova,' p. 774; and especially D.L. Mordovtsev, 'N.I. Kostomarov po moim lichnym vospominaniiam,' *Nov*, XXII, 15, 16, XXIII, 17 (St Petersburg, 1888), no. 15, pp. 109–21.

35 According to L.V. Domanovsky, 'K Saratovskim vzaimo-otnosheniiam N.G. Chernyshevskogo i N.I. Kostomarova (Iz istorii "Saratovskogo kruzhka"),' in *N.G. Chernyshevsky: Stati, izsledovaniia, i materiialy*, vol. III (Saratov: Izdatelstvo Saratovskogo Universiteta, 1962), pp. 213–32, it was Chernyshevsky who drew Kostomarov's attention to Stenka Razin and the general theme of peasant/Cossack revolts. However, Domanovsky provides no evidence in support of this statement, and it is unlikely that the young radical Chernyshevsky could have had a profound influence on his older friend, who was already an accomplished historian with well-formed views. Rather the influence probably flowed in the opposite direction.

36 Iudin, 'Kostomarov v ssylke.' Iudin notes that many years later Prudentov spoke with great pride of his business relationship and friendship with the famous historian.

37 Chernyshevsky, 'Po povodu "Avtobiografiia" N.I. Kostomarova,' p. 775, concluded: 'It was a mean trial. So the Senate decided ... [Kostomarov's] participation in the trial was a deplorable episode in his activities. But he did not think to regret it when he dictated his autobiography. In spite of my knowledge of all his unhealthy faults, I never expected that from him. I had thought that he would regret it and be ashamed of himself.' Compare the editor's note, ibid., pp. 818–19, which gives further information about the affair, with Kostomarov's accounts in 'Avtobiografiia–1885,' no. 6, p. 26, on which Chernyshevsky was commenting, and 'Avtobiografiia,' pp. 494–5, which is Kostomarov's fullest statement. There is also a brief discussion of the affair in Papazian, 'Nicholas Ivanovich Kostomarov,' p. 264.

38 'Avtobiografiia,' pp. 495–6, describes the affair of the *Saratovskie gubernskie vedomosti* most fully. In his 'Avtobiografiia–1885,' no. 6, p. 27, Kostomarov

states that the matter went all the way to Tsar Nicholas I, who condemned the verses in the strongest terms.

39 On Mordovets (Mordovtsev in Russian), see V. Bieliaiev, 'Zhyttia i tvorchist Danyla Mordovtsia,' in Danylo Mordovets, *Tvory v dvokh tomakh*, vol. I (Kiev, 1958), pp. 5–38, and the Mordovets memoir of Kostomarov, 'N.I. Kostomarov po moim lichnym vospominaniiam.'

40 'Avtobiografiia,' pp. 499–500.

41 'Bogdan Khmelnitsky i vozvrashchenie Iuzhnoi Rusi k Rossii' appeared in *Otechestvennye zapiski* in various numbers for 1857. For the details of Kostomarov's various troubles with the censor, see I. Butych, 'M.I. Kostomarov i tsarska tsenzura,' *Arkhivy Ukrainy*, no. 6 (Kiev, 1967), 64–6, and the brief remarks of S. Velychenko, 'Tsarist Censorship and Ukrainian Historiography, 1828–1906,' *Canadian-American Slavic Studies*, XXIII, 4 (1989), 398–9.

42 My analysis is based on the considerably revised first book edition of *Bogdan Khmelnitsky*, 2 vols (St Petersburg: Kozhanchikov, 1859); note the simplified title. For Khmelnytsky's speech to the Cossacks at the start of the rebellion, see vol. I, pp. 111–12.

43 Ibid., II, 143–44.

44 Ibid., II, 407–8.

45 Chernyshevsky's major review was of the *Otechestvennye zapiski* edition and appeared in *Sovremennik*, no. 1 (1857). It was followed by other positive comments in later issues. See his *Polnoe sobranie sochinenii*, vol. IV (Moscow, 1948), pp. 701–2, 821.

46 A.A. Kotliarevsky, 'Bogdan Khmelnitsky,' in *Sbornik otdelenie russkago iazyka i slovesnosti*, XL (St Petersburg, 1889), 267–85. This volume is a reprinting of Kotliarevsky's collected works.

47 *Sovremennik*, no. 12 (1859), 161–214, especially 214.

48 See the discussion in Dmitry Likhachev, *The Great Heritage: The Classical Literature of Old Rus*, trans. D. Bradbury (Moscow: Progress, 1981), p. 328. The 'Gore-Zlochaste' is now generally considered a classic of old Russian literature.

49 Mykola Kostomarov, 'Z privodu "Zapisok o iuzhnoi Rusi" P. Kulisha,' in *Etnohrafichni pysannia Kostomarova*, pp. 241–81. This work first appeared in *Otechestvennye zapiski* in various numbers for 1857.

50 'Ocherk torgovli moskovskago gosudarstva v XVI i XVII stoletiiakh' was first published in *Sovremennik* in various numbers for 1857 and 1858. It was reprinted in book form in 1862 and in *Sobranie sochinenii*, 21 vols in 8 bks (St Petersburg: Stasiulevich, 1903–6; photorepr. The Hague: Europe Printing, 1968), bk VIII, vol. XX. According to the testimony of D. Mordov-

tsev [Mordovets], 'Istoricheskiia pominki po. N.I. Kostomarove,' *Russkaia starina*, XLVI (1885), 625, his wife, Hanna, had interceded with government officials on behalf of Kostomarov during her trips to St Petersburg, and the influential Miliutin brothers and State Secretary Nikitin helped to secure his release.

51 In Pinchuk, *Mykola Ivanovych Kostomarov*, p. 91.

Chapter 5: Liberty

1 D.A. Korsakov, 'Nikolai Ivanovich Kostomarov v ego otnosheniiakh k Konstantinu Dmitrievichu Kavelinu,' *Istoricheskii vestnik*, CXLIX–CL (July–Aug., 1917), 157–66, especially 157.

2 'Avtobiografiia,' pp. 502–16, gives the most detailed account of the first European tour.

3 Ibid., p. 516; Zaitsev, *Taras Shevchenko*, pp. 214–15.

4 E. Brobrov, 'Epizod iz zhizni N.I. Avtobiografiia (Po arkhivnym doku-mentam),' *Russkaia starina*, no. 3 (1904), 604–11. Brobrov gives a detailed outline of Kostomarov's project for the teaching of old Russian social history. See also H.I. Marakhov, 'Novi storinki z biohrafii M.I. Kosto-marova,' *Visnyk AN URSR*, XXXVI, 1 (1972), 100–1.

5 For the text of 'Bunt Stenki Razina,' see *Sobranie sochinenii*, bk I, vol. II, especially pp. 412, 426–7, 505.

6 It first appeared in Kalachev's journal *Arkhiv istoricheskikh i prakticheskikh svedenii otnosiashchikhsia do Rossii* in various numbers for 1859 and 1860 and was reprinted separately in St Petersburg in 1865. For a more recent edition, see *Tvory v dvokh tomakh*, II, 7–126.

7 'Avtobiografiia,' pp. 521–2; Kostomarov, 'Lyst do vydavtsia-redaktora *Russkoi stariny* M.I. Semevskoho.'

8 Korsakov, 'Kostomarov v ego otnosheniiakh k Kavelinu,' pp. 158–9, states that the princess asked Kostomarov to write a history of the Ukrainian peasantry for her. The historian's response is unknown.

9 In Pinchuk, *Istoricheskie vzgliady N.I. Kostomarova*, p. 51, who cites a Kosto-marov manuscript from the Central Scientific Library of Ukraine.

10 'Avtobiografiia,' p. 523. For the mechanics of Kostomarov's election to the chair of Russian history at St Petersburg University, see P.L. Iudin, 'K biografii N.I. Kostomarova,' *Istoricheskii vestnik*, CXII (1908), 981–6.

11 'Avtobiografiia,' p. 524.

12 Kostomarov, 'Lyst do vydavtsia-redaktora *Russkoi stariny* M.I. Semevskoho.'

13 'Avtobiografiia,' p. 501.

14 See P. Lobas, 'Ukrainskyi literaturnyi zbirnyk,' *Arkhivy Ukrainy*, no. 2 (Kiev, 1968), 74–80, and Velychenko, 'Tsarist Censorship,' p. 398. The *Malorusskii literaturnyi sbornik* (Saratov, 1859) remains a bibliographical rarity, but Kostomarov's 'Narodyne pesni, sobrannye v zapadnoi chasti volynskoi gubernii v 1844 godu' is reprinted in *Etnohrafichni pysannia Kostomarova*, pp. 127–202.

15 Mordovtsev, 'Istoricheskiia pominki po N.I. Kostomarove,' p. 618.

16 N.A. Belozerskaia, 'Nikolai Ivanovich Kostomarov v 1857–1875 gg. Vospominaniia N.A. Belozerskoi,' *Russkaia starina*, XLIX, no. 3 (1886), 618, cited in Doroshenko, *Mykola Ivanovych Kostomarov*, p. 49.

17 Belozerskaia, 'Vospominaniia,' pp. 611–12, cited in Pinchuk, *Mykola Ivanovych Kostomarov*, pp. 104–5.

18 Mordovtsev, 'Istoricheskiia pominki po N.I. Kostomarove,' p. 691.

19 M.D. Bernshtein, *Zhurnal 'Osnova' i ukrainskyi literaturnyi protses kintsia 50–60-kh rokiv XIX st.* (Kiev: AN URSR, 1959), pp. 1–22.

20 'Avtobiografiia–1885,' no. 6, p. 38; Markevich, 'Kostomarov,' p. 310, mentions the role of the Miliutins.

21 P. Polevoi, 'Istorik-idealist,' *Istoricheskii vestnik*, XLII (1891), 501–20, especially 514–15. Polevoi later became a historian in his own right and even authored the *History of Russian Literature in Biographies*, a work which was to parallel Kostomarov's last efforts; see ch. 9, n17, below.

22 G. Vashkevich [H.S. Vashkevych], 'Iz vospominanii o Nikolae Ivanoviche Kostomarove,' *Kievskaia starina*, no. 4 (1895), 35.

23 Kostomarov's lecture was printed immediately: N.I. Kostomarov, 'Vstupitelnaia lektsiia v kurse russkoi istorii, chitannaia 22-go Noiabria,' *Russkoe slovo*, no. 12 (1859), i–xiv. See also the brief excerpts in V.A. Zamlinsky, 'Zhizn i tvorchestvo N.I. Kostomarova,' pp. 237, 241.

24 'Avtobiografiia–1885,' no. 6, p. 34.

25 Polovoi, 'Istorik-idealist.'

26 Markevich, 'Kostomarov,' p. 310. See also N. Podorozhny, 'Iz pamiatnoi knizhki: Vospominanie o N.I. Kostomarove,' *Kievskaia starina*, no. 4 (1895), 22–4.

27 'Avtobiografiia,' pp. 527–8.

28 N.I. Kostomarov, 'Russkie inorodtsy: Litovskoe plemia i otnosheniia ego k russkoi istorii,' *Russkoe slovo*, no. 5 (1860), 1–100, reprinted in *Sobranie sochinenii*, bk I, vol. III.

29 Mordovtsev, 'Istoricheskiia pominki po N.I. Kostomarove,' pp. 622–3.

30 N.I. Kostomarov, 'Zamechanie na statiu g. Soloveva "Malorossiiskoe kozachestvo do Bogdana Khmelnitskogo",' *Sovremennik*, LXXVII, 2 (1859), 51–7, reprinted in *Naukovo-publitsystychni i polemichni pysannia Kostomarova*, pp. 53–7.

31 N.I. Kostomarov, 'O kozachestva,' *Sovremennik*, LXXXII, 7 (1860), 75–92, reprinted in *Naukovo-publitsystychni i polemichni pysannia Kostomarova*, pp. 57–69.

32 N.I. Kostomarov, 'Otvet g. Padalitse,' *Sovremennik*, LXXXIV (1860), 373–82, reprinted in *Naukovo-publitsystychni i polemichni pysannia Kostomarova*, pp. 68–74.

33 In Korsakov, 'Kostomarov v ego otnosheniiakh k Kavelinu,' pp. 162–3.

34 'Rossiia i Polsha,' *Kolokol* (London), 15 January 1859. For an English translation of 'Russia and Poland,' annotated and with an analytical introduction, see my 'Herzen on Poland and Ukraine,' *Journal of Ukrainian Studies*, no. 12 (Toronto, 1982), 31–49.

35 This hypothesis was first advanced by Mykhailo Drahomanov in 1885. See *Pismo N.I. Kostomarova k izdateliu 'Kolokola,'* ed. M. Drahomanov (Geneva: Hromada, 1885), p. iii.

36 Ibid.

37 N.I. Kostomarov, 'Nachalo Rusi,' *Sovremennik*, no. 1 (1860), 5–32, quoted at length in N. Barsukov, *Zhizn i trudy M.P. Pogodina*, vol. XVII (St Petersburg, 1903), pp. 272–3.

38 Barsukov, *Zhizn i trudy M.P. Pogodina*, pp. 273–4.

39 Ibid., p. 275. Also in V.A. Diakov, 'Uchennaia duel M.P. Pogodina s N.I. Kostomarovym: O publichnom dispute po normanskomu voprosu 19 Marta 1860 g.,' in *Istoriografiia i istochnikovedenie stran tsentralnoi i iugovostochnoi Evropy*, ed. V.A. Diakov (Moscow, 1986), p. 42.

40 See, for example, L.F. Panteleev, *Vospominaniia* (Moscow: Khudozhnaia literatura, 1958), pp. 232–3, who was one of the students present at the debate, and more extensively, Vashkevich, 'Iz vospominanii,' pp. 38–9. See also N.G. Chernyshevsky, letter of 22 March 1860 to his family, in *Polnoe sobranie sochinenii*, vol. XIV (Moscow, 1949), p. 289, who wrote, 'Kostomarov's every word was greeted sympathetically by the public. At the conclusion of the debate they carried Nikolai Ivanovich out on their shoulders. The subject of the debate was very dry ... and the public attended, of course, only out of its love and respect for Kostomarov. He enjoys a fame here that no other professor has had since the foundation of the university.' See also Kostomarov's letter of 19 March to Mordovets in the latter's 'Istoricheskiia pominki po N.I. Kostomarove,' pp. 624–5, in which he says that he felt like David who had slain Goliath.

41 A.V. Nikitenko, *Dnevnik*, vol. II (Moscow, 1955), p. 113, cited in Diakov, 'Uchennaia duel Pogodina s Kostomarovym,' p. 48.

42 In Barsukov, *Zhizn i trudy M.P. Pogodina*, pp. 295–8.

43 *The Contemporary*, no. 5. See N.A. Dobroliubov, *Sobranie sochinenii*, vol. VII (Moscow, 1963), pp. 297–398, and the brief discussion in Diakov, 'Uchen-

naia duel Pogodina s Kostomarovym,' p. 51. Kostomarov later wrote to Pogodin in respectful terms dissociating himself from *The Contemporary*'s radical critics, Dobroliubov and Chernyshevsky. But on Kostomarov's admiration for the young Dobroliubov, see Podorozhny, 'Iz pamiatnoi knizhki,' pp. 23–4.

44 Mordovtsev 'N.I. Kostomarov po moim lichnym vospominaniiam,' no. 16, pagination unavailable.

45 Ibid.

46 N.I. Kostomarov, 'Misticheskaia povest o Nifonte: Pamiatnik russkoi literatury XIII veka,' *Russkoe slovo*, no. 3 (1861), 1–28.

47 Mordovtsev, 'N.I. Kostomarov po moim lichnym vospominaniiam.'

48 Ibid.

49 N.I. Kostomarov, 'Ocherk domashnei zhizni i nravov veliko-russkogo naroda v XVI–XVII stoletiiakh, first appeared in *Sovremennik* in various issues for 1860. It was reprinted in book form in 1862 and 1887.

50 See N.I. Kostomarov, 'Getmanstvo Vygovskogo,' *Osnova*, no. 4 (1861), 1–66, no. 7 (1861), 67–114; reprinted separately in 1863 and 1872, and in *Sobranie sochinenii*, bk I, vol. II.

51 Ivan Krypiakevych, 'Arkheohrafichni pratsi M. Kostomarova,' *Zapysky Naukovoho Tovarystva im. Shevchenka*, CXXVI–CXXVII (1918), 105–40.

52 Mordovtsev, 'N.I. Kostomarov po moim lichnym vospominaniiam.'

Chapter 6: The *Foundation* Years

1 Panteleev, *Vospominaniia*, pp. 235–7.

2 Zaitsev, *Taras Shevchenko*, p. 254.

3 In Arkadii Zhyvotko, *Istoriia ukrainskoi presy* (Munich: Ukrainskyi Teknichno-hospodarskyi Instytut, 1989–90), p. 44. Though the general inspiration may have come from Shevchenko, Kulish and Kostomarov were the practical organizers of the venture. A contemporary who was close to Kostomarov at the time later wrote that 'the initiative for the publication of the journal *The Foundation* belonged to that powerful warrior of the word, M.I. Kostomarov.' See Z. Nedoborovsky, 'Moi vospominaniia,' *Kievskaia starina*, 1 (Kiev, 1893), 194.

4 N.I. Kostomarov, 'Mysli o federativnom nachale v drevnei Rusi,' *Osnova*, no. 1 (1861), 121–58, reprinted in *Sobranie sochinenii*, bk I, vol. I, pp. 3–30.

5 Ibid.

6 N.I. Kostomarov, 'Dve russkie narodnosti,' *Osnova*, no. 3 (1861), 33–80, reprinted in *Sobranie sochinenii*, bk I, vol. I.

7 Ibid.

8 N.I. Kostomarov, 'Cherty narodnoi iuzhno-russkoi istorii,' *Osnova*, no. 3
   (1861), 114–65, no. 6 (1861), 1–45, reprinted in *Istoricheskie proizvedeniia.
   Avtobiografiia*, pp. 8–107.
9 Zhyvotko, *Istoriia ukrainskoi presy*, pp. 55–7, analyses the general reaction.
10 Printed as N.I. Kostomarov, 'Slovo nad hrobom Shevchenka,' *Osnova*, no.
   3 (1861), 8, and reprinted in *Naukovo-publitsystychni i polemichni pysannia
   Kostomarova*, p. 85, and in *Tvory v dvokh tomakh*, II, 398.
11 Mordovtsev, 'Istoricheskiia pominki po N.I. Kostomarove,' p. 626. Mordovets noted that of all the speeches at Shevchenko's funeral, the historian
   was most impressed by that of a young Polish student who acknowledged that the poet had not loved the Poles but had good reason for it.
12 N.I. Kostomarov, 'Vospominanie o dvukh maliarakh,' *Osnova*, no. 4
   (1861), 44–56, reprinted in his *Tvory v dvokh tomakh*, II, 399–411, and in
   Ukrainian translation in *Spohady pro Tarasa Shevchenka*, ed. Dzeverin, pp.
   130–7. Many of the same ideas, together with a statement comparing
   Shevchenko to Pushkin and Mickiewicz, appeared about a year earlier in
   Kostomarov's anonymous review of Shevchenko's *Kobzar* published in
   Otechestvennye zapiski, no. 3 (1860), 44–50, reprinted in *Tvory v dvokh
   tomakh*, II, 421–8. See Ie. Shabliovsky and V.S. Borodin, 'M.I. Kostomarov:
   Avtor anonimnoi retsenzii na "Kobzar" 1860 roku,' *Radianske literaturoz-
   navstvo*, no. 4 (1969), 70–3.
13 On Duchiński, see Ivan L. Rudnytsky, 'Franciszek Duchiński and His
   Impact on Ukrainian Political Thought,' in his *Essays in Modern Ukrainian
   History* (Edmonton: CIUS, 1987), pp. 187–202.
14 N.I. Kostomarov, 'Otvet na vykhodki gazety (Krakovskoi) Czas i zhurnala
   Revue Contemporaine,' *Osnova*, no. 2 (1861), 121–35, reprinted in *Naukovo-
   publitsystychni i polemichni pysannia Kostomarova*, pp. 75–84. However,
   Kostomarov did think that the problem of the Russians' origins and its
   Finnish angle was a very important one, the solution of which required
   great philological, archaeological, and geographical expertise. Several
   years later, he advised a young student of early Russian history to make a
   systematic investigation into Russian place-names in the hope of estab-
   lishing or contradicting their Finnish origins. See D.A. Korsakov, 'Iz vospominanii o N.I. Kostomarove i S.M. Soloveve,' *Vestnik Evropy*, CXLI
   (Sept.–Oct., 1906), 240.
15 N.I. Kostomarov, 'Pravda Poliakam o Rusi,' *Osnova*, no. 10 (1861), 100–12,
   reprinted in *Naukovo-publitsystychni i polemichni pysannia Kostomarova*, pp.
   94–101.
16 N.I. Kostomarov, 'Pravda Moskvicham o Rusi,' *Osnova*, no. 10 (1861),
   1–15, reprinted in *Naukovo-publitsystychni i polemichni pysannia Kostomarova*,

pp. 102–10. In this essay, Kostomarov went to great lengths to explain the original meaning of the term 'Rus'.' He maintained that 'Rus'' originally had two uses: as a specific geographical term denoting the land of Kiev, the Dnieper basin, and as a general political/ecclesiastical term denoting all those lands belonging to the Kievan state. This explanation is accepted by almost all present-day historians.

17 Mordovtsev, 'Istoricheskiia pominki po N.I. Kostomarove,' p. 629.

18 N. Kostomarov, *O znachenii kriticheskikh trudov Konstantina Aksakova po russkoi istorii* (St Petersburg, 1861).

19 'Perepiska I.S. Aksakova s N.I. Kostomarovym o Malorossii,' *Russkii arkhiv*, no. 12 (1906), 537–48.

20 See the summaries in Hrushevsky, 'Z publitsystychnykh pysan Kostomarova,' pp. xiii–xv, and in Roman Serbyn, 'The *Sion-Osnova* Controversy of 1861–1862,' in *Ukrainian-Jewish Relations in Historical Perspective*, P.J. Potichnyj and H. Aster (Edmonton: CIUS, 1988), pp. 85–110. On the earlier Ukrainian protest against Russian anti-Jewish sentiment, see Roman Serbyn, 'Ukrainian Writers on the Jewish Question: In the Wake of the *Illiustratsiia* Affair of 1858,' *Nationalities Papers*, no. 1 (1981), 101–3.

21 N.I. Kostomarov, 'Iudeiam,' *Osnova*, no. 1 (1862), 38–58, reprinted in *Naukovo-publitsystychni i polemichni pysannia Kostomarova*, pp. 111–23, especially 114, and Serbyn, 'The *Sion-Osnova* Controversy,' p. 99.

22 Kostomarov, 'Iudeiam,' p. 123. In the final sentence, Kostomarov stated that all religious prejudice was bad but that 'historical truth' called forth some negative statements about the Jews.

23 N.I. Kostomarov, 'Mysli iuzhnorussa: I. O prepodavanii na iuzhnorusskom iazyke,' *Osnova*, no. 5 (1862), 1–6, reprinted in *Naukovo-publitsystychni i polemichni pysannia Kostomarova*, pp. 137–40.

24 Ibid.

25 *Osnova*, no. 9 (1862), cited in Doroshenko, *Mykola Ivanovych Kostomarov*, p. 60, who gives a general outline of Kostomarov and the education question, pp. 59–62.

26 I. Zhytetsky, 'Lystuvannia Kostomarova z kharkivskymy hromadianamy pro vydannia narodnikh knyzhok,' *Ukraina*, no. 3 (1925), 69–72.

27 For the complete text of the letter, see V. Baturinsky, 'K biografii N.I. Kostomarova,' *Byloe*, no. 10 (St Petersburg, 1907), 89–93, who also comments on Kostomarov and the education question more generally.

28 Mykola Kostomarov, letter of 25 February 1863, in M. Vozniak, 'Lystuvannia Kostomarova z Konyskym,' *Ukraina*, no. 3 (1925), 72–7, especially 75.

29 Baturinsky, 'K biografii N.I. Kostomarova,' pp. 89–93; Doroshenko, *Mykola Ivanovych Kostomarov*, pp. 59–62.

30 M. Drahomanov, *Mykola Ivanovych Kostomariv: Zhytiepysnyi ocherk*, ed. I. Franko (Lviv: NTSh, 1901), pp. 26–34. It was only in the early years of the twentieth century that the Academy awarded the funds to Borys Hrinchenko (1863–1910) as a prize for the compilation of his four-volume Ukrainian-Russian dictionary (1902–9), which was based on materials collected by numerous predecessors.

31 See Mordovtsev, 'Istoricheskiia pominki po N.I. Kostomarove,' p. 628, who prints an interesting letter from Kostomarov describing the stormy relations between Kulish, 'a very honest and straightforward man, but self-centred in the extreme,' and Bilozersky, who did not want to be his underling. A disagreement between Kulish and his wife, who was Bilozersky's sister, only added to the tensions.

32 See the discussions in Zhyvotko, *Istoriia ukrainskoi presy*, pp. 62–4, and in Bernshtein, *Zhurnal 'Osnova'*, pp. 191–9.

33 Hrushevsky, 'Z publitsystychnykh pysan Kostomarova,' p. x. It was also to some extent very influential for the work of Russia's last great pre-revolutionary 'statist' historian, Vasili Kliuchevsky (1841–1911), who clearly distinguished between what he thought was a commercial and Europe-oriented Kievan Rus' and an agricultural and nationally isolated Muscovy. Although Kliuchevsky devoted the first volume of his *Course of Russian History* to Kievan Rus', he thereafter restricted his study to that of Muscovy and imperial Russia and carefully avoided writing what today would be called Belorussian or Ukrainian history. Through the medium of Kliuchevsky, Kostomarov's positive ideas on Kievan Rus' gained wide circulation and are generally accepted by most present-day Western historians of Russia.

34 Mordovtsev, 'N.I. Kostomarov po moim lichnym vospominaniiam.' Mordovets wrote these words upon the historian's death in 1885.

Chapter 7: After *The Foundation*

1 'Avtobiografiia,' p. 535; Mordovtsev, 'Istorisheskiia pominki po N.I. Kostomarove,' pp. 628–9; Doroshenko, *Mykola Ivanovych Kostomarov*, pp. 62–3.

2 'Avtobiografiia,' p. 537.

3 Printed as N.I. Kostomarov, 'O znachenii Velikogo Novgoroda v russkoi istorii,' *Otechestvennye zapiski*, CXL, 1 (1862), 84–105, and reprinted in his *Sobranie sochinenii*, bk I, vol. I, pp. 199–214. Throughout the essay, Kostomarov argued that *edinoderzhavie* had always been strengthened by foreign conquest and foreign influences, first that of the Mongols, then that of the Germans.

4 In his 'Avtobiografiia,' p. 547, Kostomarov says that one German newspaper openly accused him of stirring up discontent among the students.

5 Ibid., p. 550.

6 N.I. Kostomarov, 'Tysiacheletie,' *Sanktpeterburgskie vedomosti*, no. 5 (1862), reprinted in *Naukovo-publitsystychni i polemichni pysannia Kostomarova*, pp. 125–30.

7 'Avtobiografiia,' pp. 550–51. On Kostomarov's statements in the St Petersburg press, see Pinchuk, *Istoricheskie vzgliady N.I. Kostomarova*, p. 54, who cites *Sanktpeterburgskie vedomosti*, nos 237, 258, 262 (1861).

8 Papazian, 'Nicholas Ivanovich Kostomarov,' pp. 288–90, makes some use of the police reports. At least one of the reports, by an agent named Kastorsky, which accused Kostomarov of ridiculing autocracy while simultaneously praising 'Novgorod liberty' and 'the popular element,' even reached the desk of Tsar Alexander II, who noted: 'The general direction is terrible because it will lead straight to revolution. Given this sort of thing, it is no wonder if the youth accept these ideas. It is therefore necessary to watch such professors most closely.' See R.P. Ivanova, 'M.I. Kostomarov u suspilno-politychnomu rusi XIX st.,' *Ukrainskyi istorychnyi zhurnal*, no. 5 (1967), 31–41, especially 35, quoted in Pinchuk, *Mykola Ivanovych Kostomarov*, p. 120.

9 'Avtobiografiia,' p. 552. He continued: 'I was at first considered to be a liberal, even a revolutionary, and that was one of the reasons for that hot affection which I had enjoyed among the youth. The probable reason why the youth thought that way was my long exile for a political affair whose significance they did not fully understand.' Indeed, one of the historian's contemporaries later remarked that 'for us, Kostomarov, like Victor Hugo, like Geoffroy Saint Hilaire, was a protagonist of freedom and movement in science and in art.' In Pinchuk, *Istoricheskie vzgliady N.I. Kostomarova*, p. 54. See also Vashkevich, 'Iz vospominanii,' pp. 34–5.

10 Papazian, 'Nicholas Ivanovich Kostomarov,' pp. 292–3, citing *Protsess N.G. Chernyshevskogo* (Saratov, 1939), pp. 59–60. Chernyshevsky kept notes on his visit to Kostomarov, who later wrote to Chernyshevsky declaring the friendship at an end.

11 'Avtobiografiia,' pp. 552–3; Vashkevich, 'Iz vospominanii,' pp. 40–1.

12 See Kostomarov's three articles on the university question in *Naukovo-publitsystychni i polemichni pysannia Kostomarova*, pp. 131–6. At about the same time, he wrote to Mordovets that his relations with the 'progressive party' among the professors were becoming very strained. 'In particular,' he informed him, 'those people who form the progressive party, although they are all noble persons, have fallen out of sympathy with me, and all

of them do me ill. They have been compelled to conclude that I hold many ideas that they consider prejudices, and besides, I have never wandered away from scholarship.' See Mordovtsev, 'Istoricheskiia pominki po N.I. Kostomarove,' p. 629.

13 Papazian, 'Nicholas Ivanovich Kostomarov,' pp. 294–5, examined the Ministry of Education documents on the case but misread Kostomarov's 'Avtobiografiia,' p. 555, as saying that the Ministry had initiated the resignation. The historian clearly states that he initiated the process himself and, moreover, that Golovnin said he would keep him in mind for a future post at another Russian university. See also Pinchuk, *Mykola Ivanovych Kostomarov*, pp. 119–21.

14 'Avtobiografiia,' p. 556. Pinchuk, *Mykola Ivanovych Kostomarov*, stresses that many of the historian's student critics and opponents, who for a time included even Bilozerska, later saw the wisdom of his actions and regretted his departure from the university, even writing to him personally in respectful terms on the subject.

15 'Avtobiografiia,' p. 583. Polevoi, 'Istorik-idealist,' p. 510, for example, later accused the historian of being 'tactless,' susceptible to Polish flattery, and indifferent to the systematic extinction of Orthodoxy and the traces of 'Russian' antiquity then ostensibly being carried out by the local Polish administration.

16 See the discussion in his 'Avtobiografiia,' p. 587. For a detailed account of Kostomarov's Novgorod tour by a student who accompanied him, see Nikolai Barsukov, 'Vospominaniia o N.I. Kostomarove i A.N. Maikove,' *Russkoe obozrenie*, no. 5 (1897), 123–41.

17 N.I. Kostomarov, *Severnorusskiia narodopravstva vo vremena udelno-vechevogo uklada: Novgorod, Pskov, Viatka*, 2 vols (St Petersburg: Kozhanchikov, 1863), reprinted in his *Sobranie sochinenii*, bk III, vols VII and VIII. See also the brief remarks of Hrushevsky, 'Z publitsystychnykh pysan Kostomarova,' p. xv.

18 See chapter 4, above.

19 Nedoborovsky, 'Moi vospominaniia,' pp. 201–2.

20 N.I. Kostomarov, 'Khniaz Vladimir Monomakh i Kazak Bogdan Khmelnitsky,' *Russkii invalid*, no. 86 (1863), 1–15, reprinted in *Naukovo-publitsystychni i polemichni pysannia Kostomarova*, pp. 149–55.

21 Nedoborovsky, 'Moi vospominaniia,' pp. 200–1. Strangely, Kostomarov does not mention these meetings in his 'Avtobiografiia.'

22 N.I. Kostomarov, 'O prepodavanii na narodnom iazyke v Iuzhnoi Rusi,' *Golos*, no. 94 (20 April 1863), reprinted in *Naukovo-publitsystychni i polemichni pysannia Kostomarov*, pp. 156–9. Kostomarov ended the article by

stating that the tsar's official Holy Synod was currently reviewing a Ukrainian edition of the Gospels and that the publication of that work with ecclesiastical permission was most important.

23 For a collection of Katkov's articles from *Moskovskie vedomosti* and other papers, see [M.N. Katkov], 'Ukrainofilstvo i g. Kostomarov,' *Russkii vestnik*, CLII (April 1881), 687–725. Before the Polish insurrection and the urgings of Yuzefovich, Katkov had not been anti-Ukrainian. See, for example, the brief but perceptive remarks of Ivan Franko, 'Katkov i ukrainofilstvo,' in his *Zibrannia tvoriv u piatdesiaty tomakh*, XLI, pt 1, 484–6.

24 N.I. Kostomarov, 'Otvet "Moskovskim vedomostiam,"' *Den*, no. 27 (1863), 18–19, reprinted in *Naukovo-publitsystychni i polemichni pysannia Kostomarova*, pp. 159–60. See also Kostomarov's 'Ukrainskii separatizm,' ibid., pp. 193–6, which was blocked from publication by the Russian censor and printed only after the revolution (1921).

25 N.I. Kostomarov, 'Pismo k redaktoru,' *Den*, no. 29 (1863), 19–20; 'G. publitsistu ...,' *Sanktpeterburgskie vedomosti*, no. 164 (1863); 'Zametka,' ibid, no. 186 (1863). All this material, together with lists of financial contributors to the cause, are reprinted in *Naukovo-publitsystychni i polemichni pysannia Kostomarova*, pp. 160–7.

26 'Avtobiografiia,' p. 595. Valuev noted in his diary for this date: 'Several persons visited me including Kostomarov, who was deeply perplexed by the ban on popular publications in the *Khokhol* dialect. I gently but directly and categorically declared to him that the measures taken by me will remain in effect.' In Marakhov, 'Novi storinky,' p. 105.

27 Unsigned, 'O nektorykh foneticheskikh i grammaticheskikh osobennostiakh iuzhnorusskogo (malorusskogo) iazyka, neshodnykh s velikorusskim i polskim,' *Zhurnal Ministerstva Narodnogo Prosveshcheniia*, CXIX, 8 (1863), 45–56; reprinted with corrections based on the manuscript, which is preserved in the Central Scientific Library of Ukraine, Kiev, in *Naukovo-publitsystchni i polemichni pysannia Kostomarova*, pp. 168–79.

28 In Pinchuk, *Mykola Ivanovych Kostomarov*, p. 123. See also Marakhov, 'Novi storinky,' pp. 101–6, who prints a private exchange of letters between Kostomarov and Annenkov.

29 'Avtobiografiia,' pp. 593–4.

30 N.I. Kostomarov, 'Ivan Susanin: Istoricheskoe izsledovanie,' *Otechestvennye zapiski*, CXL, 2 (1862), 720–38, reprinted in *Sobranie sochinenii*, bk I, vol. I, pp. 267–80.

31 'Avtobiografiia,' pp. 591–2.

32 N.I. Kostomarov, 'Velikorusskie religioznye volnodumtsi v XVI veke,' *Otechestvennye zapiski*, CXLIV, 10 (1862), 317–48, reprinted in *Sobranie sochinenii*, bk I, vol. I, pp. 237–63.

33 N.I. Kostomarov, 'Kulikovskaia bitva,' *Prilozhenie k Mesiatseslovu na 1864 god* (St Petersburg: Academy of Sciences, 1864), pp. 3–24, reprinted in *Sobranie sochinenii*, bk I, vol. III, pp. 521–41.

34 N.I. Kostomarov, 'M.P. Pogodinu,' *Golos*, no. 32 (1864), reprinted in *Naukovo-publitsystychni i polemichni pysannia Kostomarova*, pp. 180–3.

35 See the polemics collected ibid., pp. 184–92. Many years later, however, Kostomarov reconsidered the matter and admitted that both he and Pogodin had read the chronicles too literally. He was thus somewhat kinder to Dmitri in his *Russian History in the Lives of Its Principal Figures*, which was written late in his life.

36 Many years later, his former student Polevoi, 'Istorik-idealist,' pp. 510–20, accused Kostomarov of writing sensational articles for financial profit and to keep himself in the public eye while receiving a government pension that he thought was inadequate for his needs. Polevoi considered Kostomarov a partisan of the 'extreme left' and called his articles on Susanin and Donskoi 'trashy and teasing.'

37 N.I. Kostomarov, 'Ob otnoshenii russkoi istorii k geografii i etnografii,' *Zapiski Imperatorskogo Russkogo Geograficheskogo Obshchestva*, XII, 2 (1863), 92–113, reprinted in *Sobranie sochinenii*, bk I, vol. III, pp. 717–31.

38 Nikolai Kostomarov, *Istoricheskie monografii i izsledovaniia*, vol. I (St Petersburg: Obshchestvennaia polza, 1863).

39 See N.I. Kostomarov, 'Otvet g. Malorossu-volyntsu,' *Den*, no. 6 (1864); [untitled article], *Golos*, no. 120 (1864); and 'Zamechanie g. Lokhvitskomu,' *Sanktpeterburgskie vedomosti*, no. 205 (1864); reprinted in *Naukovo-publitsystychni i polemichni pysannia Kostomarova*, pp. 196–203.

40 Mordovtsev, 'N.I. Kostomarov po moim lichnym vospominaniiam.'

41 Nedoborovsky, 'Moi vospominaniia,' pp. 202–4.

42 See M.I. Koialovich, *Lektsii po istorii zapadnoi Rossii* (Moscow: Bakhmetev, 1864), and N.I. Kostomarov, 'Lektsii g. Koialovich po istorii zapadnoi Rossii,' 'Otvet na otvet g. Koialovicha,' and 'Lektsii po istorii zapadnoi Rossii M. Koialovicha, 1864', in *Naukovo-publitsystychni i polemichni pysannia Kostomarova*, pp. 204–15.

43 Mordovtsev, 'N.I. Kostomarov po moim lichnym vospominaniiam,' no. 17, pp. 34–5.

44 'Avtobiografiia,' p. 603.

45 Kostomarov's revised study was first printed in *Biblioteka dlia Chteniia* in various numbers for 1865 and was reprinted in vol. III of his *Istoricheskie monografii i izsledovaniia* (1867). It was reprinted a third time in his *Sobranie sochinenii*, bk I, vol. III, pp. 619–98, and most recently in *Istoricheskie proizvedeniia. Avtobiografiia*, pp. 108–97. The reprints bear the simplified title 'Iuzhnaia Rus' v kontse XVI veka.'

46 *Vestnik Evropy*, I (1866), ix.

47 See the discussion in O.I. Kyian, 'Spivrobitnytstvo M.I. Kostomarova v istorychnykh zhurnalakh poreformenoi Rosii,' *Ukrainskyi istorychnyi zhurnal*, no. 4 (1990), 64–5.

48 N.I. Kostomarov, *Smutnoe vremia moskovskogo gosudarstva*, 3 vols (Saint Petersburg: Kozhanchikov, 1868), reprinted in *Sobranie sochinenii*, bk II, vols IV, V, VI. Kostomarov's innovative use of a wide range of new Polish and Western European sources and his lively and detailed narration of the course of events made this bulky study a significant contribution to Russian historiography. That, however, did not satisfy his critics, who could not forgive him for his severe treatment of their traditional Muscovite heroes. For example, Polevoi, 'Istorik-idealist,' p. 512, later wrote of the work: 'The exposition of the material, as one would expect of Kostomarov, was lovely and beautiful. But the links between facts turned out to be extremely weak. The author's views of the more important events were shaky and indefinite; his characterization of the more important figures was arbitrary and untrue. In comparison with his previous historical works, *Bohdan Khmelnytsky* and *Stenka Razin*, which had established Kostomarov's fame, the *History of the Time of Troubles* was a notable step back.' By contrast, the populist Semevsky, 'Kostomarov,' p. 208, considered Kostomarov's *Time of Troubles* 'masterly,' 'one of the most outstanding works of our historiography.'

49 Mordovtsev, 'N.I. Kostomarov po moim lichnym vospominaniiam,' no. 17, p. 35.

50 Ibid., pp. 35–6.

51 Hryhory Vashkevych was the technical editor of this edition. See his 'Iz vospominanii,' pp. 43–5, for the background.

52 N.I. Kostomarov, 'Lyst do redaktoriv chasop. "Slavianskaia zaria" Livchaka i Klimkovicha,' *Slavianskaia zaria*, no. 1 (Vienna, 1867), 18–22, reprinted in *Naukovo-publitsystychni i polemichni pysannia Kostomarova*, pp. 216–19.

53 Mordovtsev, 'N.I. Kostomarov po moim lichnym vospominaniiam,' no. 17, p. 41.

54 In his 'Avtobiografiia,' p. 610, Kostomarov states that enthusiasm for his work alone kept him away. However, in view of the historian's strong interest in Panslavism, that seems unlikely.

55 N.I. Kostomarov, 'Ob'iasnenie,' *Golos*, no. 218 (1867), reprinted in *Naukovo-publitsystychni i polemichni pysannia Kostomarova*, pp. 219–22.

56 Mordovtsev, 'N.I. Kostomarov po moim lichnym vospominaniiam,' no. 17, p. 37.

57 Korsakov, 'Iz vospominanii o N.I. Kostomarove i S.M. Soloveve,' p. 236.
58 N.I. Kostomarov, *Poslednie gody Rechi Pospolitoi* (St Petersburg: Vestnik Evropy, 1870); revised edition in *Istoricheskie monografii i izsledovaniia*, vols XVII and XVIII (1886), and reprinted in *Sobranie sochinenii*, bk VII, vols XVII and XVIII.
59 Ibid., pp. 378–9.
60 Ibid., p. 674.
61 D.A. Korsakov, 'Pamiati Nikolaia Ivanovicha Kostomarova,' *Istoricheskii vestnik*, XXI (1885), 72–86, especially 80.
62 Polevoi, 'Istorik-idealist,' p. 520.
63 In Pinchuk, *Mykola Ivanovych Kostomarov*, p. 127.
64 Mordovtsev, 'N.I. Kostomarov po moim lichnym vospominaniiam,' no. 17, p. 38.
65 Mordovtsev, 'Istoricheskiia pominki po N.I. Kostomarove,' pp. 630–3.
66 Semevsky, 'Kostomarov,' p. 207.

Chapter 8: The Accomplished Historian

1 Mordovtsev, 'Istoricheskiia pominki po N.I. Kostomarove,' p. 631.
2 'Nachalo edinoderzhaviia drevnei Rusi,' which was first published in *Vestnik Evropy* in various numbers for 1870, was reprinted in his *Istoricheskie monografii i izsledovaniia*, vol. XII (St Petersburg: Kozhanchikov, 1872), and reprinted again in his *Sobranie sochinenii*, bk V, vol. XII, pp. 5–94.
3 Kostomarov's 'Lichnost Ivana Vasilevicha Groznogo' and 'Lichnosti Smutnogo vremeni' are both reprinted in *Sobranie sochinenii*, bk V, vol. XIII.
4 'Avtobiografiia,' p. 621. Zabelin's attack on Kostomarov was especially fierce. He had tried to get it published in *Vestnik Evropy* and *Russkaia starina*, but the editors of those liberal journals had turned him down. Only after those refusals did he get P.I. Barteniev, the editor of *Russkii arkhiv*, who was close to the Moscow Slavophiles, to publish the piece. See the discussion in Kyian, 'Spivrobitnytstvo Kostomarova,' pp. 63–4.
5 Mordovtsev, 'Istoricheskiia pominki po N.I. Kostomarove,' p. 630.
6 Korsakov, 'Iz vospominanii o N.I. Kostomarove i S.M. Soloveve,' pp. 252–3.
7 Ibid.
8 Gennadii Karpov, *Kriticheskii obzor razrabotki glavnykh russkikh istochnikov do istorii Malorossii otnosiashchikhsia* (Moscow: Grachev, 1870).
9 N.I. Kostomarov, 'Otvet g. Karpovu,' *Beseda*, I, 2 (1871), 1–9, reprinted in *Naukovo-publitsystychni i polemichni pysannia Kostomarova*, pp. 231–7.

10 G.F. Karpov, *Kostomarov kak istorik Malorossii* (Moscow: Grachev, 1871). 35 pp.

11 N.I. Kostomarov, 'Zametka,' *Golos*, no. 130 (1871), reprinted in *Naukovo-publitsystichni i polemichni pysannia Kostomarova*, pp. 237–9.

12 N.I. Kostomarov, 'Istoricheskoe znachenie iuzhnorusskogo narodnago pesennago tvorchestva,' in various numbers of *Beseda* for 1872. It is reprinted in *Sobranie sochinenii*, bk VIII, vol. XXI.

13 N.I. Kostomarov, 'Predaniia pervonachalnoi russkoi letopisi v soobrazhe-niiakh s russkimi narodnymi predaniiami v pessniakh, skazaniiakh i obychaiakh' was first published in *Vestnik Evropy* in various numbers for 1873; reprinted in *Sobranie sochinenii*, bk V, vol. XIII, pp. 289–394.

14 'Avtobiografiia,' p. 622.

15 Vols III (1872), IV (1877), and V (1874). The full title of the collection was *Trudy etnografichesko-statisticheskoi ekspeditsii v zapadno-russkii krai snaria-zhennoi Imperatorskim Russkim Geograficheskim Obshchestvom.* I have seen a complete set of this rare work in the library of the Ukrainian Museum of Canada, Saskatoon.

16 N.I. Kostomarov, 'Malorusskaia literatura,' in *Poeziia Slavian*, ed. N.V. Gerbel (St Petersburg, 1871), reprinted in *Naukovo-publitsystychni polemich-ni pysannia Kostomarova*, pp. 240–7. Kostomarov also made the point that Church Slavonic was more comprehensible to the average Ukrainian vil-lager than modern literary Russian.

17 'Avtobiografiia,' p. 628.

18 The *Akty otnosiashchiesia k istorii iuzhnoi i zapadnoi Rossii*, which was edited by Kostomarov himself, is discussed in detail by Krypiakevych, 'Arkheo-hrafichni pratsi M. Kostomarova,' pp. 113–28, who analyses the contents of each volume. See chapter 5, above.

19 The first referee appointed by the Academy was a Russian scholar who was working on the same topic. His evaluation was highly critical and recommended Kostomarov only for the lesser prize. The Academy then turned to a German scholar, Ernst Hermann, for a second appraisal. His appraisal was considerably more positive and recommended Kostomarov for first prize. Nevertheless, the Russian public was outraged that the Academy had turned to a foreigner for an evaluation in Russian history, and, perhaps in consequence of the uproar, Kostomarov was awarded the lesser prize. But even Hermann had criticized Kostomarov for his unsym-pathetic treatment of the Constitution of 3 May and the liberal declara-tions of the Polish gentry, a position which the historian continued to defend even in his 'Avtobiografiia, pp. 630–1.

20 N.I. Kostomarov, *Russkaia istoriia v zhizneopisaniiakh ee glavneishikh deiatelei,*

3 bks in 7 pts (St Petersburg: Stasiulevich, 1873–88, photoreprinted Moscow: Kniga, 1990–1). Kostomarov continued to work on this project to the end of his life. The final sections were on personalities of the eighteenth century. Kostomarov was working on a chapter on Lomonosov when he died. See A. Kostomarova, 'Poslednie dni zhizni Nikolaia Ivanovicha Kostomarova,' *Kievskaia starina*, XLIX, 4 (1895), 1–19. See also Mordovtsev, 'Istoricheskiia pominki po N.I. Kostomarove,' p. 633.

21 This is the 'Avtobiografiia–1885.'

22 Mordovtsev, 'Istoricheskiia pominki po N.I. Kostomarove,' pp. 640–1. According to the historian's will, after his death this album, which contained photographs of some fifty-seven of Kostomarov's friends and colleagues, was donated to the St Petersburg Public Library, where it has been preserved to the present day. See Pinchuk, *Mykola Ivanovych Kostomarov*, pp. 169–70, 220.

23 From Alina Leontievna's memoirs, quoted in full in Doroshenko, *Mykola Ivanovych Kostomarov*, pp. 68–9.

24 Ibid.

25 Nikolai Kostomarov, 'Istoricheskaia poeziia i novye ee materiialy: Istoricheskiia pesni malorusskogo naroda s obiasneniiami V. Antonovicha i M. Dragomanova, Tom Pervyi,' *Vestnik Evropy*, no. 12 (1874), 573–639, reprinted in *Etnohrafichni pysannia Kostomarova*, pp. 299–334.

26 N.I. Kostomarov, *Kudeiar: Istoricheskaia khronika v trekh knigakh* was first published in *Vestnik Evropy* in various numbers for 1875. It was translated into Ukrainian and published in Austrian Galicia (1897), and again in Winnipeg, Canada (1921), by early Ukrainian immigrants from Galicia. It was long neglected by the Soviets, who probably objected to its negative portrayal of Ivan the Terrible – a figure greatly admired by Stalin – and who in general certainly eschewed the positive portrayal of Ukrainian personalities independent of Russian connections. It was missing from *Tvory v dvokh tomakh* (1967) and appeared only during the 'glasnost' era, in two separate editions, in 1989 and 1990. For Kostomarov's reply to his critics, see his 'Moe ukrainofilstvo v Kudeiare,' *Kievskii telegraf*, no. 85 (1875), reprinted in *Naukovo-publitsystychni i polemichni pysannia Kostomarova*, pp. 248–51.

27 N.I. Kostomarov, 'Tsarevich Aleksei Petrovich,' *Drevniaia i novaia Rossiia*, I, no. 1 (1875), 31–54, no. 2, 134–52, reprinted in *Sobranie sochinenii*, bk V, vol. XIV, pp. 635–79.

28 See the remarks of Korsakov, 'Iz vospominanii o N.I. Kostomarove i S.M. Soloveve,' pp. 256–60, and the observations of Doroshenko, *Mykola Ivanovych Kostomarov*, pp. 69–70, who summarizes Alina's memoir.

29 Korsakov, 'Iz vospominanii o N.I. Kostomarove i S.M. Soloveve,' p. 260. There were also some complaints about the local patriotism and 'Ukrainophilism' of the congress in the conservative newspaper *Kievlianin*; see 'Avtobiografiia,' p. 640.

30 Mordovtsev, 'Istoricheskiia pominki po N.I. Kostomarove,' p. 646.

31 'Avtobiografiia,' p. 641; Doroshenko, *Mykola Ivanovych Kostomarov*, p. 70; D. Mordovtsev, 'Nikolai Ivanovich Kostomarov v posledniia desiat let ego zhizni, 1875–1885,' *Russkaia starina*, XLVIII, 12 (1885), 638–40, recounts the story of the historian's quarrel with his mother, his illness, and his marriage to Alina. When Kostomarov first told Mordovets of his plan to marry Alina, Mordovets opposed the idea, thinking it another of the historian's impetuous flights of fantasy. However, he soon changed his mind and afterwards acknowledged that the match was a good one and that Alina was 'to the highest degree a kindly, noble, and very intelligent woman.'

32 In Fedir Savchenko, *Zaborona ukrainstva 1876 r.* (Kiev–Kharkiv: Derzhavne vydavnytstvo Ukrainy, 1930; reprinted Munich: Wilhelm Fink, 1970), pp. 376–8.

33 Ibid. passim.

34 In Drahomanov, *Mykola Ivanovych Kostomariv*, pp. 26–30. In the same letter, Kostomarov described the 'Yuzefovich law' as 'barbaric.'

35 N.I. Kostomarov, 'Ob uchastii Rossii v osvobozhdenii khrestian ot turetskogo iga,' *Novoe vremia*, no. 707 (1878), was not available to me.

36 See the discussion in Hrushevsky, 'Z publitsystychnykh pysan Kostomarova,' p. xviii. See also Mordovtsev, 'Nikolai Ivanovich Kostomarov v posledniia desiat let ego zhizni,' pp. 654–5, who quotes a letter from Kostomarov replying to his liberal critics (although not to Drahomanov). Kostomarov thought that in both Great and Little Russia the common people supported the war, that they did so both as Christians and as Slavs, and that in spite of everything they 'actually blessed their tsar.'

37 N. Kostomarov, 'Pismo v redaktsiiu,' *Novoe vremia*, no. 1650 (1880), reprinted in *Naukovo-publitsystychni i polemichni pysannia Kostomarova*, p. 266; Drahomanov, *Mykola Ivanovych Kostomariv*, pp. 32–4, criticized the dictionary project as a betrayal of the commitments for which the money had originally been donated. See chapter 6, above.

38 N.I. Kostomarov, 'Malorusskoe slovo,' *Vestnik Evropy*, I, 1 (1881), 401–7, reprinted in *Naukovo-publitsystychni i polemichni pysannia Kostomarova*, pp. 267–71.

39 See the introduction to Savchenko, *Zaborona ukrainstva*, p. xxvi.

40 In V. Zamlynsky, 'Apostol krashchoi doli Ukrainy,' *Visnyk AN Ukrainy*, no. 6 (1992), 75–81, especially 77–79.

41 N.I. Kostomarov, 'Zadachi ukrainofilstva,' *Vestnik Evropy*, I, 2 (1882), 868–900, reprinted in *Naukovo-publitsystychni i polemichni pysannia Kostomarova*, pp. 289–98.

42 Drahomanov, *Mykola Ivanovych Kostomariv*, pp. 26–34.

43 Barvinsky's position is summarized in Oleksander Barvinsky, ''Pohliady Mykoly Kostomarova na zadachi ukrainskoi inteligentsii i literatury,'' *Zapysky Naukovoho Tovarystva im. Shevchenka*, CXXVI–CXXVII (1918), 83–103.

44 Both letters are printed ibid.

45 Mykola Kostomarov, *Istorychni monohrafii*, 11 vols (Ternopil–Lviv: NTSh, 1886–96); *Kudeiar: Istorychna khronika v 3-k knyhakh* (Lviv, 1897).

46 P. Kulish's *Istoriia vozsoedineniia Rusi* was published in St Petersburg in 1873–7 and was followed by 'Kozaki v otnoshenii k obshchestvu i gosudarstvu,' *Russkii arkhiv*, nos 3, 6 (1877). There is a summary of Kulish's historical views in Doroshenko, 'Survey of Ukrainian Historiography,' pp. 146–56. See also Luckyj, *Panteleimon Kulish*, pp. 154–5, and Ihnat Zhytetsky, 'Kulish i Kostomarov,' *Ukraina*, nos 1–2 (1927), 39–65.

47 N.I. Kostomarov, 'O Kazakakh,' *Russkaia starina*, XXI, 3 (1878), 385–402, reprinted in *Sobranie sochinenii*, bk V, vol. XIV, pp. 617–34.

48 P. Kulish, *Krashanka Rusynam i Poliakam na Velykden 1882 roku* (Lviv: 1882), summarized in Luckyj, *Panteleimon Kulish*, p. 162.

49 N.I. Kostomarov, 'Krashanka g. Kulisha: Pismo v redaktsiiu,' *Vestnik Evropy*, IV, 8 (1882), 729–48.

50 P. Kulish, 'Khutorna poeziia,' *Tvory*, vol. I (Lviv, 1908). See also the discussion in Luckyj, *Panteleimon Kulish*, pp. 167–71.

51 N.I. Kostomarov, 'P.A. Kulish i ego posledniaia literaturnaia deiatelnost,' *Kievskaia starina*, V, 2 (1883), 221–34. In its original form, Kostomarov's article contained some material on Kulish's participation in the Cyril-Methodian Brotherhood, but out of fear of the censor and the negative consequences that publishing it might have for the Ukrainian journal *Kievskaia starina*, the historian himself asked the editor to omit the lines in question. See Kyian, 'Spivrobitnytstvo Kostomarova,' p. 72.

52 V.L. Berenshtam, 'Vospominaniia o poslednikh godakh zhizni N.I. Kostomarova,' *Kievskaia starina*, no. 6 (1885), 227, cited in Doroshenko, *Mykola Ivanovych Kostomarov*, p. 77.

53 Doroshenko, *Mykola Ivanovych Kostomarov*, pp. 77–8; Kyian, 'Spivrobitnytstvo Kostomarova.'

54 N.I. Kostomarov, 'Po povodu knigi M.O. Koialovicha,' *Vestnik Evropy*, IV (1885), 867–78, reprinted in *Naukovo-publitsystychni i polemichni pysannia Kostomarova*, pp. 304–21. Kostomarov also tried to defend his idea of the close relations between Novgorod and Southern Rus' against the criticism of Koialovich, but he did so much less convincingly.

55 Berenshtam, 'Vospominaniia,' p. 228, quoted in Pinchuk, *Mykola Ivanovych Kostomarov*, p. 186.

56 N.I. Kostomarov, 'Ruina: Istoricheskaia monografiia, 1663–1687' first appeared in *Vestnik Evropy* in various numbers for 1879 to 1880; it is reprinted in *Sobranie sochinenii*, bk VI, vol. XV. At first, reluctant to make historical judgments, Kostomarov had much difficulty finishing the manuscript and would not accept the advice of Alina and Mordovets to revise it. When his publisher, Stasiulevich, refused the work, however, Kostomarov was forced to rewrite it with some kind of conclusion. Such difficulties reveal, perhaps, the extent to which health problems affected the historian's judgment and impeded his later historical work. See Mordovtsev, 'Nikolai Ivanovich Kostomarov v posledniia desiat let ego zhizni,' pp. 644–5.

57 Kostomarov's study of Mazepa was published together with a shorter study of the hetman's émigré followers as 'Mazepa i Mazepintsy' in *Russkaia mysl* in various numbers for 1882 and 1884. It is reprinted in his *Sobranie sochinenii*, bk VI, vol. XVI. I have used the most recent edition published in Moscow by Respublika (1992). See especially pp. 244–5, 320–2.

58 Mordovtsev, 'Nikolai Ivanovich Kostomarov v posledniia desiat let ego zhizni,' pp. 659–62; Doroshenko, *Mykola Ivanovych Kostomarov*, p. 78. The novel *Sorok let* is reprinted in Kostomarov's *Tvory v dvokh tomakh*, vol. II. *Chernigovka* was translated entirely into Ukrainian by Borys Hrinchenko and published in Kiev in 1922.

59 N.I. Kostomarov, 'Istoriia kozachestva v pamiatnikakh iuzhnorusskogo narodnogo pesennogo tvorchestva' was first published in *Russkaia mysl* in various numbers from 1880 to 1883. It was reprinted in *Sobranie sochinenii*, bk VIII, vol. 21. Several chapters remained unpublished until the second half of the twentieth century. See my 'Mykola Kostomarov and East Slavic Ethnography,' pp. 183–6.

60 Korsun, 'N.I. Kostomarov,' pp. 218–19, and my 'Mykola Kostomarov and East Slavic Ethnography,' pp. 184–5.

61 Mordovtsev, 'Nikolai Ivanovich Kostomarov v posledniia desiat let ego zhizni.'

62 L. Hrytsyk, 'Zustrich A. Tsereteli z M. Kostomarovym: Vypadkovist chy zakonomirnist?' *Slovo i chas*, no. 6 (1990), 40–4.

63 D.K.M., 'Vospominaniia o N.I. Kostomarove,' *Kievskaia starina*, no. 7 (1891), 75–84.

64 Kostomarov's funeral is most fully described by Pinchuk, *Mykola Ivanovych Kostomarov*, pp. 201–5, who cites the necrology in *Istoricheskii vestnik*, no. 5 (1885), 13–16.

65 Halyna Mukhyna, 'Teoriia "Khatnoho vzhytku": Do stolittia smerty My-koly Kostomarova,' *Suchasnist*, no. 2 (1986), 31–41.
66 Very little is known about the personal relations between Antonovych and Kostomarov. See, for example, S. Iefremov, 'Z lystiv Kostomarova do Antonovycha,' *Ukraina*, no. 3 (1925), 77–8.
67 I.M. Hapusenko, *Dmytro Ivanovych Iavornytsky* (Kiev: Naukova Dumka, 1969), p. 5. It is remarkable, in fact, that Kostomarov seems to have given similar advice to the distinguished artist Ilia Repin, who interviewed him some time before 1880 when he made an important research trip to Ukraine in search of materials for his great painting *The Zaporozhian Cossacks Writing a Satirical Letter to the Turkish Sultan*. Kostomarov even seems to have drawn up an itinerary along the Dnieper rapids for the young painter to follow. See I.E. Repin, *Dalekoe blizkoe* (Leningrad: Khudozhnik RSFSR, 1982), p. 364.
68 In Pinchuk, *Mykola Ivanovych Kostomarov*, p. 152.

Chapter 9: Conclusions

1 M. Hrushevsky, 'Kostomarov i novitnia Ukraina,' *Ukraina*, no. 3 (1925), reprinted in *Ukrainskyi istoryk*, XXI, 1–4 (1984), 148–70.
2 Doroshenko, 'Survey of Ukrainian Historiography,' pp. 143–4.
3 For Marx's comments on Kostomarov's work, which he read in the original Russian, see 'K. Marks: Stenka Razin,' ed. D. Riazanov, *Molodaia gvardiia*, no. 1 (1926), 106–25, and the discussion in Ie. Shabliovsky and V.G. Sarbei, 'N.I. Kostomarov v istoriograficheskom nasledii Karla Marksa,' *Voprosy istorii*, no. 8 (1967), 49–59.
4 'The Traditional Scheme of "Russian" History and the Problem of a Rational Organization of the History of the East Slavs' is available in many editions and translations. For a recent edition and discussion, see Lubomyr Wynar, *Mykhailo Hrushevsky: Ukrainian-Russian Confrontation in Historiography* (Toronto–New York–Munich: Ukrainian Historical Association, 1988).
5 Barvinsky, 'Pohliady Mykoly Kostomarova na zadachi ukrainskoi inteli-gentsii i literatury,' pp. 102–3.
6 For example, after the First World War Ukrainian scholars in the West seemed almost embarrassed by Kostomarov's moderation and seemingly equivocal attitude towards Ukrainian nationality. Accordingly, Ukrainian academic institutions in both Western Europe and North America repeat-edly reprinted Hrushevsky's 1904 essay 'The Traditional Scheme' but until the 1990s ignored Kostomarov's 'Two Russian Nationalities.'

7 M. Hrushevsky, 'Ukrainska istoriografiia i Mykola Kostomarov,' *Litera-turno-naukovyi vistnyk*, L, 5 (1910), 224.

8 V.B. Antonovych, 'N.I. Kostomarov kak istorik,' *Kievskaia starina*, XII, 5 (1885), xxx–xxxi.

9 Ibid., p. xxvii.

10 Korsakov, 'Pamiati Nikolaia Ivanovicha Kostomarova,' p. 81.

11 V.O. Kliuchevsky, *Neopublikovannye proizvedeniia* (Moscow: Nauka, 1982), pp. 177–8, and quoted in full in Zamlinsky, 'Zhizn i tvorchestvo N.I. Kostomarova,' p. 240.

12 Hrushevsky, 'Kostomarov i novitnia Ukraina,' pp. 168–9.

13 See, in particular, the criticisms of Pypin, *Istoriia russkoi etnografii*, III, 178, 186–7, and M.K. Azadovsky, *Istoriia russkoi folkloristiki*, 2 vols (Moscow: Gosudarstvennoe Uchebno-pedagogicheskoe Izdatelstvo Ministerstva Prosveshcheniia RSFSR, 1958–63), II, 39–46.

14 Hrushevsky, 'Ukrainska istoriografiia i Mykola Kostomarov,' p. 225.

15 For example, by Doroshenko, 'Survey of Ukrainian Historiography,' p. 144.

16 Thus, argued Markevich, 'Kostomarov,' p. 317, of the three major Cyril-Methodians, only the historian remained true to the political ideals of the seventeenth century.

17 P.N. Polevoi, *Istoriia russkoi slovesnosti*, 3 vols in 6 pts (St Petersburg: Marks, 1890), III, pt 2, p. 590; A. Brückner, *Geschichte der Russischen Literatur*, 2nd ed. (Leipzig: C.F. Amelangs, 1909), pp. 419–20.

Bibliography

Bibliographies of Works by and about Kostomarov

There is no full bibliography of works of Kostomarov, but a very good one, and one that was used in compiling many of the publishing histories in the notes of the present work, is 'Bibliograficheskii ukazatel sochinenii N.I. Kostomarova,' in *Literaturnoe nasledie N.I. Kostomarova* (St Petersburg: Stasiulevich, 1890), pp. 493–521. A great many works about as well as by Kostomarov are given in *Ukrainski pysmennyky: Biobibliohrafychnyi slovnyk*, vol. II (Kiev: Khudozhnia literatura, 1963), pp. 464–88, although this list is incomplete and somewhat sporadic. For an analysis of works about Kostomarov, memoirs, commentaries, and obituaries, as well as studies by more modern authors, see Iu.A. Pinchuk, 'Dozhovtneva i radianska istoriohrafiia pro M.I. Kostomarova iak istoryka,' *Istoriohrafichni doslidzhennia v Ukrainskoi RSR*, no. 4 (Kiev: Naukova Dumka, 1971), 124–49.

Primary Materials

Works by Kostomarov

i. Collections of His Works
Istoricheskie monografii i izsledovaniia. Vol. I. St Petersburg: Obshchestvennaia polza, 1863.
Sobranie sochinenii. 21 vols in 8 bks. St Petersburg: Stasiulevich, 1903–6; photo-repr. The Hague: Europe Printing, 1968.
Naukovo-publitsystychni i polemichni pysannia Kostomarova. Ed. M. Hrushevsky. Kiev: Derzhavne vydavntstvo Ukrainy, 1928. Contains a valuable introduction by Hrushevsky.

Etnohrafichni pysannia Kostomarova. Ed M. Hrushevsky. Kiev: Derzhavne vydavnytstvo Ukrainy, 1930. Contains another valuable introductory essay by Hrushevsky.

Tvory v dvokh tomakh. 2 vols. Kiev: Dnipro, 1967. All references to Kostomarov's literary works are to this edition.

Istoricheski proizvedeniia. Avtobiografiia. Ed. V.A. Zamlinsky. Kiev: Izdatelstvo pri Kievskom Gosudarstvennom Universitete, 1989. All references to Kostomarov's 'Avtobiografiia' are to this edition.

Tvory v dvokh tomakh. 2 vols. Kiev: Dnipro, 1990. Contains a good introduction by V.L. Smilianska as well as the text of *Kudeiar.*

Slov'ianska mifolohiia: Vybrani pratsi z folklorystyky i literaturoznavstva (Kiev: Lybid, 1994). Published too late to be used in the research for this book.

ii. Individual Works

'Avtobiografiia N.I. Kostomarova, zapisannaia N.A. Belozerskoi.' *Russkaia mysl*, no. 5 (1885), 185–223, no. 6 (1885) 20–43. All references to 'Avtobiografiia–1885' are to this edition.

'Zapiska N.I. Kostomarova ob ego uchenykh trudakh sostavlennaia v 1870 g.' *Russkaia mysl*, no. 6 (1885), 43–54.

Slavianskaia mifologiia. Kiev: Bainer, 1847; photorepr. London–The Hague: Mlyn, 1978. In Old Cyrillic type. Hrushevsky also reprinted this work, but in modern type, in *Etnohrafichni pysannia Kostomarova*, pp. 203–40.

Knyhy buttia ukrainskoho narodu. Ed. K. Kostiv. Toronto: NTSh, 1980. Contains an English translation.

Le livre de la genèse du peuple ukrainien. Ed. G. Luciani. Paris: Institut d'études slaves de l'Université de Paris, 1956.

'Spohad pro dvokh maliariv.' In *Spohady pro Tarasa Shevchenka*, ed. I.O. Dzeverin, 130–7. Kiev: Dnipro, 1982.

'Lyst do vydavtsia-redaktora *Russkoi stariny* M.I. Semevskoho.' In *Spohady pro Tarasa Shevchenka*, ed. Dzeverin, 138–44.

Bogdan Khmelnitsky. 2 vols. St Petersburg: Kozhanchikov, 1859.

Dvi rus'ki narodnosty. Ed. Dmytro Doroshenko. Trans. Oleksander Konysky. Kiev–Leipzig: Ukrainska nakladnia, n.d. 111 pp. A useful translation into modern Ukrainian with a brief introduction by Doroshenko.

'Two Russian Nationalities.' Ed. and trans. Thomas M. Prymak. Unpublished manuscript. 82 pp.

'Vstupitelnaia lektsiia v kurse russkoi istorii, chitannaia 22-go Noiabria.' *Russkoe slovo*, no. 12 (1859), i–xiv.

Pismo N.I. Kostomarova k izdateliu 'Kolokola.' Ed. M. Drahomanov. Geneva: Hromada, 1885.

O znachenii kriticheskikh trudov Konstantina Aksakova po russkoi istorii. St Petersburg, 1861.

'Perepiska I.S. Aksakova s N.I. Kostomarovym o Malorossii.' *Russkii arkhiv,* no. 12 (1906), 537–48.

Russkaia istoriia v zhizneopisaniiakh ee glavneishikh deiatelei. 3 bks in 7 pts. St Petersburg: Stasiulevich, 1873–88; photorepr. Moscow: Kniga, 1990–1.

Mazepa. Mocow: Respublika, 1992.

'Lystuvannia Kostomarova z kharkivskymy hromadianamy pro vydannia narodnikh knyzhok.' Ed. I. Zhytetsky. *Ukraina,* no. 3 (1925), 69–72.

'Lystuvannia Kostomarova z Konyskym,' Ed. M. Vozniak. *Ukraina,* no. 3 (1925), 72–7.

'Apostol krashchoi doli Ukrainy.' Ed. V. Zamlynsky. *Visnyk AN Ukrainy,* no. 6 (1992), 75–81. A brief collection of Kostomarov's unpublished correspondence.

'Krashanka g. Kulisha: Pismo v redaktsiiu.' *Vestnik Evropy,* IV, 8 (1882), 729–48.

'P.A. Kulish i ego posledniaia literaturnaia deiatelnost.' *Kievskaia starina,* V, 2 (1883), 221–34.

'Z lystiv Kostomarova do Antonovycha.' Ed. S. Iefremov. *Ukraina,* no. 3 (1925), 77–8.

'Z lystuvannia M.I. Kostomarova z grafyneiu A.D. Bludovoiu.' *Ukraina,* no. 5 (1926), 80–90.

'Pisma N.I. Kostomarova k V.M. i N.M. Belozerskim.' *Kievskaia starina,* LIX, 10 (1897), 132–42.

Contemporary Reports, Polemics, Memoirs

Antonovich, V.B. [Antonovych]. 'N.I. Kostomarov kak istorik.' *Kievskaia starina,* XII, 5 (1885), xxvi–xxxiv.

'Arest gg. Kulisha i Kostomarova po razskazu nemetskikh gazet v 1847 g.' *Russkaia starina,* no. 9 (October, 1885), 123–5.

Barsukov, Nikolai. 'Vospominaniia o N.I. Kostomarove i A.N. Maikove.' *Russkoe obozrenie,* no. 5 (1897), 123–41.

Belozerskaia, N.A. [Bilozerska, N.O.]. 'Nikolai Ivanovich Kostomarov v 1857–1875 gg. Vospominaniia N.A. Belozerskoi.' *Russkaia starina,* XLIX (1886), 609–36, L, 327–38, 615–54.

D.K.M. 'Vospominaniia o N.I. Kostomarove.' *Kievskaia starina,* no. 7 (1891), 75–84.

Drahomanov, M. *Mykola Ivanovych Kostomariv: Zhytiepysnyi ocherk.* Ed. I. Franko. Lviv: NTSh, 1901.

Karpov, Gennadii F. *Kriticheskii obzor razrabotki glavnykh russkikh istochnikov do istorii Malorossii otnosiashchikhsia.* Moscow: Grachev, 1870.
– *Kostomarov kak istorik Malorossii.* Moscow: Grachev, 1871. 35 pp.
[Katkov, M.N.]. 'Ukrainofilstvo i g. Kostomarov.' *Russkii vestnik,* CLII (April, 1881), 687–725. A collection of articles.
Koialovich, M.I. *Lektsii po istorii zapadnoi Rossii.* Moscow: Bakhmetev, 1864.
Korsakov, D.A. 'Pamiati Nikolaia Ivanovicha Kostomarova.' *Istoricheskii vestnik,* XXI (1885), 72–86.
– 'Iz vospominanii o N.I. Kostomarove i S.M. Soloveve.' *Vestnik Evropy,* CCXLI (Sept.–Oct., 1906), 221–72.
– 'Nikolai Ivanovich Kostomarov v ego otnosheniiakh k Konstantinu Dmitrievichu Kavelinu.' *Istoricheskii vestnik,* CXLIX–CL (July–Aug. 1917), 157–66.
Korsunov, A. [Korsun, O.]. 'N.I. Kostomarov.' *Russkii arkhiv,* no. 10 (1890), 199–221.
Kostomarova, Alina. 'Poslednie dni zhizni Nikolaia Ivanovicha Kostomarova.' *Kievskaia starina,* XLIX, 4 (1895), 1–19.
– 'Nikolai Ivanovich Kostomarov.' In *Avtobiografiia N.I. Kostomarova,* ed. V. Kotelnikov, 6–116. Moscow: Zadruga, 1922.
Kulish, P. 'Vospominaniia o Nikolae Ivanoviche Kostomarove.' *Nov,* IV, 13 (1885), 61–75.
Kyrylo-Mefodiivske Tovarystvo. 3 vols. Kiev: Naukova Dumka, 1990–1. Volume I contains the material on Kostomarov.
Markevich, A. 'Kostomarov, Nikolai Ivanovich.' In *Russkii biograficheskii slovar,* vol. IX, 305–19. St Petersburg, n.d.
Marx, Karl. 'K. Marks: Stenka Razin.' Ed. D. Riazanov. *Molodaia gvardiia,* no. 1 (1926), 106–25.
Mordovtsev, D.L. [Mordovets]. 'Istoricheskiia pominki po N.I. Kostomarove.' *Russkaia starina,* XLVI (1885), 617–48.
– 'Nikolai Ivanovich Kostomarov v posledniia desiat let ego zhizni, 1875–1885.' *Russkaia starina,* XLVIII (1885), 636–62, XLIX, 323–60.
– 'N.I. Kostomarov po moim lichnym vospominaniiam.' *Nov,* XXII, no. 15 (1888), 109–121, no. 16 (1888), 210–17, XXIII, no. 17 (1888), 34–45.
Naumenko, V. 'N.I. Kostomarov kak etnograf.' *Kievskaia starina,* no. 6 (1885), xxxv–xliv.
Nedoborovsky, Z. 'Moi vospominaniia.' *Kievskaia starina,* no. 1 (1893), 189–208.
Palimpsestov, I.U. 'Iz vospominanii o Nikolae Ivanoviche Kostomarove.' *Russkoe obozrenie,* no. 7 (1895), 155–90.
Panteleev, L.F. *Vospominaniia.* Moscow: Khudozhnaia literatura, 1958.
Podorozhny, N. 'Iz pamiatnoi knizhki: Vospominanie o N.I. Kostomarove.' *Kievskaia starina,* no. 4 (1895), 20–33.

Polevoi, P. 'Istorik-idealist.' *Istoricheskii vestnik*, XLII (1891), 501–20.

Pypin, Aleksander. 'Istoricheskaia obektivnost.' *Sovremennik*, XCV, 2 (1863), 257–84. A critique of Kostomarov's concessions to the conservative Slavophiles from a progressive Westerning viewpoint.

Semevsky, V.I. 'Nikolai Ivanovich Kostomarov, 1817–1885.' *Russkaia starina*, no. 1 (1886), 181–212.

– 'Kirillo-Mefodievskoe Obshchestvo 1846–47 g.' *Russkoe bogatstvo*, no. 5 (1911), 98–127, no. 6 (1911), 50–67.

Vashkevich, G. [Vashkevych, H.S.]. 'Iz vospominanii o Nikolae Ivanoviche Kostomarove.' *Kievskaia starina*, no. 4 (1895), 34–62.

Secondary Materials

Aizenshtok, I. 'Persha dysertatsiia Kostomarova.' *Ukraina*, no. 3 (1925), 21–7.

– 'Do etnohrafichnykh planiv 1840-kh rokiv.' *Za sto lit*, IV (Kiev, 1929), 12–24.

– [Ajzensztok, Jeremiasz]. 'Romantycy ukraińscy a zagadnienia jedności słowiańskiej.' *Slavia orientalis*, no. 3 (1973), 321–34.

Andrusiak, M. 'Ukraintsi–Velykorusy–Poliaky: Iz dumok M. Kostomarova pro vidnoshennia ukrainskoho narodu do rosiiskoho i polskoho narodiv do poch. 60 rr. XIX st.' *Novi shliakhy*, no. 1 (Lviv, 1929), 124–8.

Bagalei, Olga [Bahalii]. 'Otnoshenie N.I. Kostomarova k g. Kharkovu i kharkovskomu universitetu.' *Russkaia starina*, CLX, 12 (1914), 465–80.

Barsukov, N. *Zhizn i trudy M.P. Pogodina*. Vol. XVII. St Petersburg, 1903.

Barvinsky, Oleksander, 'Pohliady Mykoly Kostomarova na zadachi ukrainskoi inteligentsii i literatury.' *Zapysky Naukovoho Tovarystva im. Shevchenka*, CXXVI–CXXVII (1918), 81–103.

Baturinsky, V. 'K biografii N.I. Kostomarova.' *Byloe*, no. 10 (1907), 89–93.

Bernshtein, M.D. *Zhurnal 'Osnova' i ukrainskyi literaturnyi protses kintsia 50-60-kh rokiv XIX st.* Kiev: AN URSR, 1959.

Bobrov, E. 'Epizod iz zhizni N.I. Kostomarova (Po arkhivnym dokumentam).' *Russkaia starina*, no. 3 (1904), 604–11.

Bushkovitch, Paul. 'The Ukraine in Russian Culture, 1790–1860: The Evidence of the Journals.' *Jahrbücher für Geschichte Osteuropas*, XXXIX, 3 (1991), 339–63. Argues that prior to 1856 Ukrainian history and culture were favourably presented in Russian journals and that tsarist censorship was very relaxed on this question.

Butych, I. 'M.I. Kostomarov i tsarska tsenzura.' *Arkhivy Ukrainy*, no. 6 (1967), 60–70.

Čiževsky, Dmitry. 'Mickiewicz and Ukrainian Literature.' In *Adam Mickiewicz in World Literature*, ed. W. Lednicki, 409–36. Berkeley and Los Angeles: University of California Press, 1956.

Diakov, V.A. 'Uchennaia duel M.P. Pogodina s N.I. Kostomarovym: O publichnom dispute po normanskomu voprosu 19 Marta 1860 g.' In *Istoriografiia i istochnikovedenie stran tsentralnoi i iugovostochnoi Evropy*, ed. V.A. Diakov, 40–56. Moscow, 1986.

Domanovsky, L.V. 'K Saratovskim vzaimo-otnosheniiam N.G. Chernyshevskogo i N.I. Kostomarova (Iz istorii "Saratovskogo kruzhka").' In *N.G. Chernyshevsky: Stati, izsledovaniia, i materiialy*, vol. III, 213–32. Saratov: Izdatelstvo Saratovskogo Universiteta, 1962.

Doroshenko, Dmytro. *Mykola Ivanovych Kostomarov.* (Kiev–Leipzig: Ukrainska nakladnia, 1920. Brief but valuable.

– 'A Survey of Ukrainian Historiography.' *Annals of the Ukrainian Academy of Arts and Sciences in the U.S.*, V–VI, no. 4 (New York, 1957), 132–45.

Fedchenko, P.M. 'Shevchenko, Kulish, i Kostomarov u Kyrylo-Mefodiivskomu Tovarystvi.' *Radianske literaturoznavstvo*, no. 7 (1989), 29–36.

Flynn, James T. 'The Affair of Kostomarov's Dissertation: A Case Study of Official Nationalism in Practice.' *Slavonic and East European Review*, LII (1974), 188–96.

Hrushevsky, Mykhailo. 'Ukrainska istoriografiia i Mykola Kostomarov.' *Literaturno-naukovyi vistnyk*, L, 5 (1910), 209–25.

– *Istoriia Ukrainy-Rusy.* 2nd ed. Vol. VIII, 213–21. Kiev–Lviv, 1922. Contains a discussion of the place of Kostomarov's *Bohdan Khmelnytsky* in Ukrainian historiography.

– 'Kostomarov i novitnia Ukraina.' *Ukraina*, no. 3 (1925); repr. in *Ukrainskyi istoryk*, XXI, 1–4 (1984), 148–70.

– 'Z publitsystychnykh pysan Kostomarova.' In *Naukovo-publitsystychni i polemichni pysannia Kostomarova*, iii–xxi; repr. in *Ukrainskyi istorychnyi zhurnal*, no. 4 (1992), 113–32. Important. All references are to the original edition.

– 'Etnohrafichne dilo Kostomarova.' In *Etnohrafichni pysannia Kostomarova*, ix–xxiv.

Hrushevsky, Oleksander [Grushevsky, A.S.] 'Malovidoma statia Kostomarova z 1846 r.' *Zapysky Naukovoho Tovarystva im. Shevchenka*, LXXXIX (1907), 161–4.

– 'Iz kharkovskikh let N.I. Kostomarova.' *Zhurnal Ministerstva Narodnogo Prosveshcheniia*, n.s. XIV, 4 (1908), 233–95.

– 'Novi materiialy do biografii Kostomarova.' *Zapysky Ukrainskoho Naukovoho Tovarystva*, I (1908), 72–81.

– 'Ranniia etnograficheskiia raboty N.I. Kostomarova.' *Izvestiia Otdeleniia Russkogo Iazyka i Slovestnosti*, XVI, 1 (1911), 77–120.

- 'Do statti Kostomarova pro federatyvnyi lad staroi Rusi.' *Ukraina*, no. 3 (1928), 50–7.
- 'Istorychni statti Kostomarova v "Osnovi".' *Ukraina*, no. 1 (1928), 73–90.

Hrytsyk, L. 'Zustrich A. Tsereteli z M. Kostomarovym: Vypadkovist chy zakonomirnist?' *Slovo i chas*, no. 6 (1990), 40–4.

Iudin, P.L. 'K biografii N.I. Kostomarova (Pismo grafa Orlova M.L. Kozhevnikovu).' *Istoricheskii vestnik*, XCIV (1903), 562–4.
- 'N.I. Kostomarov v ssylke.' *Istoricheskii vestnik*, C (1905), 136–53.
- 'K biografii N.I. Kostomarova.' *Istoricheskii vestnik*, CXII (1908), 981–6.

Ivanova, R.P. 'M.I. Kostomarov u suspilno-politychnomu rusi XIX st.' *Ukrainskyi istorychnyi zhurnal*, no. 5 (1967), 31–41.

Kolesnyk, Ie. 'Biblioteka M.I. Kostomarova.' *Ukrainskyi istorychnyi zhurnal*, no. 10 (1967), 156–7.

Kozak, Stefan. 'Knyhy Bytija Ukrainśkoho narodu Mykoły Kostomarova i Księgi narodu i pielgrzmystwa Polskiego Adama Mickiewicza.' *Slavia orientalis*, no. 2 (1973), 177–88.

Krypiakevych, Ivan. 'Arkheohrafichni pratsi M. Kostomarova.' *Zapysky Naukovoho Tovarystva im. Shevchenka*, CXXVI–CXXVII (1918), 105–40.

Kyian, O.I. 'Spivrobitnytstvo M.I. Kostomarova v istorychnykh zhurnalakh poreformenoi Rosii.' *Ukrainskyi istorychnyi zhurnal*, no. 4 (1990), 63–72.

Lobas, P. 'Ukrainskyi literaturnyi zbirnyk.' *Arkhivy Ukrainy*, no. 2 (1968), 74–80.

Luckyj, G.S.N. *Between Gogol' and Ševčenko: Polarity in the Literary Ukraine, 1798–1847.* Munich: Wilhelm Fink, 1971.
- *Panteleimon Kulish: A Sketch of His Life and Times.* Boulder: East European Monographs, 1983.
- *Young Ukraine: The Brotherhood of Saints Cyril and Methodius, 1845–1847.* Ottawa–Paris: University of Ottawa Press, 1991.

Marakhov, H.I. 'Novi storinky z biohrafii M.I. Kostomarova.' *Visnyk AN URSR*, XXXVI, 1 (1972), 99–106.

Miiakovsky, Volodymyr. 'Kostomarov u Rivnomu.' *Ukraina*, no. 12 (1925), 28–66.
- 'Liudy sorokovykh rokiv: Kyrylo-Metodiivtsi v ikh lystuvanni.' *Za sto lit*, II (Kiev, 1928), 33–98.
- 'Shevchenko i Kostomarov.' *Shevchenko*, no. 7 (New York: UVAN in the USA, 1958), 16–30.
- 'Knyha pro Kyrylo-Metodiivske Bratstvo.' *Suchasnist*, no. 3 (Munich, 1963), 85–96. Important.

Mukhyna, Halyna. 'Teoriia "Khatnoho vzhytku": Do stolittia smerty Mykoly Kostomarova.' *Suchasnist*, no. 2 (1986), 31–41.

Myhul, Ivan M. 'M.I. Kostomarov in Recent Soviet Ukrainian Historiography.' *Laurentian University Review*, X, 1 (1977), 85–95.

Mykhailyn, Ihor. 'Etiudy pro Kostomarova.' *Zbirnyk Kharkivskoho Istoryko-Filolohichnoho Tovarystva*, ns. I (Kharkiv, 1993), 51–64.

Ocherki istorii istoricheskoi nauki v SSSR. Ed M.V. Nechkina et al. Vol. II, 129–46. Moscow: Akademiia Nauk SSSR, 1960.

Papazian, Dennis. 'Nicholas Ivanovich Kostomarov: Russian Historian, Ukrainian Nationalist, Slavic Federalist.' Unpublished Ph.D. diss., University of Michigan, 1966.

– 'N.I. Kostomarov and the Cyril-Methodian Ideology.' *Russian Review*, XXIX, 1, (1970), 59–73.

Petrov, N.I. *Ocherki istorii ukrainskoi literatury XIX stoletiia*, 235–57. Kiev: Davidenko, 1884.

Pinchuk, Iu. A. *Istoricheskie vzgliady N.I. Kostomarova: Kriticheskii ocherk*. Kiev: Naukova Dumka, 1984.

– 'Do otsinky naukovoi i hromadskoi diialnosti M.I. Kostomarova.' *Ukrainskyi istorychnyi zhurnal*, no. 3 (1992), 3–11.

– 'Ideoloh Kyrylo-Mefodiivskoho Bratstva.' *Kyivska starovyna*, no. 5 (1992), 5–18.

– 'M.I. Kostomarov u Kyievi (1844–1847 rr.).' *Ukrainskyi istorychnyi zhurnal*, no. 5 (1992), 3–15.

– *Mykola Ivanovych Kostomarov, 1817–1885*. Kiev: Naukova Dumka, 1992.

Polukhin, L.K. *Formuvannia istorychnykh pohliadiv M.I. Kostomarova*. Kiev: Vydavnytstvo AN URSR, 1959.

Popov, A.I. 'N.I. Kostomarov: Prepodavatel rovenskoi gimnazii.' *Istoricheskii vestnik*, no. 3 (1917), 716–35.

Popov, P.M. *M. Kostomarov iak folkloryst i etnohraf*. Kiev: Naukova Dumka, 1968. Good.

Prymak, Thomas M. 'Mykola Kostomarov and East Slavic Ethnography in the Nineteenth Century.' *Russian History*, XVIII, 2 (1991), 163–86.

Pypin, A.N. *Istoriia russkoi etnografii*. 4 vols. St Petersburg: Stasiulevich, 1890–2; photorepr. Leipzig: Kubon and Sagner, 1971. Volume III contains most of the Ukrainian material including a lengthy essay on Kostomarov.

Rubach, M.A. 'Federalisticheskie teorii v istorii Rossii.' In *Russkaia istoricheskaia literatura v klassovom osveschenii*, ed. M.N. Pokrovsky, vol. II, 3–120. Moscow: Izdatelstvo Kommunisticheskoi Akademii, 1930.

Rubinshtein, N.L. *Russkaia istoriografiia*. Moscow: Gospolizdat, 1941.

Saunders, David. 'The Kirillo-Methodian Society.' *Slavonic and East European Review*, LXXI, 4 (1993), 684–92. A review article.

Savchenko, Fedir. *Zaborona ukrainstva 1876 r*. Kiev–Kharkiv: Derzhavne vydavnytstvo Ukrainy, 1930; photorepr. Munich: Wilhelm Fink, 1970.

Serbyn, Roman. 'Ukrainian Writers on the Jewish Question: In the Wake of the *Illustratsiia* Affair of 1858.' *Nationalities Papers*, no. 1 (1981), 101–3.

– 'The *Sion-Osnova* Controversy of 1861–1862.' In *Ukrainian-Jewish Relations in Historical Perspective*, ed. P.J. Potichnyj and H. Aster, 85–110. Edmonton: CIUS, 1988.

Shabliovsky, Ie. 'Shevchenko i Kostomarov.' In *Zbirnyk prats 15 shevchenkivskoi konferentsii*, 23–50. Kiev: AN URSR, 1968.

– 'N.I. Kostomarov v gody revoliutsionnoi situatsii.' In *Revoliutsionnaia situatsiia v Rossii v 1859-61 gg.*, vol. V, 101–23. Moscow, 1970.

– , and V.S. Borodin. 'M.I. Kostomarov: Avtor anonimnoi retsenzii na "Kobzar" 1860 roku.' *Radianske literaturoznavstvo*, no. 4 (1969), 70–3.

– , and V.G. Sarbei. 'N.I. Kostomarov v istoriograficheskom nasledii Karla Marksa.' *Voprosy istorii*, no. 8 (1967), 49–59.

Tolochko, Petro. 'Vydatnyi istoryk Ukrainy i Rosii.' *Kyivska starovyna*, no. 5 (1992), 7–14.

Tsamutali, A.N. *Borba techenii v russkoi istoriografii vo vtoroi polovine XIX veka.* Leningrad: Nauka, 1977.

Velychenko, S. 'Tsarist Censorship and Ukrainian Historiography, 1828–1906.' *Canadian-American Slavic Studies*, XXIII, 4 (1989), 385–408.

– *National History as Cultural Process: A Survey of the Interpretations of Ukraine's Past.* Edmonton: CIUS, 1992.

Vozniak, Mykhailo. *Kyrylo-Metodiivske Bratstvo.* Lviv, 1921.

Zaionchkovsky, P.A. *Kirilo-Mefodievskoe Obshchestvo (1846–1847)* Moscow: Izdatelstvo Moskovskogo Universiteta, 1959.

Zaitsev, Pavlo. *Taras Shevchenko: A Life.* Ed. and trans. George Luckyj. Toronto: University of Toronto Press, 1988.

Zamlinsky, V.A. 'Zhizn i tvorchestvo N.I. Kostomarova.' *Voprosy istorii*, no. 1 (1991), 234–41.

Zhytetsky, Ihnat. 'Kulish i Kostomarov.' *Ukraina*, nos 1–2 (1927), 39–65.

Zhyvotko, Arkadii. *Istoriia ukrainskoi presy.* Munich: Ukrainskyi Teknichno-hospodarskyi Instytut, 1989–90.

Zlupko, S.M. 'Zv'iazky M.I. Kostomarova iz zakhidnoiu Ukrainoiu.' *Ukrainskyi istorychnyi zhurnal*, no. 5 (1967), 31–41.

Index